SUNDOWNERS AT DAWN

SUNDOWNERS AT DAWN

A Banker's Tale

Geoffrey Bignell

The Book Guild Ltd
Sussex, England

First published in Great Britain in 2004 by
The Book Guild Ltd
25 High Street
Lewes, East Sussex
BN7 2LU

Typesetting in Baskerville by
Keyboard Services, Luton, Bedfordshire

Printed in Great Britain by
CPI Bath

A catalogue record for this book is
available from the British Library

ISBN 1 85776 811 6

To my wife Diana for her love and forbearance and Guy and Adrian for providing the motivation

CONTENTS

LIST OF PHOTOGRAPHS

The original Nairobi branch in 1904

The chief Nairobi branch in 1964

Nita Decker – Malindi 1956

The Bank house – Gulu 1957

The Bank house – Nairobi

Philip and Vivian Percival – Machakos

Crossing the Nile en route to Gulu 1957

The 'unrecognisable swing' – Kisumu 1959

Relay racing Aden 1961

Water ski-ing – the barren rocks of Aden in the background

Fancy dress – Aden 1963

Anthea Legge — Nairobi 1964

Lord Aldington meeting local dignitaries – Nairobi 1965

High jinks – Nairobi Polo Club

Tying the knot – Nairobi 1967

Elizabeth on honeymoon — Malindi 1967

Water ski-ing – Brighton

Lining up against the President's Bodyguard – Karachi 1968

The winners' enclosure – Karachi 1969

Elizabeth modelling at a charity show – Karachi 1969

View from the terrace of the Bank penthouse – Beirut 1970

Lord Gore-Booth, Colin Kerr and author with secretaries at the opening of the Tokyo office 1971

'Three Merry Maids' – Tokyo 1973

The hazardous drive to Simla – a rocky landslide prior to our arrival on the scene

A remarkable scene outside Kanpur branch

Winter scene – Srinagar, Kashmir

Shikaras at Srinagar

Lower Stonehurst Farm

William and Amanda Bond Elliot

Royal Ashdown Forest G.C. outside the Southampton Club, Long Island

Geoffrey Kent lifting the ultimate polo trophy at Palm Beach

Ashdown House Under Eleven cricket team. Guy and Adrian seated on left

The author and wife in retirement

ACKNOWLEDGEMENTS

Certain historical data was gleaned from *100 Years of Banking in Asia and Africa* – the history of National and Grindlays Bank Ltd published in 1963. A number of photographs have been reproduced from *Minerva,* the house magazine of the Grindlays Bank Group.

'I shall be telling this with a sigh
Somewhere ages and ages hence:
Two roads diverged in a wood, and I –
I took the one less travelled by,
And that has made all the difference.'

Robert Frost 1874–1963

PROLOGUE

Over the years I have subjected friends to tales of my exploits traipsing round the world pursuing a banking career. At their suggestion, and in my mind, grew an intention to chronicle these adventures, however irreverent – not least for my sons, Guy and Adrian. I have never kept a proper notebook. Accordingly, some names may have been misspelt and some dates might be slightly askew.

From chatting with acquaintances it seems commonplace that with age one has 'senior moments' and forgets events that have occurred in the recent past; but surprisingly, the human mind can recall with some clarity, if prompted, scenes and happenings many years ago. Aided by trip reports, letters home – which my late mother lovingly retained – and old diaries, the following tale evolved with reasonable accuracy, even if some events have become slightly fudged with the passage of time. Evocative images have been brought to life by recourse to old photographs and slides – the latter were in fashion at the time. While certain incidents, stashed away in one's memory, have been recounted here, I am sure there were some more interesting anecdotes which, alas, have faded into oblivion.

In this description of my life and times I have omitted any dialogue as this would have been superfluous to the main theme. I could have peppered the story with many pages of historical summary and political argument but this too would have distracted the reader from what, after all, is a simplistic tale.

Also, as one grows older, and becomes afflicted by arthritic joints and unforeseen ailments, I felt the urge to leave for the younger generation a taste of what it was like to travel the

1

world at somebody else's expense. When I began my career the globe was mainly coloured pink, indicating the strength and influence of the British Empire. Today, in many of these ex-colonies visas are in force, which restrict movement, and the need for a work permit imposes further restrictions.

To remember what one can of experiences and record a way of life no longer available is, I hope, a modest contribution to a bygone era. I have allowed myself the luxury of leaving out boring details of failed business deals; needless to say, where there has been the odd success this has been given some prominence.

Many people have meant a great deal to me but there is simply no room on this stage to mention them individually. However, I trust I will be forgiven if I give prominence to some notable personages as they provide added diversity and may engage the attention of a wider public. Soul-searching revelations and unfettered honesty could, possibly, cause offence in certain quarters. I have, accordingly, endeavoured to steer a path and use the wide and varied memories that crowd the years in question without, I hope, upsetting my family and friends. If I have been less than critical in glossing over my own shortcomings my excuse is that I intend to provide a narrative which keeps pace with changing times rather than to expose my own frailties.

Banking has provided me with a worthwhile career, even if at times this journal may read like a censored version of Lothario's progress abroad.

For the sake of interest I have confined my circumspect scribblings to the time spent overseas and the following pot-pourri of recollections is drawn together sequentially in terms of when and where my tours of duty took me.

When exchanging gifts at Christmas, invariably I receive an autobiography of some description – quite often that of a sporting personality who has used a 'ghost' writer. These have varied in quality from the excellent to the humdrum. Spurred on by the challenge that I should be able to produce something more readable than the latter I have been tempted to try my hand.

Everyone has a past and if that past has been as varied and eventful as mine it is surely worth writing down. If, in so

2

doing, one can share the pleasure and interest with others then the exertion will have been worthwhile. In any case sitting in the comfort of my study with a view stretching across the South Downs with the trees stripped of their leaves and the comforting sound of Test Match Special droning in the background, what better way to while away a winter's day.

As PG Wodehouse wrote, 'As in sprint races – the start is everything'. Here goes.

I

The Beginning

The slate-grey clouds and the bent shoulders of City workers hunched against the sleeting rain spurred me along Bishopsgate; I knew I had made the right decision. It was one of those days when a cold dampness seeped into one's bones, no prospect pleased and everything looked dismal and dispiriting.

Early in 1956, at the tender age of 21, I was answering an advertisement which, apart from offering a banking career in the colonies, held out promise of adventure and, as I fondly hoped, an escape to blue skies and sun-kissed beaches. I had not at that early and naïve stage factored into the equation mosquitoes, deprivation, searing heat and life-sapping humidity.

I duly arrived at my appointed time at No. 26, the head office of the National Bank of India. I was to be interviewed for a job as a junior officer on the overseas staff. Togged out in a smart overcoat (borrowed), three-piece suit, stiff white collar and highly polished shoes I hoped would create the right impression and camouflage my lack of a suitable professional qualification.

My interview was with the Accountant, in those far off days one of the more important positions in the Bank. The fashion where just about everyone nowadays has a rather grandiose title had not yet taken hold. His office was somewhat Dickensian and his countenance suitably ascetic. I was quizzed on my ability to pass Part I of the Institute of Bankers exams but, more importantly, on my prowess on the games field. Having satisfied him on both counts I was promptly recruited as a trainee on the Bank's eastern staff, with an offer of residential accommodation at the Bank's Sports Club at Blackheath. My fellow trainees were a cheerful eclectic bunch with a range of backgrounds and mostly from north of the Border. Historically, the Bank was a conduit for the sons of executives of trading houses, banks, tea companies, etc. who had dealings with the National Bank of India in some shape or form.

Blackheath was a convivial base where the emphasis on games and social activities tended to preclude studying for the banking exams. Thus some of the more talented extroverts fell by the wayside. One such, possibly the best rugby player in residence, was Charlie (Angus) Sharp, a mainstay of a strong Blackheath side when they won the Middlesex 'sevens' at Twickenham.

In the '50s the message if one wanted to improve one's financial circumstances was to 'go east, young man'. Christopher Ondaatje, a fellow trainee and one of the better cricketers, decided to buck the trend, resigned from the Bank and went west. He pitched up in Canada, where with a handful of dollars in his pocket he used his financial acumen to amass a not inconsiderable fortune and has become a successful author, philanthropist and generous patron of the arts. He is now well-known for being a major benefactor to Somerset Cricket Club, the National Portrait Gallery, the Royal Geographical Society, the Labour Party and other good and – depending on one's political leanings – not so good causes.

Apparently, T.S. Eliot was extremely interested in a career in banking and his friends spent their time plotting as to how they could get him out of this unbefitting drudgery. His wife wrote to his sister, 'Now that Tom has taken so extraordinarily to the City, he is considering, to my great astonishment, taking up banking as his money-making career! We are all very much surprised at this development, but not one of his friends has failed to see, and to remark upon, the great change in Tom's health, appearance, spirits and literary productiveness since he went in for Banking.'

Training at the Bank for an executive job overseas was, in retrospect, ludicrously irrelevant. I was allocated a high stool in front of one of those long old-fashioned Victorian sloping benches, all in mahogany, under the eagle eye of the departmental manager. One's time was spent filing and marking off in a ledger expired letters of credit. The latter documents being financial devices for facilitating trade between various countries

5

in which the Bank operated. At the end of it all I was none the wiser, but by burning the midnight oil found sufficient time to study for, and pass, my banking exams which comprised five subjects: English, Commercial Geography, Economics, Basic Principles of Law and Accountancy. The first three were a doddle but for the uninitiated, the latter two required considerable study. To this day I still remember the Carbolic Smoke Ball Company featuring somewhere in the law of contract. Having achieved the requisite qualification I was, much to my pleasure, posted to Nairobi, to embark on a career which eventually encompassed places about which at the time I knew very little. The National Bank of India in those days were bankers to the Government in such diverse places as Aden, Uganda, Kenya, Somaliland and Zanzibar, operating throughout East Africa and the Indian sub-continent.

The Bank's terms of service were financially attractive with a first tour of three years followed by six months furlough, interspersed with a month's local leave. We were provided with a first class air fare and an outfit allowance of £150. In those days there were a number of tropical outfitters who specialised in lightweight suits, ant-proof trunks and wardrobes to cater for every social and climatic contingency. I seem to recollect that Alkits of Cambridge Circus was a recommended source. Resisting the temptation of blowing the lot on a mobile 'thunder box' I was nevertheless seduced by a fetching maroon cummerbund. Fortunately, as I was already in possession of a soup-stained dinner jacket and bespoke suiting there was a sufficient surplus after this modest expenditure to clear my debts and throw a somewhat drunken farewell party. Another attraction, although not of immediate appeal, was the Bank's retirement scheme offering a generous pension plus provident fund payable at the age of 55. The latter benefit, in those far-off days, was of sufficient magnitude to buy a decent size farm in Kenya, if one so chose.

My parents travelled to Heathrow to see their son and heir off but owing to an enormous crush at the first class check-in counter our farewells were somewhat truncated. Apparently Liberace was catching the same flight; he was off to Rome to have an audience with the Pope. I was thus swept through most of the departure formalities with his entourage, fending off hordes of adoring fans (his, not mine).

After Rome the flight was fairly uneventful, although Khartoum proved a shock as I disembarked into what felt like, on account of the humidity, warm soup. Having been led to believe from my history lessons at school that General Gordon had decreed that the centre of Khartoum be laid out in the shape of a Union Jack I was disappointed to see that from the air it was just a hotch-potch of architecture with no apparent grid system.

Not having travelled first class before, I found one of the delights of the trip was having an attractive air hostess at one's beck and call. In those halcyon days the hostesses' job was to be in constant attendance and not confined to pushing a trolley up and down the aisle. The chap in the next seat to me was a geologist with Shell Co. who spent the whole trip peering out of the window seeking some geophysical fault promising vast oil reserves. Conversely, I contented myself with chatting up the air hostess and reading Robert Ruarks' *Something of Value*.

II

East Africa

Having left a drab grey London one's spirits were soon lifted as we came into land at Nairobi early Saturday morning with a bright sun shining out of an azure sky and the distant Ngong hills a purple smudge on the horizon.

After a couple of bone-shaking bounces the aircraft touched down and shuddered to a halt, to the relief of all concerned. As the aircraft doors were opened one was met by the intoxicatingly alien smells of Africa. More surprising was the diamond sunlight and the cool invigorating air which made it easy to forget that one had landed virtually on the equator.

Embakasi airport in the '50s was an oasis of tranquillity and calm. In those pre-charter-flight days there were probably, at the most, two international flights a day, with the smaller private aircraft diverted to Wilson's airport, situated the other side of Nairobi. It was at the time when British passports were issued sparingly and companies operating in Kenya were obliged to lodge deposits equivalent to the cost of a return airfare with the colonial authorities in case their employees 'misbehaved' and had to be repatriated for unseemly behaviour. With all these disciplines in place, one was greeted with a degree of courtesy verging on deference by smartly uniformed immigration officials, usually of Asian extraction, Europeans holding the senior jobs.

The old airport at Embakasi was a cheerful well ordered place and what it lacked in modern facilities it made up for in colonial charm. There was none of the chaotic clamour of today with travel weary passengers swarming everywhere. As such it was a relatively easy matter locating the Bank's representative deputed to meet me.

He duly materialised – a bronzed, good-looking but somewhat disinterested individual. It transpired that his insouciance was due to the fact that he had other, more important, matters to attend to – my arrival coincided with his picking up his girlfriend some 20-odd miles away at Thika. Having duly made this detour, despite being completely exhausted from the trip, I was whisked straight off to the Nairobi Agricultural Show, where the Bank had a stand dispensing liquid refreshment, mainly to our farming customers. Introduced to Messrs Horsfield and Cowmeadow, I wondered if I was still suffering from the hallucinatory effects of jet lag. As dusk fell the showstand closed and, along with some very inebriated young bank officers, I wound my way back to the Bank Mess/Chummery, located in one of the more salubrious suburbs, where I was allocated a bedroom. Much to my relief I was then allowed to unpack and get some sleep.

Nairobi in the 1950s, whilst not exactly a one-horse town, was but a shadow of the modern city it is today. The only buildings of note were the banks, some government establishments and the three main hotels, namely the New Stanley, Torrs Hotel and the Norfolk – the latter of Lord Delamere fame.

If history is any guide, Nairobi as an important commercial and administrative centre seems to have evolved by accident. By 1901 the Uganda railway, starting in Mombasa, had reached Kisumu. The building of the railway was fraught with many problems, not least the debilitating effects of dysentery and malaria on the indigenous workers compounded by the havoc wreaked by man-eating lions which further decimated the workforce.* Half way up the line the small shanty town of Nairobi was deemed an appropriate place to establish its headquarters, despite the fact that it was virtually in the middle of nowhere on land teeming with game of all kinds. The camp followers – a motley crew of traders, adventurers, 'remittance' men from aristocratic families and settlers – followed suit and made the railway construction camp of tents and tin shacks their base. Most of the workers on the railway were of Asian origin, having been shipped over from the sub-continent. They

---

* For anyone interested in this particular episode, *The Man-Eaters of Tsavo* makes for an edifying read.

complemented the established traders and, at the turn of the century with characteristic enterprise, the Indian shopkeepers were already beginning to dominate local trade. The National Bank of India was the first bank to open its doors in 1906 in a tin shack, which was at least in keeping with the then current architectural trends. By the time I arrived the Bank's main branch was one of the most impressive buildings in Nairobi. On a clear day, normally at the end of the rainy season, one could, with luck, when standing on the roof parapet, see both Mounts Kenya and Kilimanjaro, their snow-capped peaks glistening in the sunshine.

In the 1950s Nairobi was a pretty cosmopolitan place and despite being only a hundred or so miles south of the equator, as it was situated at about 5,500 feet above sea level it enjoyed a freshness of atmosphere and near perfect climate. First impressions were of avenues ablaze with colour from the tropical bushes and trees. All in all Nairobi was one of the most attractive and healthy cities in Africa with malaria and related diseases generally confined to the coast. It still had the spirit of a growing frontier town, the side walks of the streets being protected by canopies stretching out from the shops, mainly Asian owned, to protect pedestrians from the sun and seasonal rains. The most common roofing material was corrugated iron and the odd hitching rail was in evidence.

My first week at the Bank was spent learning the ropes, buying a car – in my case a new MGTF – and joining suitable clubs. The Nairobi Club and the Royal Nairobi Golf Club were deemed acceptable and appropriate places to hobnob with business acquaintances and friends. The Nairobi Club offered comfortable residential accommodation, a first class restaurant and a comprehensive library. It catered for most sporting activities, having a cricket ground, tennis and squash courts, bowling rinks and, latterly, a most attractive swimming pool. Importantly, it had reciprocal arrangements with a large number of London clubs, many of which, sadly, no longer exist. The membership in general comprised senior government officials and leading members of the business community. Then the more exclusive Muthaiga Club – renowned for its nefarious activities – was off limits to junior Bank executives, and was mostly the preserve of the settler/farming community, many of whose families stemmed from the British aristocracy. Its membership boasted a fair smattering of dukes, earls, lords and other titled personages who formed part of, or were on the fringes of, the bacchanalian excesses of the original Happy Valley Community. Many of the secondary nobility were 'remittance men'. The errant offspring of distinguished families packed off to the colonies to 'earn a crust' and escape scandals. Kenya seemed the preferred choice. Nairobi was not known as a 'place in the sun for shady people' for nothing.

I had hoped that on my arrival in Nairobi I would have projected an image of suave civility but this was frustrated by the repercussions of the Suez crisis, as a result of which my sea luggage with most of my wardrobe was diverted on a long and tortuous journey round the Cape.

My dilemma was heightened as my first made-to-measure shirt, tailored by Messrs Esquire (outfitters to the nobility), survived but one day. Having exercised the precaution of getting it carefully washed by hand, I was sunbathing in the garden of our bungalow watching with admiration as it fluttered on the washing line, only to see a passing African hop off his bicycle, leap over the fence, grab it and fast disappear in a cloud of dust. My insurance claim for 90 East African shillings was unsuccessful as, not having read the small print, I discovered I was liable for the first 100 shillings.

Fortunately, I had the presence of mind to pack my most prized possessions – records of Bill Haley and his Comets and Doris Day's *Once I had a Secret Love* in my hand luggage. With these discs, not yet available in Nairobi and rock 'n' roll all the rage, I was in immediate demand to attend otherwise inaccessible parties.

I remember with some embarrassment that I actually had the temerity, along with a compliant partner, to enter the Nairobi Rock 'n' Roll championship at Torrs Hotel. We were spurred on by a bet made in an alcoholic haze. Needless to say, despite the latest techniques learned at the Humphrey Lyttleton Jazz Club in Oxford Street, we came last.

My first job in the Bank was Cash Officer, which put me in charge of fourteen cashiers and coding and decoding telegrams. The latter was the most onerous task as, in addition to a complicated test key, every word had to be coded up or

11

deciphered – a long and tedious procedure, particularly as the Manager expected to receive the incoming telegrams decoded on his desk first thing in the morning. One had to get in early and, invariably, one was the last to leave in the evening. To this day I remember the code word for 'AND' was 'IMIET'. I also had to initial as correct numerous vouchers which flowed across my desk. Here I was guided by a grizzled peon (messenger boy) who sat at the opposite corner. Not only did he keep me copiously supplied with a constant flow of vouchers, but also with coffee and sticky cakes from the staff canteen. After several days happily signing away, I thought it wise to enquire from the peon what I was doing and called him round to explain. He looked nonplussed and eventually admitted he had not the vaguest idea viewing documents from this angle, as for the past 40 years he had read them upside down!

The dangers of getting into debt at the start of one's career were graphically illustrated at an early stage. A practice very much in force, and probably inherited from India, was the 'chit' system whereby credit was obtained from local emporia simply by signing a form of IOU. It was also the standard method of paying for drinks and meals at the various clubs. Rather like credit cards today it was a seductive ruse for tempting one into debt.

An early encounter with a by-product of the procedure was at the end of my first month in the office when an unseemly rumpus arose not far from my desk. A junior colleague in charge of another department was surrounded by a posse of irate Asian storekeepers baying for blood. Apparently, the individual concerned had run up a considerable number of unpaid bills in the bazaar. Not being able to settle, in order to buy time, he had come up with the novel idea of putting all the unpaid 'chits' into a basket, shuffling them around and then drawing one with a flourish, which he paid on the spot. If any creditor became 'too noisy' his unpaid account would not be eligible for the following month's lottery. By adopting this method he staved off the inevitable for a considerable time until it finally got out of hand and he was reported to senior management. The Bank then cleared the outstandings and sent the errant officer back to the UK where, no doubt, disciplinary action was taken.

At the time, the Bank was anxious to build up its deposit base and had adopted an aggressive marketing ploy of encouraging many of the newly formed farming cooperatives, particularly the coffee-related ones, to open accounts with our up-country branches. While seeming a good idea on paper it did not in practice make economic sense, as thousands of cooperative workers opened accounts for their monthly pittance to be paid in and, on the following day, formed enormous and quite often chaotic queues to take their money out. With all transactions carried out by hand and many of the new customers not being able to sign their names, thumbprints became the only means of identification. These were not the easiest of formalities and quite often the subject of abusive argument, or so I presumed as the dispute invariably was conducted in Swahili through an interpreter. The whole rigmarole was a time-consuming exercise. As the most junior officer, I was shunted off at an early stage to help out at Thika and its then sub-branch at Fort Hall – both dusty shanty towns – some thirty miles north of Nairobi in the heart of the Kikuyu reserves where, not long previously, the Mau Mau had exercised considerable influence. Even at this embryonic stage of my banking career I considered the policy ill-judged. It seemed even more pointless when, at the end of the day, the books did not balance and one had to scour the day's entries late into the night with the aid of a Tilley lamp in an attempt to discover where the odd shilling had gone astray.

Elspeth's Huxley's book, *The Flame Trees of Thika*, had somehow conjured up in my mind a somewhat more romantic visual image than the actuality. In her day the countryside held for the early settlers a certain appeal. However, in the '50s it had mostly been turned over to coffee and sisal and, towards Fort Hall, native shambas in the Kikuyu reserves were a patchwork of thatched huts and unsightly maize. Apart from the Bank, a relatively modern building, and some grubby Asian shops selling everything under the sun, there were no buildings of note in Thika; open drains added to the generally depressing effect. Life for the expatriates was, however, reasonably tolerable. The Thika Club, complete with an eighteen-hole golf course, and the Ruiru Club with a nine-hole golf course, tennis courts, etc. catered for the drinking and sporting needs of the European coffee farmers. The Blue Posts hotel, sited just outside Thika, was near some quite dramatic waterfalls and Hollywood contrived to use the location for a Tarzan film – *Tarzan and the Trappers*. The offspring of Allen Oldham, a Bank colleague, was cast as the double for an American child actor playing the son of Tarzan. While the part did not lead to fame and fortune it at least saved his father forking out pocket money for the duration.

Virtually all of the senior executive staff were seasoned bankers from north of the Border and models of financial rectitude and probity – the NBI had a recruiting officer who went round the Scottish schools and banks. As such, the régime within office hours was strict and uncompromising. It was, for example, a sackable offence to leave the Bank keys unattended. As these were weighty in the extreme it was the practice to attach them to a chain, looped into one's trouser belt. We were also subject to surprise inspections from London to ensure the Bank's rules and regulations were strictly adhered to.

On one such occasion the inspectors set off the Bank's alarms which, amongst other procedures, necessitated the closure of the vaults and the breaking of the combination on the locks. Unfortunately, at this particular moment the Manager and his assistant were inside the vault checking some items in safe custody. One of my colleagues, on hearing the alarm go off, dashed down and slammed shut the vault doors, imprisoning the Manager and his assistant (who held the code to the top combination) inside. They could not be released for several hours as access to the combination in question was locked away in the Standard Bank of South Africa in Delamere Avenue – some miles away. They eventually emerged in no little discomfort and were not amused. George Shand, the colleague who had caused this fracas, could not be accused of dereliction of duty and escaped censure. He did, however, go up in the esteem of all the junior officers, which was quite difficult as he was already highly regarded through having been offered professional terms to play soccer for Aberdeen. George (no relation to the band leader) was not really cut out for a career in banking, and was dismissed when he got a local girl pregnant and was subsequently caught cooking the books for an inconsequential amount at our Masaka branch. Personally, I was sorry to see him go.

In the course of presenting the telegrams to the Manager I

14

met and fell in love with his secretary. In those days the bank not only recruited a nucleus of female staff from the UK but also hired local European girls, normally the daughters of bank clients. Nita Decker was a local girl – her parents were coffee farmers – and, as I quickly found out, she was an outstanding athlete. She represented Kenya at swimming (holding a number of records) and hockey, and she was no mean performer at squash and golf. Rather remarkably, she did not have the stature or androgynous looks of Babe Zaharias (the legendary American sportswoman) but was modelled along the lines of Esther Williams: a nubile figure with a pretty face and sunny smile to hone the finished product. The perfect girl, a combination of sexy and sporty, a titillating tomboy.

Despite some strong competition from her established swains, the combination of a reasonable golf handicap and a new MGTF prevailed and got me to the front of the queue. It also nearly put both of us six foot under. With no drink-driving rules in force alcohol was consumed without restraint at most parties. After one such function, held at Hoppy's Inn just outside Karen, I was racing a Ford Zephyr home when a roundabout suddenly appeared. The MG's brakes worked well but not those of the Ford Zephyr which hit the back of the MG, sailed over the roundabout and after a couple of somersaults, came to rest. Fortunately, the driver miraculously escaped with but a broken leg and, having felt the draught of air as the Ford passed over our heads, we knew we had literally had a brush with death. Hoppy, incidentally, was the public hangman; he owed his name to the fact that he had only one leg. Whether or not this was the result of a miscue in his rôle as the public executioner, history does not relate but, despite this handicap, with capital punishment still in force he was regularly in demand.

Space prevents me recounting all the other 'prangs' we had.

In retrospect this courtship was my undoing (or possibly my doing) as it was the Bank's strict policy that no new officer could get married on his first tour. This rule was based on the supposition that young, newly-recruited expatriates were expected to maintain certain standards, which quite often entailed living beyond one's means. Accordingly, it was not deemed appropriate to marry until the requisite lifestyle became affordable when

15

one could indulge and participate in all the social activities which went with the job. Apart from supporting a wife, the arrival of a family was very much an added expense as in most outposts of the Empire local schools were not up to the mark and convention dictated that children were sent back to the UK to be privately educated. While I could see the logic of the Bank's stance, it did little to quell my ardour and I was optimistic that my case might prove to be the exception to the rule. Being thus precluded at that stage from taking the honourable course we did the next best thing and, in today's parlance, became 'an item'. This provoked the understandable ire of the authorities and I was dispatched post-haste on relief duties to Zanzibar.

Zanzibar at that time was ruled by the Sultan – an Arab of Omani origin. It is considered the birthplace of the Swahili language and the island has a rich and romantic history. From here Livingstone started on his last great journey into the interior of Africa. Noblemen and Arab traders from the Persian Gulf regularly plied their trade in slaves and ivory and their influence can be seen in the architecture of the quaint narrow streets and the heavy brass-studded doors of the houses. The streets presented a lively scene and, for reasons which I did not delve into, men of high degree walked about in pairs hand in hand – a practice which I later discovered was commonplace in the Arab states.

Zanzibar was planted with acres of clove trees and copra palm, it also had an abundance of coconuts which formed the basis of the island's prosperity and rendered the administration self-supporting. The highly efficient colonial service neatly counterbalanced the cultured, rather decadent Omani Arabs who made up the Sultan's court. I had the chance to visit the adjacent island of Pemba which is very much a microcosm of Zanzibar.

My job was to help promote the export trade of cloves to Indonesia where, apparently, they are used to spice up the local cigarettes. It was my first experience of working in a relatively small branch. The allocation of labour predictably fell heavily on the most junior officer. At times I was close to despair as a mountain of work piled up, some of it incomprehensible, while the Manager pushed off early to play

16

his evening game of golf or tennis. Fortunately, senior Asian supervisors were on hand to help guide and instruct. They were remarkably loyal and helpful, bearing in mind the considerable disparity in remuneration.

Conditions in the office verged on the Neanderthal. Partly to combat the oppressive heat the fans were turned up several notches and, at full blast, revolved at such a speed that anything unattached flew in all directions. The comparatively simple task of checking shipping documents became in itself a hazardous business with 'bills of lading' having to be firmly anchored down.

If working conditions were primitive, the safe installed in 1893 was positively archaic. With the passage of time, coupled with the baking heat, the heavy steel door was no longer a perfect fit. Accordingly, the approved method of closure entailed backing up against it and giving it a firm heel kick, assisted by a shove from the other key-holder. This method had claimed a number of casualties over the years so I quickly volunteered to be a 'shover' rather than a 'kicker'. All part of the learning curve, so I was told!

While the Manager's house was situated out of town, the accountant's flat was above the Bank, which, in turn, was next to the English Club. It was an extremely pleasant apartment. Scarlet bougainvillaea trailed round the edge of the terrace, and clumps of white oleander, massed just below it, stood out against the dark blue of the sea dotted with the white sails of dhows going into port. Once a week the Sultan's band in their full regalia played on the lawn behind the club while members enjoyed their sundowners. Accordingly, it was a useful ploy to invite guests to the Bank to coincide with the band's performance. One could not wish for a more romantic setting than to be dining on the balcony at dusk, the band playing on the lawn below framed by rustling palm trees and, as the monsoon wind died, a huge African moon rising to beat a silver path across the Indian Ocean. All it needed was a 'young' Elizabeth Taylor and gypsy violinist to make it complete.

That said, Zanzibar was hot – very hot. At night I used to lay under the mosquito net streaming with sweat and dreaming, amongst other things, of the cooler climes of Nairobi.

Pre-independence, the National Bank of India's Manager was

17

virtually the Finance Minister and a permanent member of the Legislative Council. If one played one's cards right and completed a full tour of duty (i.e. three years) one invariably ended up with an OBE. My sojourn, alas, lasted only a month and I ended up with nothing more than a better appreciation of trade finance, a love for the beauty of the island and the wonderful Arab-style camphor chests, one of which resides in my study today. The revolution in 1964 saw the overthrow of the Sultan and not long thereafter the Bank was nationalised.

On my return to Nairobi I found that I was again facing fierce competition for the hand of N.D., so sold the MGTF and purchased a rather smart blue TR2, the first car I had owned which could exceed 100mph. While getting me back in favour in the right quarter it subsequently proved a grave liability. Senior management were again displeased and, despite my protestations, I was shunted off to Entebbe the week before Christmas. Somehow the TR2 survived the 450-odd mile trip, completed in one day over some of the worst roads in East Africa, which apart from the odd stretch of tarmac were mostly dusty, rutted murram tracks.

The drive in itself was quite an adventure. Leaving Nairobi, one progressed higher through the tea plantations of Limuru and fertile dairy farms nestling in the rolling green hills punctuated by orange flame trees. Along the way, I passed groups of Kikuyu women with heavy luggage (often firewood) on their backs supported by a strap round their foreheads; their ears were slit and ornamented and their clothes dun-coloured, unattractive shifts. The menfolk were easily recognisable: they strolled behind, idly chatting as they herded their womenfolk forward.

Eventually, I reached the edge of the escarpment with the shadows of the clouds sweeping across the mighty Rift Valley, which stretched out below. This mysterious geological fault in the earth's surface begins in what was Portuguese East Africa in the south and terminates in the Dead Sea. I then descended rapidly to Naivasha passing on the way a shrine carved into the rock face by the Italian prisoners of war who, although conscripted, provided their considerable expertise in constructing this dramatic sector of the highway – no mean engineering feat. Naivasha was a recognised watering hole where, if my memory serves me right, I stopped for a beer at the Bell Inn situated in the main street lined by fever trees augmented by purple jacaranda in full bloom. Then onwards past the shallow soda lakes of Elmenteita and Nakuru where a multitude of flamingos nested. If disturbed they rose like dust beaten from a carpet in a not-to-be-forgotten pink cloud of flapping wings. After Nakuru the tarmac finished and the corrugated red murram took over on the steady climb up again to Eldoret and the fertile 'white' highlands. There you knew the world was round with the countryside dropping away in all directions as far as the eye could see. Thence, a meandering bone-shaking drive downwards to Tororo on the Uganda border. In those days there were no frontier formalities and, even if there were, I was travelling at such a speed I would have been oblivious to them.

Possibly the most treacherous parts of the journey occurred when overtaking the vehicle in front which invariably threw up an impenetrable choking cloud of red dust in its wake. Unable to see any car or lorry approaching from the other direction, the usual strategy was to press the accelerator at the critical moment and pray. I was lucky. This technique does not always pay off, however, and there were frequent fatal collisions.

Rather surprisingly, the road to Jinja and onwards to Kampala, the commercial capital, improved with stretches of tarmac placating the TR2's overworked suspension. When not avoiding interminable potholes, I found the journey provided incomparable sightseeing: valleys and peaks, lakes and forests, rivers and waterfalls and an abundance of wild life.

On arrival in Entebbe I was more than pleasantly surprised by the place, shimmering picturesquely on the shores of Lake Victoria. Entebbe, despite being the administrative centre of Uganda was no more than one main street, with a few Asian-owned stores and the Bank. It was a most lovely 'town', built on a horseshoe of hills overlooking the lake, vivid with flowering trees. At that time the Botanical Gardens were a famous feature. Sporting facilities were first class: a splendid golf course, picturesque cricket ground and active club with beautifully maintained lawn tennis courts and a swimming pool sited on rocks above the lake. Although Lake Victoria looked an inviting prospect in terms of aquatic pursuits, along with most other

19

freshwater lakes and rivers in East Africa it was dangerous bathing as bilharzia was rife. Other than swimming pools, the only safe place was down at the coast. 'Safe' is a word that rarely features in the African lexicon and the ocean outside the reef teemed with sharks while within jellyfish, spiked sea urchins and other 'nasties' were in themselves hazardous.

Entebbe boasted many splendid colonial bungalows with impeccably kept gardens, alive with colour. Apart from Government House and the Chief Secretary's House the other residences varied in size depending on the rank of the occupants. It was a very status-conscious station and the Government officials soon knew their place in the pecking order by where they were housed – the more exclusive the area, the higher the rank. Fortunately, by dint of working for the Bank one did not experience these social distinctions. There was also a splendid hotel which I quickly found out served a sumptuous and scrumptious buffet lunch on Sunday where one could fill up for the rest of the week for the princely sum of ten shillings – 50p in today's currency. The airport achieved notoriety when the Israelis aborted an attempted hijacking there.

I received a most hospitable welcome from the Manager and his wife, Andrew and Jess Aitchison and their lovely teenage family. Apparently, I had been called up at short notice as my predecessor, Vic Sword, had been despatched back to the UK. I was led to understand that he had taken a black girl as a mistress – a sackable office in those less enlightened days.

While one might question his judgement, his taste was understandable as the Buganda women were far more attractive than their Kenya counterparts. Not only were they more colourfully attired but, under their flowing robes, more statuesque and with wonderful deportment. It was rumoured that, to achieve the right dimensions, they not only balanced plates on their heads but also their bottoms! Sword had compounded the offence by stating in his defence that '...if the Kabaka could sleep with a white girl he saw no reason why he should not sleep with a black girl...'

The Kabaka (King Freddy) had just returned from exile, along with a bevy of white girlfriends of suspect pedigree. King Freddy was a dapper figure, educated at Cambridge and commissioned in the Grenadier Guards. Much as he tried, he was not really cut out for the hurly-burly of African politics and with the granting of independence he was yet again posted back to the UK where, if my memory serves me right, he was reduced to living in comparative poverty.

Jess was a real character and no stranger to Entebbe. She originally arrived in Kampala in 1937 to visit her brother, Sir Beresford Craddock, a prominent Uganda businessman and latterly a Conservative MP. There she fell in love with Andrew, got married, bore two children and, thereafter, followed the National Bank of India flag to such exotic places as Ceylon, Kenya (during the Mau Mau) and back to Uganda. In keeping with her status as a sister of a Ugandan Grandee Jess was a great stickler for appearances. Come high days and holidays, she would retrieve her beloved fur stole from where it was kept in a plastic bag in the freezer and, once defrosted, suitably adorned she would sweep down to the Entebbe Club and make a grand entrance – no difficult thing as it was quite a sight in equatorial Africa. But she was even better known for her culinary prowess – very much a legend in her own lunchtime, the Fanny Cradock of East Africa. While she could hardly be described as a 'domestic goddess', she was certainly an earlier version of Nigella Lawson. A curry prepared by Jess was a repast of beauty, not just your standard take-away from the local Tandoori. Apart from the usual ingredients of chicken, prawns, rice and curry powder, she threw in mangos, nuts, raisins, avocados, bananas – a miasma of flavours. If after the third helping she detected any sign of movement amongst her guests, this was quickly snuffed out by the introduction of a selection of delicious puddings and cheeses. When Andrew retired from the Bank, Jess's fame was such that he was head-hunted to take over as secretary of the Mombasa Club and subsequently the Kiambu Club. Under their stewardship the size of the membership expanded in every sense of that word.

Both the son and daughter were good news and the parents anxious to keep them in Entebbe. I was, accordingly, delegated to play golf with the son most afternoons – Iain had a single figure handicap – and escort his lovely sister, Anne, to parties in the evenings in Entebbe and Kampala. On one trip to Kampala, wedged into the TR2, when taking a corner fast a cyclist suddenly appeared from out of the bush and we were forced off the road into a swamp and thence, miraculously, back onto it again – the skid marks were still in evidence six months later. On regaining terra firma we were cruising along at about 90mph thanking our lucky stars we were still alive when we hit a chicken, causing considerable damage to the car and more to the chicken. We eventually limped into Kampala where running repairs were done to both the car and our spirits. On another occasion I gave a lift to two nuns seeking transport to Kampala. Needless to say, it was a tight fit in a cockpit designed for two and rumour has it they were seen to cross themselves when disgorged at their destination, to the amusement of my bank colleagues.

I fondly imagined the TR2, with a glorious feral howl as the engine revved up, to be the most potent vehicle in Uganda until I accepted a challenge from the owner of a Chevrolet Corvette, which left me firmly in its wake when racing along the runway at the airport – having first been cleared by traffic control!

Regular sorties were made into Kampala, whether to sample the night life at the Black Cat, play golf or, with romance in the air, attend a clutch of weddings. A good friend and banking colleague, Robin Baillie, had won the hand of an attractive doctor, Liz Ordish. She was part of the medical fraternity at Makerere University (Mulago Hospital) which in those days had an enviable reputation as one of the major seats of learning in Africa. The wedding reception gave one a chance to chat up the European secretaries recruited by the Bank. They were housed in flats above a new impressive head office which had been built in the city centre and was now a major landmark. Kampala itself, being the commercial hub of Uganda, was not unattractive built, like Rome, on seven hills; the streets of mainly Asian shops were lined by flowering trees. The Bank's bachelor accommodation was in the aptly named Baskerville Avenue and the incumbents' reputation was fully justified by its canine connotations.

News of 'La Dolce Vita' had got back to Nairobi, and my intended, for once in her life, was obliged take the offensive and duly pitched up in Entebbe. Unfortunately, her fame as a 'star of the sporting scene' proved disadvantageous as her visit was reported in the Uganda Argus. This further displeased the

Executive in Nairobi and I was promptly despatched to Gulu where we had recently opened a branch on the Uganda-Sudan-Congo border. N.D., God bless her, followed in hot pursuit and we spent an idyllic weekend exploring the Murchison Falls National Park, mostly on board a dilapidated paddle steamer – shades of *The African Queen*, redolent of Humphrey Bogart and Katharine Hepburn. This area was, and still is, one of the wildest in Africa, with an abundance of game. The falls are a dramatic sight: here the River Nile, compressed into a narrow gorge, plunges through a series of roaring cascades to a river pool approximately 160ft below. Many species of game – including elephant, hippo and crocodiles, can be seen watering, feeding and sunning themselves. The crocodiles looked particularly sinister as they slid towards the steamer seeking discarded offerings from the lunch table, of which there were many. The standard of the food produced from the bowels of the boat by the African stoker-cum-cook was predictably crisp, overdone and barely edible.

Some years earlier I had stayed with the Percival family in Machakos, where Ernest Hemingway was putting together some thoughts for an American magazine outlining the times he had spent on safari and deep-sea fishing at the coast. Hemingway was a great admirer of Philip Percival, the legendary white hunter, and while I was staying in Machakos I copied some notes Hemingway had made which are reproduced here as they epitomise his elegiac prose.

'Philip Percival is the finest man I know. This statement covers very much ground, and is not intended to offend good friends. Most of us good friends know we are not as fine as we would wish, and are good friends anyway. Philip has only one defect. He is going to die, as all of us will. But no man will do it better or give it less importance. He has been retired for three years, and never intended to take out a Safari again. He had no need to. With many forms of the true physical suffering, from sciatica, which is a pain men cannot bear, down through the simpler tortures, he was always cheerful, sound, solid, efficient and exemplary. He was also more fun to be with than anyone I know from any war or any peace. He loves the animals, and respects and knows them, as few other people ever can. And when things start to be bad, he is as young as when he galloped lion fifty years ago on the lovely broken hill at Wami.'

At the time Hemingway was rather battered in appearance, having spent a dissolute life; his prodigious capacity for alcohol and womanising (sometimes with the local Wakamba girls) now taking its toll. Shortly after leaving Machakos he took on an even more battered appearance when he and his wife miraculously escaped from their light aircraft when it crashed at Murchinson Falls. Fortunately, a privately chartered boat was on hand to take them on to Butiaba where an enterprising pilot, who had discovered their plight, was available to ferry them back to civilisation. In a remarkable turn of events the rescue plane crashed on take-off and, even more remarkably, the Hemingway party escaped yet again – although by this time Hemingway was not just battered and shaken but severely injured. Somehow they managed to make it to Masindi and then on to Entebbe. News of the first crash had already spread around the world and the passengers were assumed dead. Hemingway was subsequently much amused and delighted to read his own flattering obituaries which may well have played a part in his later receiving the Nobel prize for literature. This episode is covered in greater detail in Christopher Ondaatje's scholarly book, *Hemingway in Africa*, which is a compulsive and entertaining read for anyone interested in this genre.

Gulu was a one-horse town (or a typical colonial outpost) at the time the Bank opened a branch in 1958. There was no electricity (unless you were fortunate enough to have a generator) no telephone (at times a blessing) and contact with the outside world restricted to a weekly mail drop, delivered by an antiquated aircraft which, with luck, landed on a hazardous airstrip. Travelling from Kampala, one was obliged to traverse the mighty Nile at 'Packwach'. Here it was not quite so mighty – a broad flow of water bounded by rank swamps, swollen, murky brown and devoid of any beauty or interest. There were two methods of crossing – the main ferry was cranked back and forwards with a series of chains and carried the heavier cargo. This was supplemented by a make-shift paddleboat. They both had their disadvantages. With regard to the first there was invariably a long queue which often took hours to clear as too did the dense clouds of mosquitoes in attendance. The drawback of the smaller version was that it tended to list and, at times, sink if overloaded – a not uncommon occurrence. With a need to make Gulu before nightfall I gambled on the paddleboat and to my surprise made the far bank without any undue alarms and excursions. Once reached, Gulu township was distinctly unappealing: a single main street lined with some ramshackle shops owned and serviced by the local Asian community. Despite the rather seedy appearance of these emporia the owners could not be faulted on their versatility, stocking a vast array of items ranging from Huntley & Palmer's biscuits, maize, curry powder and tinned peaches to bolts of cloth, Bata flip-flops and, surprisingly, somewhat rusty tins of Andrews liver salts – a commodity not much in demand. Their medical counterparts, boasting suspect qualifications like MD, BSc Bombay (failed), were equally versatile, offering every conceivable assistance. Services were provided for dentistry, advanced surgery, a cure for venereal diseases and treatment for baldness. Somewhat incongruously, if custom was slack, those not afflicted with tonsorial problems could have their hair cut in a manner producing the then fashionable Elvis Presley quiff. While the Europeans were obliged to patronise the emporia they wisely gave the medical practitioners a wide berth, except in the most desperate of circumstances. In my case the need for an urgent consultation did arise as I was afflicted, shorty after my arrival, with the most diabolical attack of diarrhoea. Amazingly the prescribed dosage of copious amounts of sulphanilamide seemed to do the trick, at least temporarily.

Nevertheless, like most outposts of the Empire, it had its compensations. The members of the expatriate community were generally interesting individuals in their own right. The government sector was headed by a Provincial Commissioner supported by the usual complement of district officers, medical functionaries and public works department officials, added to which there was an entertaining smattering of BAT executives. Tobacco along with cotton being the main cash crops which sustained the local economy. Shortly after arrival I was privileged to be introduced to the Provincial Commissioner, Christopher Powell-Cotton. When I congratulated him on his feat of having shot an elephant with record breaking tusks, he modestly said I had got the wrong man. After three gin and tonics he was more forthcoming and mentioned that his father, late in the nineteenth century, had virtually shot his way across Africa, starting from the West Coast and finishing up in East Africa. He had bagged every conceivable type of game, breaking records en route. To celebrate his feats he had most of the creatures stuffed and shipped back to the UK. This animalistic Madame Tussaud's survives today and a museum has been built to house the collection attached to the family home in Kent. This esoteric monument to his life is still a popular attraction and was recently the subject of a TV documentary.

George Cook was in charge of the bank and, being on his second tour, had received permission to marry a Swedish beauty who was working in Kampala. They were the most entertaining and glamorous couple in Gulu and we became firm friends. Like most friendships forged in hardship postings the relationship has stood the test of time. Invariably, the Government Rest House was filled with eccentric characters attempting to wend their way from Cairo to the Cape, ensuring that the Gulu Club was always a lively watering hole in the evening. Drink, liar dice and a skiffle group provided the entertainment, with Scottish country dancing thrown in for good measure. A lack of females tended to confuse matters if two eightsomes were organised. However, one of the Agricultural officers had married 'Miss Troon 1957' which stimulated interest. Occasionally, BAT executives based in Juba in the Southern Sudan came down for some rest and recuperation. For these bachelors to make the lengthy and arduous trek to sample the questionable delights of Gulu would suggest that facilities in Southern Sudan were bleak indeed. I found it amusing when, in a TV travelogue, that intrepid explorer, Michael Palin, gave the impression he was a latter day Livingstone when he 'discovered' Juba, as though no white man had been there before.

The nine-hole golf course was designed to keep the mosquito population down and was maintained by denizens of the local prison – known locally as the 'King Georgey Hotely'. It was quite a daunting sight to see fifty unsupervised prisoners sweeping down the fairway, swatting at offending clumps of sunscorched grass with razor sharp pangas when one was playing a delicate approach shot over their heads to the green. However, in those pre-Amin days one's life never felt threatened, although my own nearly came to a premature and undignified end in somewhat unusual circumstances. One of our Asian customers had decided to open the first petrol station and, having acquired a site, dug a number of pits twelve foot in depth to accommodate the tanks. Prior to installation of the pumps the owner hosted a celebratory party and primed the attendant guests with copious amounts of neat whisky – unboiled water was suspect. Unfortunately, having imbibed enthusiastically, I was one of the last to leave. The night was pitch black. I lost my bearings and disappeared down one of the newly-dug holes. I must have knocked myself out for when I regained consciousness dawn was breaking. My initial cries for help attracted the attention of some curious dogs but otherwise my plight remained unnoticed until mid-morning when some workmen arrived. I was extremely lucky to emerge unscathed.

During my time in Gulu I was invited to dinner by one of the BAT executives, Robin King. Although at the time a bachelor he had just moved into spacious, newly-built married quarters. In keeping with the modern trend a serving hatch had been designed to facilitate the movement of dishes from the kitchen to the dining-room. Robin amusingly recounted the possibly apocryphal tale of his inaugural dinner party. While entertaining guests in the drawing room he was interrupted by strangulated cries emanating from the kitchen. Fearing that his cat had got caught in the mangle he dashed through to find his cook/houseboy firmly wedged in the serving hatch, still clasping a soup tureen. What had been designed as a time-saving device proved anything but as a lengthy debate ensued as to whether to push or pull. The solution, duly implemented, was partially to disrobe the houseboy and provide alternative directions.

The obligatory squash court, with no roof, was regularly patronised and a high lob shot, into the backhand corner, though seeming to disappear into the black African night sky, invariably produced a winner. The club swimming pool, such as it was, had been commandeered by large African toads. For those brave enough to take a dip it was rather like swimming in warm jelly, among the dollops of spawn not far from the surface. Certainly my digestive tract has never been the same since.

The Bank looked after the accounts of the White Fathers Mission near Lira. Most of the catholic priests were not averse to a glass of whisky in the evening and I was invited out to share a dram at their settlement. Judging by some of their helpers they also seemed to have struck up a close and friendly relationship with some of the local girls. The main mission building was a most impressive cathedral-like edifice, the ceilings depicting, along the lines of Michelangelo's frescoes in the Sistine Chapel, murals of the Good Shepherd herding his flock across green pastures. When I mentioned to one of the artists that the scenes looked strangely familiar, he admitted that they had drawn inspiration from a label on a packet of New Zealand butter.

As government bankers we acted as the local currency board, which controlled the issue of banknotes and coin. This was a tedious business for everything had to be carefully counted by hand and balanced. The low denomination coins had a hole in the middle which involved tying them up with string in bundles of ten – all very unproductive, unprofitable and time consuming. A more interesting diversion in those circumspect days was provided by the fact that in our efforts to educate the local populace into adopting the banking habit we had not factored into the equation the type of customer seeking an account. In the '50s in Northern Uganda clothes were considered a hindrance rather than a fashion statement and it was not unusual to find semi-naked clients presenting their 'credentials'. In such circumstances the act of taking a thumb impression, in lieu of a signature, had to be handled with some delicacy.

After a couple of frustrating months I received instructions to return to Entebbe. I looked forward to my departure anticipating, after the deprivations of Gulu, the more civilised delights that I hoped Entebbe had in store.

Having driven into Gulu in the TR2 with a bit of a flourish, I was obliged to leave in disrepair. Unbeknown to me the cotton lorries, allied to the rainy season had, on their convoys south, created a ridge down the centre of the murram road higher than the clearance of the TR. I was thus obliged to leave my pride and joy with my replacement and, after protracted negotiations, managed to hitch a lift on one of the offending lorries returning to Kampala. Here there were the usual delays as the African driver made a last minute tour of the township in an endeavour to round up additional passengers. They in turn were obliged to pay some form of fare, either in money or kind – bunches of bananas were normally the prescribed currency. Once accepted they were subjected to an uncomfortable journey, precariously perched on bales of cotton at the back. As the lorry belonged to one of our clients I was fortunate enough to be safely ensconced in the driver's cab. Whether our full complement of passengers survived the journey was debatable – certainly unheeded cries of distress emanated from the back as we careered headlong over the most rutted of roads.

I eventually arrived safely in Entebbe which was bliss after the deprivations of Gulu. Lawn tennis, swimming parties and golf now occupied the non-banking hours. An added bonus was that BOAC quite often changed crews at Entebbe, the aircrew recuperating at the Lake Victoria Hotel. For the transient visitor Entebbe had little to offer by way of entertainment, so an offer of a lift to the fleshpots of Kampala normally fell on receptive ears and my arrival at the Black Cat with a bevy of glamorous air hostesses was always greeted with relief by the Bank's allegedly deprived bachelors. In those days, when long distance air travel was still a luxury enjoyed by the fortunate minority, the job of an air hostess was much in demand and the selection criteria rigorous. Good looks and a helpful manner were not sufficient qualifications in themselves; the successful candidates also needed a 'proper' education backed up by some linguistic ability. As such the 'chosen few' were jealously chaperoned by their male counterparts. A date cadged, however tenuously, with one of these exotic creatures was always considered a major 'scalp'. Was Nirvana as good as this?

Unfortunately, my contentment was short-lived for I was designated a 'relief officer'. This entailed spells at such exotic places as Fort Portal (Mountains of the Moon), Jinja, where I had the misfortune to play rugby against Idi Amin – then a sergeant in the King's African Rifles – Kampala, Mbarara, Soroti, Masaka and Kericho. On this Cook's tour I was introduced to some of the idiosyncrasies of our managers. In Kericho, for example, the incumbent had an ancient kettle on a hob next to his desk which I presumed was used for brewing up his morning 'cuppa'. In fact, he spent most of the morning not in promoting the tea trade but steaming off the foreign stamps from the incoming mail. He proudly informed me that, over the years, he had accumulated one of the finest stamp collections in Africa.

On another occasion I was invited by a friend from Barclays D C & O Bank to play golf on a makeshift course at Thomson's Falls and stay at the now defunct Barry's Hotel. Our match was evenly poised when daylight virtually skipped twilight and the swift tropical night fell. It was my first realisation that dusk was a fleeting affair on the Equator. One minute the flagsticks were visible against a darkening sky, the next they were gone in the Stygian gloom, the first stars gleaming brightly above. Thomson's Falls was a small 'town' situated in the old 'White Highlands', not far from the Aberdare Mountain Range, and as night drew in so did the cold, making log fires a necessity at night. In the morning, with the sun rising behind the mountains and the ground covered by a hoar-frost, the air was like champagne and it was difficult to believe one was on the Equator. It was no wonder that many of the early settlers chose this area in which to pitch their tents and develop their farms.

The 'White Highlands' derived their name from the fact that the land in question was set aside for the white settlers. Up-country most of the dukas (shops) were Asian owned, although the better hotels were run by managers/owners of European stock. Prior to independence the majority of Africans were farm labourers or worked in the designated reserves. Even after independence there was no obvious change in the pecking order, although the black élite took over the governance of the country, their personal bank balances being bolstered by an influx of foreign aid.

It is a little-known fact that at the beginning of the twentieth century, in response to a plea from a leading body of Zionists, Joseph Chamberlain offered to make a tract of land available in East Africa to establish a prototype Jewish state. At the time a vast number of Jews were being subjected to and escaping from anti-semitic violence in Russia and Eastern Europe. Turkey had apparently refused to sell them Palestine! An exploratory visit was made to Kenya but the 'white settlers' under the leadership of Lord Delamere campaigned against an influx of 'undesirable aliens' and the idea of 'Jewganda' was dropped. The Block family, however, defied the odds and under their patriarch Abraham, founded a dynasty that at one time owned most of the prestigious hotels in Kenya.

I insert this aside as, unlikely as it may have been, had this proposal been accepted and followed through, many of the events and experiences described in this book would not have taken place.

My disorderly existence was thrown into further confusion when, 'out of the blue', I was instructed to proceed to Bombay post-haste. Apparently the local staff were out on a prolonged strike and assistance was needed to man the pumps. I duly packed and was driven to the airport by a colleague, Ken McLeod, in his new, prized Vauxhall. Here an alert official spotted that my yellow fever certificate was out of date. I was accordingly debarred from leaving and, after much to-ing and fro-ing the 'powers that be' decreed that poor old McLeod should take my place. He duly departed for India – never to be seen again. I think he finished up in Cochin. I was instructed to sell the Vauxhall, which I did at some considerable loss, and remit the proceeds to London. Had I finished up in Cochin no doubt this tale would have been very different.

Whilst I was roaming around Africa flying the National Bank of India flag, the Bank back in the UK was going through a metamorphosis. It purchased Grindlays, a long established but ailing institution with branches on the Indian sub-continent and Rhodesia. Along with Grindlays came their dynamic chairman, Lord Aldington, whose family had, over the generations, been strongly involved. After the merger, Lord Aldington was put in charge and the institution's name changed, firstly to National Overseas and Grindlays (NOG – unfortunate) and then to the more acceptable National and Grindlays which was ultimately shortened to Grindlays, along with the stylised elephant logo. This rapid change of identity not only confused the Bank's clients but also the staff. Some of our small branches in the outback lacked sophisticated facilities, so the manager himself was often obliged to shin up a ladder with a pot of paint or re-jig some already shaky lettering. I know – I was there!

One of the perks of working for the Bank was free accommodation, fully furnished to a very high standard. Senior managers were even entitled to a baby grand piano, an item which presented tuning problems in remote outposts like Hargeisha (Somaliland). The Manager's House was invariably the finest property on the station; the more junior officers normally lived in spacious premises above the Bank. During my time in Gulu, however, the Manager's House was a tin uniport with a thatch over the roof and the office located in an Asian duka, though in due course this was replaced by an attractive bungalow and properly designed premises. (How these structures survived the trauma of Idi Amin's régime I know not.) The Bank's main residence in Muthaiga (Nairobi), a 'Surrey Tudor style' mansion, eventually became the private home of the Vice President of Kenya.

While I was on relief duties in Entebbe there was no bank accommodation available and I took up residence in a compound of twenty small bungalows, specifically built to house the female secretaries/administrative staff seconded from the UK to work for the British Administration. These ladies were of varying ages, abilities and talents. Until I arrived the only other male in residence was an Agricultural Officer who could not believe his good fortune. Here were the potential ingredients for a salacious novel, possibly entitled *Confessions of a Bank Clerk* – but, alas, I was otherwise engaged.

One of my more important 'executive' jobs at the Entebbe branch was over-stamping cheque books with the Bank's new name. In those days a cheque book was considered a valuable instrument and in the wrong hands open to misuse. To ensure these were kept under close control I was duly locked away in the sombrous gloom of the cash safe to complete this onerous task. To break the monotony I found time to sift through the archives. Some of these proved absorbing reading as records stretched back to 1906 when the branch was opened. There was one particularly plaintive letter from an overworked manager who, after an extended tour of duty, found his relief had gone missing in Marseilles, presumably seduced by the local counter

32

attractions. As all this took place just prior to 1914 the records did not indicate whether a replacement was ever found. Nor did they mention what happened to the incumbent, who would have been in danger from bombardment by the Germans who then had partial control of Lake Victoria.

Most of the duplicates of correspondence were made by imprinting the originals on to a dampened copy by means of a press which was screwed into place. Carbon sheets were still not in vogue, even in the '50s and I have recollections of the manager's secretary screwing away at the close of business – in the nicest possible way.

Other than catering for the few Asian shops in the High Street the Bank's business revolved around looking after the Government accounts and those of expatriate officials brought out to administer the country. Unlike Kenya, Uganda was a protectorate and, apart from a few tea planters in the vicinity of Fort Portal and mining engineers at the copper mine at Kabale, very few Europeans had any stake in the country. Most of the coffee, sugar, tobacco and cotton plantations, if not in the hands of African cooperatives, were owned by wealthy Asians, although, predictably, BAT had a firm say as to how the tobacco was planted and marketed. In the '50s there still existed some ruling dynasties: the Kabaka was 'King' of Buganda and Princess Elizabeth of Toro was the offspring of the family who reigned around Fort Portal. She subsequently achieved fame as an international model – and some unwanted notoriety for frolicking in a public lavatory in Paris.

George Shand, en route to Masaka with his pregnant girlfriend, decided, under some pressure, that the time was right to get married. The ceremony was hastily arranged to take place at Entebbe church, picturesquely sited by the seventeenth green of the golf course. On discovering this George requested that I take time off and make up a four-ball on the morning of the wedding. It proved a tight match with substantial wagers on the side. To my embarrassment, but not to George's, with the game still all square at the sixteenth we saw the bride – incongruously decked out in white – with her parents and a few friends, standing impatiently outside the church. George insisted on completing the match, saying it was the time honoured tradition to keep the bride waiting. It is not often one putts out on the eighteenth green with one of the players in formal garb in front of a gallery composed of a despairing bride to be, apoplectic parents and a growing crowd of curious bystanders. I was not invited to the service, but George got married, in due course sacked, and is probably now enjoying a comfortable retirement in his beloved Aberdeen. Did the marriage survive? History does not recount.

One trip remains in my memory. Having regained the TR2 I set off for Nairobi on a Bank Holiday weekend departing late Friday evening from Soroti (Northern Uganda). Suddenly, the heavens opened. The windscreen quickly became awash with mud and the headlights pierced only a few feet of darkness. Having driven for at least an hour I encountered a 'roundabout' in the middle of nowhere. Edging round this I carried on for a further hour and eventually, espying some lights, thought that at last I had arrived at Mbale, the next port of call. Everything looked strangely familiar until I realised I was way off course and back in Gulu! Unable to telephone to explain my absence, I set off again the next morning and finally made Nairobi two days late. After a frosty reception I was allowed some brief R & R before returning to Entebbe by train. That was the end of the TR2 which I managed to sell at some considerable loss, investing the balance that remained in a Peugeot 403, a much more practical, though less glamorous, vehicle.

In Entebbe, as one of the few Europeans not connected to the Government, I was summoned on a regular basis to play golf with the Governor, Sir Michael Crawford, who played off a three handicap, which in turn helped me improve my own game. I rarely won, although I was able to take my revenge on his ADC at squash, having perfected the Gulu drop shot.

While in Entebbe my regular four-ball of John Budden, Leslie Price, Len Hendry and myself came to the easily reached conclusion that the standard of our golf was never going to merit winning any tournament of note. We were particularly envious of a magnificent trophy, 'The Prince of Wales Cup', presented by the Duke of Windsor when he played the course on one of his visits to East Africa.

To overcome this problem we clubbed together and purchased the largest trophy we could find in Kampala. It was duly christened the 'Lake Cup' and we had our names engraved in silver on the mahogany base. It was agreed that it should be played for on an annual basis. Being the first winner I lugged it around for a few years but after we all went our separate ways it was never played for again. Some 25 years later we met once more for lunch in London when the cup was ceremoniously handed over to Len for safe keeping. Sadly, John and Leslie have now shuffled off this mortal coil. I understand, however, that Len, as captain of Rosemount Golf Club, Blairgowrie, invites friends round to see his trophy cabinet, where a highly polished Lake Cup dominates a collection of EPNS monthly mugs and other assorted trivia.

During this time the late Queen Mother's aircraft developed an engine fault during her tour of East Africa and she was forced to stop over for a week at Entebbe. She, needless to say, was accommodated at Government House and I was privileged to meet her at some hastily arranged functions. In her late fifties (recently widowed) she was most attractive and charmed everybody she met.

It was at this point I was allowed to take some local leave in Mombasa. I buttered up the Hon. Sec. of the Entebbe Club and he penned a letter to the Mombasa Club under a reciprocal arrangement introducing 'Mr & Mrs Bignell'. A party of four was then gathered together in Nairobi and we set off in high spirits, firmly in the holiday mood. The drive of 300-odd miles was mostly through a landscape of unrelieved desolation – giant, flat-topped acacias, colourless scrub and ant hills – which petered out in a haze of heat. It was certainly thirsty work and, having consumed a fair quantity of Tusker beer, we decided to discard the empties, while driving at some speed, just outside Tsavo. Unfortunately, the doors of the Fiat in those days opened the 'wrong way round'. Thus, when we decided to ditch the empties one door flew off and disappeared down a deep gorge, never to be seen again. With the exception of the car's owner we all thought this hilarious and, in our inebriated state, wobbled our way into Mombasa. At the Mombasa Club, a most splendid edifice screened by palm trees overlooking the Indian Ocean, we were, despite our imposing letter of introduction, given a pokey room on the ground floor under the band-stand. When we complained, the manager, in view of our marital status, apologised and relocated us to a grand suite on the top floor, in the process turfing out my golfing partner from Kampala, Len Hendry. He took it in good spirit and whenever we meet now, normally in Cape Town, we have a good laugh.

Mombasa is undoubtedly one of the most beautiful and picturesque of all tropical ports and has the historic background that Nairobi lacks. The Club, which in those days served magnificent food, is next to the great pink-walled, battle scarred, Fort Jesus which stands above the harbour as a silent reminder of previous generations of Portuguese domination. Apart from the Club pool, the beach at Nyali was a major attraction with snorkelling and other aquatic pursuits to the fore. Although down at the coast mosquitoes were a problem at night there was something comforting about sleeping under a net which gave a great sense of security as it kept at bay a whole host of marauding insects. The downside was if the netting was penetrated one was kept awake trying to swat the offender – not the easiest manoeuvre. Rampaging ants too, presented a problem as once on the move they devoured virtually everything in their path. A simple safeguard was to place the legs of the iron bedsteads in tins of water. This acted as an effective repellent.

While on my stint of relief duties I had previously had a spell working in the Mombasa office having made the trip down from Nairobi by train, run then by the efficient East African Railways and Harbours (EAR&H). It was an exciting trip in itself. On this particular occasion, having pulled out through the tawdry native suburbs in the early evening, the air was clear after an unseasonable downpour. As the train rattled southward across the Athi plains the view stretched on forever and I was fortunate enough to catch a glimpse of the snow-capped crater of Mount Kilimanjaro rising above low-lying clouds and pink in the evening sun. It was commonplace to see herds of zebra, gazelle and families of giraffes. Occasionally one of the 'big five' could be spotted and it would be exciting to see lion on the prowl and elephants chewing on the thorn trees. One also might, if lucky, witness Masai herdsmen in their ochre red cloaks guarding their scrawny cattle.

The odd patch of dark green stood out against the parched straw-coloured plains. Looking out of the carriage window, as the night closed in one could occasionally see clusters of thatched mud huts lit with flickering oil lamps surrounded by a circle of cultivated maize and a few trees. The inhabitants invariably, either out of habit or curiosity, emerged to watch the train clatter by. Within the confines of the compartment there was a comfortable feeling of security, outside was the starkness and seemingly vast emptiness of Africa. Out on the plains there is no twilight and the sun goes down abruptly on the horizon affording five or ten minutes of golden glory – then darkness, the refracted fragments of light having disappeared.

There were two sittings for dinner. These were announced by a splendidly turned out attendant in a starched white uniform, gleaming EAR&H buttons and smart red fez. The impeccable ensemble was somewhat let down by the absence of shoes. He patrolled the first class corridors striking a gong. Not as resonant as the gong struck by the Charles Atlas figure heralding the old J. Arthur Rank films but nevertheless struck with sufficient gusto and a fine enough timbre to have the passengers scurrying to the dining carriage. Dinner was a splendid three course repast served with an acceptable wine.

Each compartment was equipped with a small hand basin and ceiling fan. In our absence the seats were converted into two bunks, one above the other, with welcoming fresh linen and downy pillows. Replete with a good meal and anaesthetised by the effects of the alcohol one then normally slept the deep sleep of the innocent – or otherwise, depending on one's companion.

The next morning one awoke to a cool pearly dawn with the heat of the day still hours away and the sound of the breakfast gong giving a wonderful feeling of well-being.

While it was a relatively simple matter looking out of the window, opening and shutting it threw up a number of complicated options. The addition of a 'mosquito screen' and a wooden slatted blind to keep out the sunlight permitted numerous and time-consuming variations on what should have been a simple manoeuvre. Once mastered the passing scene was worth the effort. Other than my travelling companion, all around was stirring and one looked out on a timeless world. Palm trees, mangrove swamps, citrus bushes and banana fronds had replaced the barren plains interspersed with thorn trees.

37

Also, more interestingly, the fashion of going topless was prevalent and semi-naked dark beauties could be seen going languorously about their ablutions. Some statuesque – forming a tableaux reminiscent of a Russell Flint painting. Others, aged and bent, from years of carrying firewood on their backs, were not so pleasing to the eye, with drooping milkless breasts.

There was nothing better on the journey than the breakfast of sizzling bacon and eggs, fresh Kenya coffee and warm buttered toast and lashings of locally made marmalade from the farms at Machakos. On rounding the final bend, as glimpses of glistening inland waterways gave promise of the Indian Ocean beyond, one was filled with the same sense of excitement and anticipation one got as a child when visiting the seaside.

During our stay we were privileged to be invited by the manager of our Mombasa branch and his wife (Louis and Peggy Gillespie) to sundowners at the Bank House. This was a most splendid residence built in the 'Riviera' style perched on a cliff overlooking the golf course, with the sparkling Indian Ocean beyond and the entrance to Kilindini harbour to the right. As we watched various cargo ships and cruise liners slipping by, with iced cold Tusker beers slipping down I thought what a perfect world. In terms of seniority being in charge of our Mombasa branch was not particularly high on the scale and at that moment I knew where my ambitions lay. To finish up as a successful failure and end one's career in such idyllic circumstances was no bad thing.

Unfortunately for the Gillespies they got caught up in a major coffee scam involving the Moshi Trading Company and, with the Bank suffering hefty losses, he was retired early and they settled down in Cooden Beach, a far cry from their tropical paradise. Louis, regrettably, died shortly thereafter but Peggy soldiered on and I heard at some stage she was President of the Sussex Ladies' Golf Union.

At the end of an ideal holiday, carless, we returned overnight to Nairobi by train (EAR&H) which was in itself a pleasure with the spotless carriages, clean linen, comfortable bunks and decent food and wine rounding off a perfect break – although the owner of the Fiat may have thought differently.

Just as life was returning to normality I was despatched back to Kenya – namely Kisumu – on permanent transfer. The drive to Kisumu was spectacular with some marvellous vistas unfolding. While the scenery in Uganda was in parts awe inspiring, generally speaking, traversing the country by car was visually dull, with tall elephant grass lining the roads, such as they were, and blocking out the panorama which lay beyond.

Kisumu was a pleasant surprise, not as pretty as Entebbe, but situated on the shores of Lake Victoria it boasted a thriving yacht club with GP14s and Hornets regularly raced. Also in those days a superb golf course having just recently hosted the Kenya Open Championship. Subsequently, the level of the lake has risen, permanently flooding the most demanding holes. One interesting local rule in force was that if a ball landed in the vicinity of a hippopotamus it could be replaced and dropped no closer to the hole.

Golf at Kisumu was nevertheless a pleasure. The course, aesthetically, was most attractive. Playing nine holes after work was always a close run thing as an African sunset is breathtaking but brief; the sun virtually drops from the sky and dusk turns to night within the hour. In the dusk distances become incalculable: flag sticks come suddenly near and yardages are thrown into disarray – the perfect excuse for the resulting incompetence.

A sunset seen with the flamboyant trees aflame with flowers against the glorious background of Lake Victoria was a spectacle not easily forgotten. Particularly so after the rains, when islands not previously visible made a purple frieze on the horizon framed by a canopy of storm-ridden clouds. As the sun made its rapid exit these turned from pink to orange to lamp black, a palette of colours not easily described which in turn were reflected in the molten gold of the lake. The last rays of natural light went as though someone had thrown the switch. Magical moments to entrance even the most disgruntled of golfers.

Being the capital of Nyanza Province there was a comparatively large expatriate community with all the banks, trading houses, oil companies, etc. having some form of presence. The various government departments were well represented. This, as always, contributed to an active social life. There was a considerable reservoir of acting talent and the local amateur theatrical society (KADS) put on many notable productions.

Life in Kisumu fell into a pleasant rhythm. I was provided

with accommodation above the bank which I shared with an immediate colleague Bill Irvine. The flat was spacious and comfortably furnished with three bedrooms adjoining bathrooms, a large sitting room, dining room and kitchen. It was surrounded by a wide verandah enclosed by gauze netting which overlooked a not unattractive floral roundabout at the top of the main street. The servants' quarters were at the rear. The manager lived in a rather grand residence on the outskirts of the town overlooking the lake.

Our executives were not best served by their initials. The manager K. Weir Smith was invariably know as Queer Smith and W.C. Irvine as 'Bogs' although on occasion some less sanitized soubriquets were bandied around. Bill, a canny Scot, very rarely played above his golf handicap of seven.

The day's routine followed a pattern. After a hefty breakfast of papaya, eggs and bacon, buttered toast and marmalade washed down with copious amounts of coffee we went downstairs, opened up the safes and tackled the morning's work. At lunchtime I repaired with packed sandwiches to the Kisumu Club for a swim and to practise my 'jack knife' dive which was designed to impress Nita on her next visit. Then back to the Bank to check the day's work. Provided everything balanced we locked up just after five and shot down to the golf club to try and squeeze in nine holes before dusk. Thereafter a 'few' drinks and back to the flat or the neighbouring Kisumu Hotel – a rather run-down hostelry – for a slap up supper. Tilapia, a local fish, was a favoured dish.

It was the laid down procedure that stocks hypothecated (pledged) to the Bank by way of security for loans granted, were subject to surprise inspections. This I found a rather fruitless exercise as most of the Asian owned stores were full of merchandise of obscure value to the uninitiated. Apart from bags of maize, tins of cooking oil and cans of kerosene there were a variety of items of indeterminate value. One shopkeeper produced a vast quantity of Christmas puddings which he said were 'very priceless and fully matured', the latter assertion evidenced by the rusty tins. After much totting up and debate, with soft drinks supplied at regular intervals, if there was any apparent shortfall fresh supplies were immediately brought in by circuitous means to make up the margin required. Normally from a neighbouring shop

40

where the missing items were said to be in 'safe keeping'. Very rarely did the Bank call up an overdraft in such circumstances as all were aware that a forced sale would be disastrous. Most managers lived in hope that they would have moved on or retired before precipitous action need be taken. Over the years many dodgy accounts survived or became prosperous depending on swings in the economy and the generosity of the Bank.

Saturday afternoons were invariably spent at the golf club or playing cricket and sometimes tennis. One of the better young tennis players, who in the school holidays participated in the Nyanza championships, was Shiraz Malik Noor, a student at Millfield School who had played as a junior at Wimbledon. Shiraz went on to pass his law exams and some thirty years later we were involved in financing a number of successful property deals in the UK. By then he was 'circular in circumference' and while on a health binge purchased Royal Jelly, a rejuvenating elixir derived from bees. He enlisted the unlikely combination of Major Ronnie Ferguson, Barbara Cartland and the Millwall Football Club to help promote the product and sponsored a number of polo tournaments. Alas, the company folded in a welter of recrimination and law suits and Shiraz died from a sudden stroke. Whether it was from stress or overweight was never established. Over the years he had proved a good friend and his death at a relatively young age was a sad loss.

The formula was changed on Sundays when, after a curry lunch, we were in demand at the yacht club to crew for the better helmsmen who raced their Hornets.

Regular dances were held at the club on Saturday nights and, while they were lively affairs, apart from a few nurses from the local hospital, there was a severe shortage of single females. In the holidays things tended to look up when daughters at boarding school in England came out to join their parents. Bill was particularly attracted to a pert young girl whose father worked for the Nyanza Cotton Board. With loving letters arriving on a regular basis from Nita I kept firmly to the straight and narrow.

As befitting its status Kisumu boasted a small hospital, outside which a group of forlorn patients regularly squatted swathed in bandages. They never seemed to move and in their mummified

41

guise it was difficult to know whether they were permanent fixtures or replaced at regular intervals by fellow sufferers with similar infirmities. I never found out.

In those days EAR&H's steamers plodded round the lake servicing ports with strange sounding names such as Bukoba and Mwanza in Tanganyika. Their expatriate captains were glamorous figures smartly turned out during the day in immaculate white uniforms dripping gold braid. Sartorial standards were such that they were obliged to change into blue and gold in the evenings even when calling at such outlandish placed as Kigoma and Musoma. Some were not sufficiently glamorous, however, to fend off bored bachelors who preyed on their equally bored wives. A friend working for Shell Co. had struck up a comfortable liaison in this regard and confided that in addition to affording much needed rest and recuperation it was a relatively safe arrangement. The designated love-nest provided commanding views across the lake. As soon as a puff of smoke appeared on the horizon heralding the return of the cuckolded husband, there was plenty of time to restore order and dispose of any incriminating evidence and make a safe retreat.

For my sins I was put in charge of the mobile bank (a reinforced Land Rover) which served the outlying districts. The most interesting stopover was Kakamega which many years before had experienced a mini gold rush. A few aged prospectors lingered on and every so often they pitched up at the Bank with specks of gold dust which we carefully weighed and advanced them a few shillings which allowed them to carry on eking out their meagre existence. Kakamega was quite beautiful, situated in pine clad hills high above Kisumu. In the 1930s it was something of a health resort and in keeping with most out-stations had a well kept and demanding golf course. The downside to this particular operation was that during the rainy season it was the most hazardous drive. On leaving Kisumu mist and drizzle reduced visibility and with the rain sluicing down as one drove higher the murram road turned to cloying mud and even driving in bottom gear with the four wheel drive engaged slithering around hairpin, rock strewn bends was extremely tricky. Precipitous drops did not help one's sang-froid. Occasionally, in conditions of scarcely conceivable asperity, the engine would stall and we would have to sit disconsolately by the roadside until it cooled down or help arrived from base. Sometimes a long and uncomfortable wait. As one navigated through this sunless world under lowering skies risking life and Land Rover to maintain some non-profitable business it did bring into question the Bank's advertised policy of 'Serving the Community'.

The mobile bank was an interesting concept. While on relief duties in Jinja I took over the run from Desmond Burnie, who was taking a spell of local leave. On arriving at the various ports of call I was invariably greeted by pretty, if disappointed, African girls anxiously enquiring the whereabouts of the said Desmond. It did not take me long to realise that the Bank's publicised slogan of 'Serving the Community' was open to different interpretations.

The manager of our Jinja branch at the time was a rather aloof individual, Commander Jack Ballardie RN (he had served in the navy during the war). When I enquired from a colleague what the Bank House was like, he admitted that despite having been at the branch for over a year he had never stepped across the portals. To remedy this situation we hatched a 'cunning plot' whereby we would kidnap Ballardie's prized and much loved Scottish terrier. We optimistically thought that if we returned the hound after a reasonable interval we would be welcomed in by the grateful owner, hopefully with a glass of whisky thrown in for good measure. All nearly went according to plan. The upside was that the 'dognap' was carried out with some success. The downside was that in burrowing through the thick and prickly hedges surrounding the Bank House we had been scratched to ribbons. The wretched dog having sensed blood then resisted our blandishments to come quietly and sank in his fangs at every opportunity. We eventually secured the hound and it was handed over to John Hutt at Barclay's Bank for safe keeping overnight. Having first concocted a feasible story of finding the beast lost and forlorn on the golf course, the next day we returned it to his, by then distraught, owner. Our thanks as we stood on the doorstep was a brusque 'Well done, boys' and we never got to see the interior. What did we get out of our tale of derring-do? Not much beyond some rather painful anti-rabies injections. There must be a moral in the story somewhere.

Most of the branch's activities in Kisumu centred around the Government accounts and running the Currency Board, where old notes were exchanged for new under the strictest security. The Bank had a fair slice of the commercial business which was mainly in the hands of the Asian Community. A large proportion of the surrounding terrain had been planted out with sisal. This was a crop that could endure climatic changes and was virtually disease free and was the fibre from which rope was made until synthetic substitutes were invented. Large areas, not necessarily fertile, needed to be set aside to make it profitable and it was predictably a tough crop to harvest. It did not have the glamour or attractiveness of coffee, tea or arable farming and normally the estates were owned and run by Greeks or Asians, who in Colonial times seemed to draw the short straw as far as land distribution was concerned. While the Asians formed their own clubs, ran their own schools, etc., the Greeks, although in some cases being relatively well off, were caught in 'no man's land' and were rarely accepted into the British clubs which formed the hub of the social life for the expatriate community.

Virtually every outpost in East Africa, however insignificant, boasted a club which was the meeting place for local farmers, government officials and the expatriate commercial community. It was the convivial centre of the social scene and normally provided facilities for 'games' of all kinds. On the sporting front swimming, tennis and squash featured and most had some form of golf course, however basic. The larger clubs provided residential and catering facilities and all contrived a monthly dance, if only to the accompaniment of gramophone records. Most had a sea-mail subscription to glossy magazines such as *The Tatler, Country Life, The Field*, etc. These were invariably a month out of date and were devoured by the old hands on arrival. However, for some newly arrived brides of English officials the nostalgia evoked by these periodicals as they attempted to cope with the privations of living in the 'sticks' made them envy their counterparts at home snug in their country vicarages. As a result quite a few did not last the course and packed their bags and returned to the UK shortly thereafter – with or without husbands.

In the 1950s, amazingly, there were 28 golf courses in operation in Kenya. Many of the smaller ones were maintained and tended by local farmers and their labour force. Ruiru was unique in having the same captain for 20 years and the Highlands Golf Club at Molo boasted the highest tee in the British Empire at over 9000 feet. Interestingly, I was later to play at Gulmarg in Kashmir which claimed a similar distinction; although on doing some research Molo appears to have the edge.

At Kisumu golf club I was introduced to the most lethal pastime I had yet encountered, the dreaded 'twenty-one aces' played with poker dice. After a round of golf a number of players, some willing, some unwilling participants, were invited to join in. The format was that the person throwing the seventh ace ordered the drinks, the fourteenth paid for them and the twenty-first drank them. The danger arose with the choice of drinks which could range from a pint of beer to a measure from every bottle on display behind the bar, mixed into a lethal cocktail. Other than the drinker, no-one else during the course of the game could touch a drop. Thus, one could finish up with the majority of the players stone cold sober and the remainder gibbering wrecks under the table. Fortunately, there were no fatalities, however, with stomach pumps being brought into play – the 'game' was subsequently banned on the grounds it could be injurious to one's health!

After one such escapade I was being driven back from the club late in the evening by my golf partner, Bill Irvine. Both of us were feeling the worse for wear when we ran into the back of an unlighted timber lorry which had broken down by the wayside. When I came round I found myself pinioned in the back seat by a large tree trunk – the fork of which had fortunately become wedged against the front pillar of the nearside windscreen. Without this obstruction I would have been decapitated. Bill in the driver's seat had escaped relatively unscathed, although the same could not be said for his car. Other than a severe headache I seemed OK and went into work the next morning notwithstanding the fact that my breathing was somewhat laboured. This condition persisted and the local doctor decided that a heavy dose of Friar's Balsam would do the trick. The diagnosis did not work and I was eventually x-rayed which revealed a broken nose requiring my nasal passages to be drilled. This was no bad thing as I was sent back to Nairobi for the operation which necessitated some rest and recuperation under the tender care of Nita. In retrospect Bill and myself were extremely lucky to get away without serious injury as only weeks later there was a fatal accident in similar circumstances.

It was at the Kisumu Club I had my first foray into public speaking. Much to my consternation I was dragooned into responding for the lassies at the Burns Night dinner hosted by the Caledonian Society for Nyanza Province, a formal function to which dignitaries had been invited from far and wide. Most of the Scots present were dressed up in their full regalia with family tartans to the fore. A piper was on hand to pipe in the haggis and the occasion was treated with the seriousness and reverence it deserved. Being my first Burns Night I was unprepared for the pomp and formality. As one of the later speakers my trepidation was increased by the fluency, erudition, sagacity and wit of the senior pillars of society who spoke prior to my slot. In those days most of the Colonial Service had graduated from either Oxford or Cambridge and there was no shortage of talented performers whose speaking skills had been honed in the groves of Academe. I realised rather late in the proceedings that my jokey and somewhat uncouth script was not suitable for the august assembled company and had to make some radical last minute revisions. I thus had the embarrassment of reducing a fifteen minute speech into five minutes of incoherent gabble. Fortunately, on such occasions, there was no shortage of the golden fluid and my shortcomings were forgiven in the ensuing alcoholic bonhomie.

During this period the 'powers that be' in Nairobi, probably bored with my shenanigans, unexpectedly gave permission for me to get married. N.D. duly arrived in Kisumu to celebrate but, strangely, with the restrictions removed we decided we were not ready to take the ultimate step and, after some soul-searching, went our separate ways. Possibly I should have seen the light earlier, bearing in mind the humiliation I suffered when swimming at the local pool. To keep abreast with Nita I was subjected to the mortifying experience of having to don flippers as she regularly swam her routine thirty lengths. Fortunately, we remain friends to this day.

Away from banking, I got thoroughly involved on the sporting front. Kisumu's main rivals were Kitale (situated on the slopes of Mount Elgon) and Kericho, populated by tea planters working for James Finlay and Brooke Bond. On long bank holiday weekends a contingent of us sallied forth equipped with golf clubs, cricket bats, hockey sticks, rugby balls (depending on the seasons) and challenged our opponents to at least three different games spread over three days, interspersed with heavy drinking. In retrospect some of the antics we got up to verged on the juvenile but it forged a collective team spirit and produced a great feeling of camaraderie. Some of the friendships formed have endured to this day.

When it came to leaving Kisumu at the end of my tour friends at the Club threw a swingeing farewell party. When I protested that I would miss the train taking me to Nairobi I was firmly given another drink. Unbeknown to me my luggage had been transferred to another car and the manager of East African Railways, Kisumu, had arranged for the train to be stopped as it climbed the escarpment to Eldoret, to await my arrival. Delays were not uncommon on this leg of the journey so I doubt if any of the other passengers were aware of the reasons for the hold up. Such was the 'devil may care' – some would call it 'arrogant' – attitude of the white population in Kenya post Mau Mau pre-independence.

Although this journal may suggest a travelogue of unadulterated leisure and pleasure, life was not all a bundle of laughs. The hours of work for the junior management were often long and demanding and at times unbearably tedious. All the ledgers were hand posted (except for Nairobi and Kampala) and should, at the end of the day, the books not balance by as little as a shilling all the entries had to be cross checked until the error was found. This could keep everybody stuck in the office until late at night with the inevitable disruption of one's social life. It was particularly annoying on New Year's Eve when the Bank, in keeping with tradition, balanced its books for the year. This involved a considerable amount of ancillary work, particularly if the books did not balance! On at least two occasions we turned up at the club's festivities some time after the witching hour, stone cold sober while the rest of the assembled merrymakers were well into their cups.

There were, nevertheless, subsidiary benefits as in my case, unwittingly, I was absorbing a wealth of knowledge and experience which stood me in good stead on future assignments.

In Nairobi I stayed with old friends, Liz and Robin Baillie (Robin rose to dizzy heights as a director of Standard Chartered Bank and a number of other companies) and then down to Mombasa where, prior to my sailing home on the MV *Africa* (Lloyd Triestino line), I lodged with the, as ever hospitable, Aitchison family who had decamped there from Entebbe.

On board I was delighted to learn that I would share a first class cabin with a friend from BAT, ex-Kampala.

Thus ended my first tour of duty with the Bank. Having been subjected to a whole gamut of experience and emotions I thought that from then on I would lead a well-ordered and humdrum existence – I could not have been more wrong.

III

Home Leave and Aden

To keep this tale of adventure moving forward sequentially I would mention that the voyage home was the ultimate in cosseted luxury with fabulous food served morning, noon and night. Fellow travellers in first class consisted of wealthy settlers, senior government officials and mercantile executives returning for a spell of 'Home Leave'. While the former providing splendid company, alas the female talent in the shape of secretaries, daughters etc. tended to travel economy class and, unlike the *Titanic*, intermingling was strictly forbidden and the lower decks were out of bounds. There was also a large contingent of Belgians on board fleeing the atrocities in the Congo; the army officers looked particularly splendid at dinner resplendent in their ceremonial dress uniforms. I did, however, pull off one coup. Having been coerced by John and Liz Fowler (John became president of the Kenya Farmers Union) to join their group at a fancy dress party, I was duly made up by Liz as a pregnant member of the 'Fishing Fleet' – those girls travelling to the colonies to find a husband. As such I unexpectedly entered the winners' enclosure waving a banner declaring: 'I should have danced all night'!

As befitting a motor vessel flying the Italian flag our first port of call was Mogadishu, then the capital of Italian Somaliland. We were warned by some of the seasoned travellers not to go ashore for fear of catching 'something nasty'. Like most warnings, the more adventurous amongst us saw it as a challenge. However, after encountering some particularly malodorous customs officials who came on board to check passports, etc. we decided discretion was the better part of valour. Our decision to stay within the luxurious confines of the MV *Africa* was justified when we witnessed the subsequent comings and goings.

49

Anchored, as we were, approximately half a mile off-shore, to get onshore involved being lowered overboard in a canvas contraption to a tender heaving on the swell below. This was all well and good but on the return trip, much to our satisfaction and amusement, some unfortunate passengers got caught standing astride the circumference of the canvas as it was abruptly hauled up. It was apparent that even if one survived the vexations of Mogadishu, the venture could still result in considerable discomfort.

In any event, from what we gathered, the town itself, other than having an imposing Catholic cathedral, was a grave disappointment with the dust and heat reflecting off some humdrum government buildings and no emporia worthy of inspection. Also, there was not sufficient time to catch 'something nasty'.

Apart from the 'unfortunates' consigned to the ship's surgery, most of us gathered on deck that evening for a sociable drink as we raised anchor and set sail. I joined up with some of the Belgians who, having been driven out of the Congo, were percipient in forecasting the demise of British rule in Africa. At the time, I argued, I thought convincingly, that the Government would hang on to its colonies – I couldn't have been more wrong. The monsoon winds which swept in from the Indian Ocean that night could well have been the 'winds of change'. While Africa would remain forever Africa, many of the names with connotations of the Empire would shortly disappear. At the time, however, all seemed well as we sipped our cocktails and watched the sun drop sharply into the ocean and the lights of Mogadishu fade away astern. For some there was a sense of nostalgia as it could well be their last look at colonial Africa; for others the feeling of well-being was heightened by the sense of anticipation of the delights ahead.

On arriving at the entrance of the Suez Canal the facility was offered to take a tour to Cairo and see the Pyramids and rejoin the ship a couple of days later at Port Said. The majority of passengers took the opportunity for a prolonged land excursion but the remainder opted for the comfortable air-conditioned grandeur of the MV *Africa*. I decided on the latter and, despite the slight inconvenience of having the duty crew employed in renewed exertions of cleaning, polishing and painting, it was on the whole an ordered and peaceful existence.

Goan stewards patrolled the decks serving iced lime-juice, and in the morning offered reviving cups of bouillon. To ensure prompt and efficient service some 'old hands' adopted the practice at the beginning of the voyage of tearing an East African 100-shilling note in half and giving it to the deck steward with a promise of the remainder on disembarkation. From what I could see, the procedure seemed to work.

Sailing through the re-opened Suez Canal was most interesting, with the hulks of sunken ships still awaiting clearance following the abortive conflict and feluccas with their billowing white sails an attractive distraction. When bored with deck games we occasionally took wagers and tried our hand at pelting unsuspecting pedestrians with oranges. But while, as a result of being high up on deck, we seemed relatively close to the road alongside the canal, it was always further than we thought and even the strongest arm failed to register a hit.

At Port Said those passengers who had taken the excursion rejoined the ship, hot, dusty and disgruntled. Most had found it uncomfortable, particularly the ride to the Pyramids by camel and considered the locals depressingly oppressive, thrusting all sorts of services and goods upon them at inflated prices. The locals had obviously won as those who had stayed on board looked with derision at the rather tasteless souvenirs loaded back on to the ship, most of which would probably never see the light of day again.

The 'Guli Guli Man' came on board at Port Said to amaze us with his magic, producing cheeping day-old chicks from some most unlikely places. Bum-boats attempted to hook up alongside, peddling everything from leather 'pouffes' to carved cigarette boxes inlaid with mother of pearl. If a buyer was tempted and a satisfactory price negotiated after much arm waving a complicated pulley system came into force with goods and money transferred up and down in baskets. Those passengers staying on board kept themselves amused throwing their spare coins into the water, where small boys expertly dived from the surrounding flotilla and retrieved them before they disappeared into the murky depths.

We duly went ashore to shop for souvenirs at Simon Artz – the Harrods of Egypt – and were predictably accosted by hawkers selling 'dirty postcards' and Spanish Fly. Although not put to the test, I was assured that the latter product was, despite its unappealing name, some form of aphrodisiac which had rejuvenating properties akin to Viagra. I contented myself with buying at an extortionate price a novel with an inflammatory wrapper, promising a stimulating read. Having got it safely back to the confines of my cabin, on breaking the seal I found I was about to embark on the *Official Tourist Guide to Alexandria* for the year 1950.

Port Said was as in the films, but sailing across the curve of the desert as the sun set was a new experience, with camels resembling a frieze against the rose and green sky.

Before turning in at nights the practice was to take a stroll round the decks invariably finishing up at the stern. If in a reflective or romantic mood there was something fascinating about gazing at the foaming wake luminous with phosphorescence.

The rest of the voyage drifted by in a haze of indolence (apart from competitive deck tennis) until we disembarked at Venice (culture to the fore) and wended our way back across Europe by train. At Paris we connected with the Gold Arrow with its comfortable wagon-lits and plush dining facilities – polished wood everywhere, shaded table lamps and liveried waiters evocative of a bygone era.

Arriving back on a cold, wet, overcast October day in England was somewhat anticlimactic. Having changed trains, the view from my compartment as we pushed out through the suburbs with grimy terraces drenched with rain, barely relieved by the dripping skeletons of trees, did nothing to dispel the gloom. After the crystal clear sunlight of Africa, possibly I was drawing invidious comparisons.

Well and lovingly as I was received by my family and friends, with the Mau Mau receding into history, East Africa was no longer a topic of interest and those I met were focused on pursuing their lives and careers in the UK. Conversely after the excitement of Africa I found the quality of life predictable and humdrum. Most of my chums had, in the interim, with a few exceptions, got married and generally worked in accountancy, Lloyds insurance or banking. Those with families were already finding it a financial strain to maintain a reasonable standard of living – by comparison on my inflated overseas salary I was well off.

Even the more adventurous of my friends seemed cocooned in their work or sport – with the odd bit of scandal to set the pulses racing. After the diversity of Africa it seemed a fairly insular existence.

While my parents politely attempted to show interest in my new life, overall they were more involved in showing me changes to the garden and were increasingly concerned about the possible repercussions of Gary Powers being shot down over the Soviet Union in a U-2 spy plane. I seem to recollect that *My Old Man's a Dustman* by Lonnie Donegan was top of the hit parade and we all enjoyed seeing the film *The Apartment*, which had just been released. Considerable ballyhoo was being given to a new contraceptive pill, which was being made available to the general public. The scaremongers predicted a collapse in moral standards, a view reinforced by the emergence of a cult following for a funky pop group from the Cavern club in Liverpool named the Beatles. At the time I had more compelling things to think about.

The highlight of my six month furlough was a month spent in Sweden at the invitation of some coffee planter friends whose family home was in a lovely village just north of Stockholm. With all their friends speaking impeccable English, and plenty of introductions to eligible daughters, it was great fun. With strict drink-driving laws in force it was quite often the practice to skate across the frozen lakes to parties at neighbouring homes. Predictably, this was incredibly painful for someone unaccustomed to this form of locomotion. Sprained ankles and similar injuries meant that interesting opportunities were lost by not being able to take to the dance floor.

It was just as frustrating on the return journey; while others skimmed gracefully I stumbled. Occasionally, however, I got up a head of steam and discovered inadvertently that to stop I needed to turn abruptly and grate the skates sideways. This expedient threw up a spectacular spray of powdered ice and was sufficiently impressive, I thought, to disguise my other inadequacies. The only downside was that my 'stop-start' technique left me trailing firmly in the wake of the delectable Sonja Henies gliding ahead.

However, once the basics were mastered, the ability to skate home on a crystal clear night, with the moonlight reflecting on the ice was indescribably beautiful and an experience not easily forgotten.

The sea trip back to Harwich I would prefer to forget. Shortly after setting sail I went along to the bar for a reassuring drink and fell into conversation with a rather distinguished looking gent who insisted that I kick off with a martini at his expense. My fellow traveller was a Mr Larsen who, as I found out later, had the Rootes concession for Scandinavia, which in those distant days was a profitable franchise and encompassed Humber, Hillman and Sunbeam cars. It transpired he had been on a number of hunting expeditions to Kenya, so we had something in common. After a few drinks he suggested that I join him for dinner as he always travelled with his 'manservant' who personally supervised the serving of food in his private suite. It seemed a good idea at the time as, with only the slightest suggestion of a roll, we glided out to sea. Dinner was a remarkably civilised affair with champagne and a dozen oysters for starters, followed by grilled steak and a decent claret. I eventually repaired to my cabin full of goodwill to all men. My feeling of repleteness was not to last for long. I was awoken shortly after midnight when all hell seemed to have broken loose with the ship pitching and rolling in the mother of all storms. In a semi-drunken state, thinking that the lifeboats offered the best hope of survival, I staggered up on deck only to see, as the lightning flashed and the rain lashed down, mountainous seas washing over the lower decks. Remarkably, no-one else seemed unduly concerned and, after contemplating a watery grave, I lurched back to my cabin. Alas, my exertions, along with the ship's, had taken their toll – every time the bow came thumping down, so too did my bowels and I was sicker than I have ever been. Fortunately, after several hours, the maelstrom abated but I was still a distinct shade of green as dawn broke. At last land could be seen through the mist and drizzle. Never had I thought that the flat, rather dull Essex coastline would provide such welcome relief.

Larsen predictably had a chauffeur-driven Humber car waiting to pick him up at the dock. I took up his kind offer of a lift into London. The Humber was a splendid limousine – all polish, chrome, leather seats and plenty of real walnut panelling to boost one's ego as we sailed through customs without undue hindrance. I was thereafter transported to my station in transport above my station. I also took him up on his even kinder offer of a discounted Sunbeam Alpine sports car – the first sports car to be produced with wind-up windows! He generously insisted that this was part of his allocation and surplus to requirements. Everything worked out extremely well as I was able to take delivery and ship it to Aden without paying tax. It was a long time before I touched oysters again and that was the last time I had contact with Mr Larsen.

The six months slipped by amazingly quickly and I was soon re-packing for my next tour of duty in Aden. I sailed from Tilbury on a wet, dank spring evening, it felt more like October. There are few sensations better than the irrepressible and involuntary smugness one feels when one is about to leave Britain on such a day and sail towards the sun. Even smugger when the vessel in question was the SS *Uganda*. A fine ship with the first class accommodation oozing mahogany and brightly burnished brasses and quality, if somewhat dated, fittings. Having unpacked I went up on deck for a last lingering look at the departing scene. Screeching gulls fought over refuse on the oily surface of the river. Further out cargo ships and tugs hooted and tooted as they jostled for position. There were the reflected lights of luxury liners and even the odd sailing ship as they rode at anchor. Tilbury was vigorously alive and its future as a commercial port of some significance looked secure, despite its much publicised labour problems.

Feeling the rain on my face with the ship's ensign drooping forlornly, the murky river and the grey and ugly warehouses, gaunt cranes silhouetted in the gathering dusk, and drably clad dock workers pushing off home, or on strike – in those days one was never quite sure – the sun-dappled barren rocks of Aden took on an added appeal. However, as the squat tugs pulled us clear into the mouth of the estuary, the sun suddenly broke through the leaden skies and turned the water to a liquid gold. As we navigated our way into the channel trailing smoke, the gleaming river ruffled by a breeze, the water whispering at the bow, the darkened fields replaced grimy terraced houses and England did not seem such a bad place after all – particularly with the cricket season in the offing.

The voyage was everything one could have wished – I was

put on the Chief Engineer's table. In those class conscious days the etiquette of travel was strictly observed. Along with the Captain's table – a much sought after slot and usually reserved for the 'high and mighty' – there were normally four other designated tables reserved for, and hosted by, the ship's senior officers. These tables aside, the allocation of seats at dinner seemed to be on a fairly random basis. All concerned, as far as I was aware, accepted where they were placed without demur. There was none of the unseemly jostling for the best tables, as appears to be the case today. Being on the Chief Engineer's table – according to the passenger list – was reasonably high up the pecking order. Ours was a particularly friendly and compatible group. We all got on so well that quite often and, unusually for a Scottish Chief Engineer, he invited us all up to his cabin in the evening for pre-dinner drinks at his own expense.

Loitering across a sunlit Mediterranean to Malta was a refreshing experience with a regular diet of Singapore Slings keeping our spirits up. One of our number, David Beatty, was the author of several bestselling books: *Wind off the Sea*, *The Proving Flight* and *The Cone of Silence* – which was subsequently filmed.

Shipboard romances were a predictable feature of every voyage. During lifeboat drill and while ashore at Malta I exchanged confidences with a particularly attractive girl en route to Rhodesia. Regrettably, she was travelling tourist class and 'never the twain shall meet'. However by dint of bribing a steward to leave one of the connecting doors open we arranged a tryst the night before docking at Aden. All was going according to plan and we were just getting to grips when my name came echoing over the ship's tannoy system. Apparently, having won the table-tennis competition and as the only passenger disembarking at Aden the Captain had arranged the presentation of the prize at that night's gala dinner. My unexplained absence resulted in one of his officers knocking on my cabin door with somewhat embarrassing results. Such was the officiousness of the system in force in those days that my misdemeanour was reported to the Bank's head office. I duly received a stern warning that my conduct was unbecoming and that I should at all times think of the Bank's good name, let alone that of the lady in question – how times have changed!

Approaching Aden from the sea, leaving aside the burning heat, one was immediately struck by two very different impressions. On the one hand, I was confronted with a panorama of newly built flats along the Ma'alla esplanade, displaying their pale-washed green, blue, cream and terracotta façades against the dark, forbidding aspect of the black volcanic hills. The stark, barren crags, with not a tree or flower or blade of grass to be seen spring straight from the desert sands and jut out into the sea as though daring the stranger to approach. And yet this apparent menace but thinly veils a welcome, for in the shelter of these same crags lay one of the busiest harbours in the world and, as I quickly discovered, a diverse and hospitable community.

Aden's then prosperity was based on being one of the largest oil bunkering ports situated, as it was, on the major sea routes between Europe, Africa, India, the Far East and Australia. These facilities attracted a large number of ocean-going ships and, in consequence, Aden became the centre of an important entrepot trade. This, allied to duty-free facilities, made it a mecca for shopaholic tourists disembarking from the liners. Being bankers to the Government plus a thriving import export business justified National and Grindlays Bank having five branches in the Colony. The main branch was situated in the central volcanic crater, now extinct, with a palatial manager's residence situated on its own peak nearby. I was fortunate to be seconded to the branch at Steamer Point, which catered for most of the various consular accounts and senior civil and service dignitaries, including the Governor. This provided an ideal springboard for getting óne's social life into action.

Aden had a full complement of banks – National and Grindlays, Chartered (now Standard Chartered) and the British Bank of the Middle East (now HSBC). The oil companies were prominent – BP, with a full-blown refinery at Little Aden, and Shell. There was also a full hand of international mercantile companies, BAT, Mitchell Cotts, Cable and Wireless, P & O, to name but a few. Added to this were entrepreneurs who had located themselves in Aden, since it had evolved as a major port – for example, Luke Thomas, Besse & Co., Athanas Bros and Paul Ries & Sons. The latter group acted as agents for a spectrum of goods ranging from Alfa Romeo cars to zebra skins from Kenya. Tony Besse's father had in fact generously endowed St Anthony's College, Oxford in celebration of his son's birth. Count Davico who ran the Aden Cold Store featured as one of our clients. It was an extremely profitable business, importing lamb from New Zealand, Upland Pork Sausages from Kenya and many other foodstuffs. He had a rather gruesome secondary trade – Aden being an extremely busy port, quite often ships arrived with passengers who had 'popped their clogs' en route to the Far East or Australia. With an inhospitable climate the bodies had to be frozen before returning them to the UK for burial if that was the family's wishes. Using his initiative Davico had set aside a special chamber for this purpose.

Most countries were represented by consulates of varying importance; Her Majesty's Government had the full range of colonial officials with the Governor, Sir Charles Johnston, at the helm. Most importantly Aden was a key strategic base for the three services with Air Marshal (later Marshal of the Royal Air Force) Sir Charles (Sam) Elworthy in overall command.

Apart from manoeuvres in the hinterland and quelling various local uprisings (the Communist revolution was but a distant prospect) the armed services, particularly the army, added considerable colour to an already hyperactive social scene. In keeping with established tradition and for reasons of climate all business activity took place in the morning. For example, most bank staff arrived at the office around seven in the morning and closed the doors just after midday. Thus, afternoons could be spent sleeping off the effects of the night before or indulging in the numerous sports on offer, ranging from the aquatic to the equine. To cater for all tastes there were numerous clubs – bathing facilities at Gold Mohur and Tarshyne (surrounded by shark nets), the Golf Club and Polo Club at Khormaksar, ideal sailing, tennis courts and various clubbable watering holes – the Union Club at Steamer Point and the Sweepers Arms in Crater.

Other than for the most dedicated of players, particularly during the blistering heat of summer, golf was put 'on the back burner', so to speak. The course was not a place of beauty, totally devoid of grass, scrub or shade of any description. Hummocks and mounds of hard baked earth were sufficient hazards in themselves, added to which rocky outcrops could destroy the best disciplined of rounds. I found the most humiliating part was putting on the oiled browns or 'greens' as they were euphemistically described. Being flat as pancakes, any putts way off line were embarrassingly evident as the 'trail' could be seen clearly in the sand. Fortunately, all the browns were carefully brushed on completion of the hole, so at least those following could not dwell on one's incompetence.

During the time of my tour three cavalry regiments were stationed in Aden: 17th/21st Lancers, 16th/5th Lancers and the 11th Hussars. They tended to set the tone with polo, race meetings, roulette parties and formal balls enlivening the scene – particularly when they brought their wives and girlfriends from the UK. At these parties we usually danced until the band packed up in the small hours when the sky began to turn grey and then yellow as dawn broke. We were quite often invited back to join General 'Jim' Robertson for a lavish Anglo-Indian breakfast. Such invitations were relayed through his ADC, a fellow Ghurka (Captain Robeson, if my memory serves me right). The General, a bachelor, enjoyed lively young company and plied us with mulligatawny soup, bacon and eggs, hot coffee and cold 'bloody Marys', aptly described as 'sundowners at dawn' or 'early morning nightcaps'. Thereafter, with the benefit of a second 'wind', we went off to change for an early morning ride along the beach at Khormaksar or water-skiing at Gold Mohur. Not a bad life!

Equally sociable were the King's Own Scottish Borderers commanded by Alastair Thorburn (who is still winning golf tournaments aged over 80!) and with 'private, l/c, sergeant' Speakman VC in their ranks. Being a traditional Scottish Regiment their mess evenings were different from the norm with dinner enlivened afterwards by Scottish dancing (all male) bridge and music supplied by a piper from the regimental Pipes and Drums in full regalia. I seem to recollect that they, or possibly one of the other Scottish regiments, recorded *Amazing Grace* and *The Barren Rocks of Aden*, both discs making the UK hit parade.

Incidentally, one of the Bank's executives, John Cruickshank, had as a Flight Lieutenant been awarded the Victoria Cross in 1944. While on anti-submarine patrol his plane was hit by U-boat flak which killed or injured his crew. Despite suffering extensive wounds he somehow managed to sink the U-boat with depth charges, and pilot his plane home, passing out several times en route. Typically, John never spoke of or publicised his award.

Most of the married service personnel brought out their families where and when suitable quarters were available. In those days before there was an awareness of skin cancer there always seemed an abundance of delectable bikini-clad daughters sunning themselves at the various bathing clubs. For some unknown reason their male offspring were left behind in the UK – probably boarding school or university being deemed more important. As a bachelor I was extremely fortunate. Equipped with an air-conditioned apartment, a new red TR3 (I had by then traded in the Sunbeam Alpine), speed boat (shared) and the use of two polo ponies I had a distinct advantage over the competing service personnel. By living in barracks and being only semi-mobile, reliant on their transport officer's generosity, they started at a distinct disadvantage. The icing on the cake was that I lived next door to the Aden Airways (AA) air hostess residential block, situated as it was in the rather grandly named Dolphin Square. While the accommodation was pretty good, the square itself was a sandy patch surrounded by some forlorn trees badly in need of water. The hostesses were a mixture of army officer's daughters, Italian and Lebanese nationals and some most attractive girls from Asmara – the offspring of Italian fathers and Eritrean mothers, a combination hard to beat. Their somewhat flamboyant motto was 'Always Available' or 'Alcoholics Anonymous', depending on the time of day and circumstance.

For a short time during this period I was obliged to share the flat with a fellow banking colleague, Morton Todd, whom I still see from time to time. Fortunately, our 'social lives' did not cross as Morton spent most of his time in Little Aden where he managed our branch and dated an attractive lady doctor seconded to the BP refinery.

Aden was a very friendly environment – and a pot-pourri of race and culture although the Arabs, Indians and Europeans tended not to mix (apart from the air hostesses!). I was lucky enough to share some great experiences, along with a speed boat, with two steadfast and most amusing pals, Hugh Freeland (Spinneys) and Ted Stanley (Commercial Union Assurance).

Water-skiing skills were quickly honed as the RAF helicopter pilots used to point out with some satisfaction, no doubt born from envy, that the surrounding waters were heavily infested with sharks. These fearsome denizens of the deep were no doubt attracted by the refuse discharged from the many ships at anchor in the port.

We jointly threw some rollicking parties and, to ensure that in turn we got invited to everything that mattered, scattered our invitations to all and sundry. On the basis that we could muster the most attractive bevy of beauties in the colony to grace our soirées, not surprisingly we got very few refusals.

A memorable diversion was the visit of the most attractive Princess Alexandra of Kent, who took the time to stop over in Aden for a few days on her way home from an official tour of the Far East.

The Governor gave a ball in her honour at Government House which, thanks to the Princess's personality, went with a swing. An enormous effort had been made to make this a special occasion with brightly lit lanterns, surrounded by historic cannons, a sumptuous buffet and the moonlit sea lapping below. I know Tony Boyle, the Governor's senior ADC, was totally smitten and remained so for many months afterwards. I had the privilege of meeting the Princess recently when she said she remembered the occasion well and how much she had enjoyed herself, but did not wish to be reminded that it was over forty years ago!

I played the odd round of golf with Mark Cato, now a 'popular' figure at Royal Worlington Golf Club. Mark subsequently achieved some notoriety on the radio and TV by playing popular melodies on his teeth! Although I water-skied most afternoons I was lucky enough to be taken under the tutelage of Bryan Tayleur, a senior cavalryman, who schooled me in the finer arts of horsemanship. Colonel Tayleur was very keen to promote and coach a service polo side capable of beating the civilians who, invariably, had the better mounts. With seven keen subalterns he needed an eighth to compete in the various practice matches and I was able to slip under the net. With reasonable ability and an acceptable handicap this enabled me to compete later in various countries and meet a mix of people I would not otherwise have met.

I was also extremely fortunate that the two senior managers I served under, Eric Williamson and Douglas Forbes, were, out of office hours, not only indulgent but actively encouraged their staff to enter into the Colony's social scene. Particularly if the contacts made resulted in business for the Bank.

One morning while I was quietly beavering away at my desk, a rather diffident American came into the office at Steamer Point and sought to open an account by depositing a cheque for US$10,000. This was a not inconsiderable sum in those days and, while assenting to his request, I mentioned that we would require suitable references. This was readily agreed and we duly got in touch with the originating bank in Texas. Their response came whistling back instructing us to accede to the client's every need as he was their major shareholder. The gentlemen in question turned out to be the legendary American oil tycoon, John L. Mecom, who in the '60s, unbeknown to me, was on a par with Paul Getty. Apparently, he and his team had decided to investigate the potential for seeking oil concessions in the Aden Protectorate. They presumably drew a blank – whether or not they had better luck in the Emirates I am not sure. To the uninitiated it nevertheless appears surprising that the discovery of oil seemed to grind to a geological halt on the borders with Saudi Arabia. Had oil been discovered in Aden, the advance of communism might well have been frustrated.

An advantage of working in the Steamer Point Office was that one met and assisted transient clients of the Bank introduced by head office. One such couple was Brigadier Myles Smeeton and his wife Beryl who achieved a measure of fame and are regarded with affection by yachtsmen all over the world. Their background and indeed their exploits were extraordinary by any standards. Before the war they had climbed into the Himalayan kingdom of Zanzkar and later climbed with the young Sherpa Tensing to 23,000 feet in the Hindu Kush – at the time higher than any woman had climbed in history. In the war Myles Smeeton was a distinguished soldier, having made a name for himself during the Burma Campaign. After the war as inveterate explorers they sought pastures new and despite virtually no yachting experience bought *Tzu Hang* a 46 ft ketch built in Hong Kong. The name derived from the

Chinese goddess 'Tzu', the protector of seafarers and 'Hang', loosely translated as 'family group'. In 1955 they set sail for 'anywhere that took their fancy' and finished up in Melbourne for the Olympic games. They then embarked on a voyage, both in their 50s, which became the subject of their famous book *Once is Enough*. Crossing the southern ocean the *Tzu Hang* during a violent storm 1000 miles from Cape Horn lost both her masts, the tiller and the entire cabin. As the yacht somersaulted Beryl was thrown into the water, but managed to swim back to the boat with a crushed vertebra. After baling for twelve hours and with an improvised rig, some five weeks later they reached the Chilean coast. Being gluttons for punishment, nine months later in her second attempt going round the Horn the *Tzu Hang* was again dismasted and rolled over west of the Magellan Strait – somehow again the Smeetons brought her safely to port.

I have described the foregoing at some length as, having sorted out a somewhat complicated transfer of funds, I was privileged to be invited to sail on the *Tzu Hang* up the coast as far as Abyan. The Aden Government considered the Smeetons sufficiently important to accede to their request to lay on a Land Rover to get me back to base. For me a unique experience and even more so after I had had the opportunity of reading their book. I believe they eventually retired to New Zealand.

A further introduction from H.O. instructed me to look after the daughter of the Maharaja of Faridkot. I had visions, if I played my cards right, of finishing up as an advisor to some princely state. The lady in question, however, turned out to be middle-aged, plump and, being highly intelligent, did not see me filling any advisory capacity. The reward for my services was a Christmas card, heavily embossed with the Faridkot coat of arms, which I received on a regular basis for the next decade.

Another sortie had some of us venturing north by Land Rover into the hinterland, ostensibly to shoot duck – we were accommodated overnight at Shuqra, courtesy of the Abyan Cotton Board. At the time, the long staple cotton was in great demand and proved a profitable source of income. Not finding any duck and somewhat inebriated, we recklessly and abortively discharged our shotguns at anything that moved. We soon discovered the error of our ways when there was a burst of answering gunfire from the surrounding hills. Some recalcitrant tribesmen were obviously as bored as we were – we quickly beat a hasty retreat without casualties, although the Land Rover bore testimony to their marksmanship.

On occasion, seeking a change of scenery, we visited Lahej, a province on the coastal plains whose boundaries to the north bordered the Yemen. The Sultan was a client of the Bank. Here the contrast to the starkness of Aden could not have been more marked. Colourful gardens, shade trees, citrus orchards and bananas grew in profusion along with the ubiquitous qat – more of which later. During our visit this apparent oasis of tranquillity was only disturbed by the buzzing of bees busily darting amongst the various flowering plants. On returning to their hives they produced an acceptable if distinctive flavoured honey. With the locals dressed in flowing robes and the odd cow mooching around it was very much reminiscent of a biblical scene – a land 'flowing with milk and honey'. All was not peace and calm, however, with fractious tribesmen regularly engaged in skirmishes with officialdom. These tribal grievances grew in number and were a precursor of the more lamentable altercations to come which eventually threw Aden into turmoil and the disastrous imbroglio of communist rule.

During my tour in Aden National and Grindlays Bank celebrated its centenary with various cocktail parties for staff and customers. Interestingly, the Bank, in the guise of the National Bank of India, had opened a branch in Hong Kong in 1869 to get itself into the main stream of China trade. Having recruited 'an old China hand' from the Chartered Bank and allocated £100,000 in capital to get the operation off the ground the said Manager 'displayed the most reckless disregard of his instructions and the most ordinary rules of banking'. The resultant losses shook the confidence of the Board in London and despite soldiering on the Hong Kong office was closed in 1880 and in 1884 the Shanghai branch was discontinued. Paradoxically, the Bank thought Aden a better bet following the opening of the Suez Canal in 1869 and commissioned a branch in 1894. It virtually had the field to itself until 1951 when the Eastern Bank opened a branch. The Bank's activities in Aden were reasonably profitable, assisted by being bankers to the Government. However, it hardly bears thinking about what might have transpired had Grindlays persevered in the Far East, where our main rivals, the Hong Kong and Shanghai Bank and the Chartered Bank, laid the foundations of their future prosperity. Also, of course, had Aden not been seduced by Communism, there is no reason why it would not have succeeded and developed an infrastructure along the lines of Dubai which depends not on oil but the far-sightedness of its rulers promoting both its trading links and opportunities for tourism.

Having expected to dislike it, after the glamour and rich beauty of Kenya, I thoroughly enjoyed my time in Aden and it is sad to reflect that now it is but a shadow of its former self and better known for its links with terrorism.

Certain events stand out in one's memory. One evening while sitting on the diving platform at Gold Mohur as the sun plunged quickly in a blaze of glory into the purple depths of the Arabian Sea I was idly chatting to the American Consul. We in turn were watching what we thought was some poor swimmer attempting the 50 yard haul from the beach to the platform. At one time he looked close to drowning as he gesticulated between flailing strokes. Just as we were about to take remedial action, the Consul recognised the waterlogged figure as one of his staff. Sadly, he was bearing the appalling news of President Kennedy's assassination.

My major sporting triumph was winning the Aden equivalent of the Grand National. This was much to the chagrin of some fairly experienced point-to-point riders entered by the cavalry regiments. Fortunately, I was mounted on a steed that managed to go through the brush fences at a speed faster than those who took the more recognised route. Shortly thereafter BP hosted a charitable event at their refinery compound in Little Aden. Several thousand spectators turned up to witness the main attraction, a relay race featuring teams consisting of a camel, horse, donkey and bicycle. The event proved utterly chaotic. I thought I had the good fortune to ride the donkey but taking over the baton from a camel in full flight, travelling at approximately 40mph, proved problematical. The bicycle 'ran' the final leg but pedalling 50 yards on a surface of churned up sand proved equally difficult. I still cannot recollect if our team finished, or for that matter whether any of the other teams passed the line, but judging by the noise as the camels ploughed out of control into the crowds, the paying public thoroughly enjoyed themselves.

Once a fortnight, in the winter, we repaired to the forces' open air cinema at Khormaksar. Normally it was turned into quite a social occasion with supper parties arranged before or after depending on the time and length of the film. Thus, most of the audience were smartly turned out, many of the men in mess kit or dinner jackets. I am not sure if certain nights were set aside for the different ranks but I have vivid memories of cigars glowing under a night sky and hip flasks produced at regular intervals. All very smooth and civilised. We watched such epics as *A Taste of Honey*, *Greengage Summer* and *Billy Liar* – the latter featuring a stunningly beautiful Julie Christie, making, I believe, her début. In the right company it made for an unexpectedly romantic setting, the cool night brilliant with a myriad stars.

For others, depending on one's dining habits or the attractions, or lack of attractions, of the film, the ambience had a snooze-inducing effect. On occasion the Army Kinema Corp's new stereophonic sound system was hard pushed to compete with the cacophony of snores generated by Aden's top brass. This fluctuating and at times unequal battle was brought to an abrupt halt with the playing of the National Anthem, which provided a rousing finale. The contestants, duly jolted out of their slumbers, leapt to their feet and stood rigidly to attention, pretending they had been awake throughout the proceedings.

Aden was the 'Friendly Station' and it would be a drawn out exercise to list by name the numerous individuals of both sexes who made my stay so memorable and enjoyable. I did at one stage have a girlfriend of unadorned pulchritude who will remain nameless christened 'Balloons' by Hugh Freeland – whether this was a structural observation born out of envy I was not quite sure but she certainly acted as a useful ballast on our speedboat. It would be invidious, however, not to mention two brothers, Christo and Stelios Athanas, scions of the Greek trading house bearing their name who featured strongly in my social life. With their swarthy good looks and sleek speedboats their beach parties in remote coves, inaccessible by road or track, were legendary. Predictably, they were always able to muster the cream of the crop and, as an assiduous 'hanger on', one benefited in more ways than one from their generosity.

An incident I would prefer to forget, but will nevertheless recount, transpired when a somewhat elderly Greek tanker broke down prior to being loaded up with oil. To avoid other shipping it was parked just outside the harbour. The requisite spare part took some time in arriving and a disconsolate and bored crew decided to throw a party on board. The Athanas brothers, the ship's agents, thought this would be an entertaining diversion and rustled up eight of us, the sexes evenly split, to enjoy the gaiety of the occasion. Initially, I was a willing participant. However, on arrival we had to climb a fifty-foot rope ladder which had been slung over the side and which dangled dangerously in the wind. The tanker, being empty, was riding high with the superstructure well out of the water. Until then I had not realised that I did not have a head for heights. I nevertheless bravely kept going, spurred on upwards by the miniskirted attractions of the girl directly above me, which helped keep my mind off the vertigo-inducing climb. She, unlike me, was oblivious to the dangers and found it all rather exciting.

Once on board there was not much entertainment other than copious amounts of food and some doubtful Greek wine. The crew were cosmopolitan in character, being made up of lascars of various hues and even the officers, other than the captain, looked a villainous bunch and not to be trusted with our, by then, inebriated female companions. A few gramophone records were put on but, unsurprisingly, the crew had other things on their minds than listening to *Michael Row the Boat Ashore* and *Zorba the Greek*. In fact, their only outstanding characteristic was their inability to make a party go with a swing. After a desultory couple of bibulous hours we decided to risk the rope ladder and return to the more fetching entertainments of Aden. As it turned out, the hazards of the ladder were avoided as we were released through a hatch somewhere in the bowels of the ship. Unfortunately, this was only a momentary period of relief. On the return journey, the ship's launch also needed a spare part and it could not be induced out of reverse gear. By then the sea was decidedly choppy and, what with the diesel fumes from the engine being blown back into our faces and the Greek food and wine also coming back with a vengeance, it all made for the most sick-making and uncomfortable of trips. An experience not to be forgotten or repeated.

Although not in keeping with the accepted yule-tide scene, Christmas in Aden was celebrated in the traditional manner. Either for nostalgic reasons, or purely out of greed, we managed to rustle up turkeys and plum pudding courtesy of Aden Cold Store and with wives and girlfriends providing all the accepted trimmings the subsequent feast was consumed with gusto (and Bisto). Boxing day was very much 'cold turkey'. There was the usual New Year's Eve fancy dress party at the Union Club where various groups of friends went to inordinate trouble to compete for the champagne prizes on offer. In my case, by now a willing conscript to such frivolities, I joined up with Mark Cato, the ultimate party organiser. He in turn mustered ten couples and, after much debate, we chose as our theme 'Fings aint wot they used to be'. We were togged out as a large Edwardian family replete with servants, a modern couple, the pill and 'the mistake', a fearsome child in nappies. Ted Stanley and myself featured as Little Lord Fauntleroys and, looking distinctly precious, somehow carried off first prize. The champagne was consumed before we had time to blink or for that matter register ownership. Mark Cato, regardless of his saturnine good looks, had drawn the short straw. Despite having orchestrated our triumph, he had the misfortune to miss out on the uninhibited dancing which followed as, encased in a capsule (as the pill), he found few, if any, attractive partners willing to smooch round the dance floor.

Spirits were revived on New Year's morning as, without any discernible break, once changed we started with a ride along the beach followed by breakfast, washed down with a mixture of Guinness and champagne. It all seemed totally blissful at the time although memories now of what ensued thereafter are distinctly hazy.

I disturbed this Utopian existence to take a spot of 'local' leave in Kenya and re-charge the batteries. All most enjoyable, looking up old friends in Nairobi and spending a fortnight

68

'topping up the tan' at the coast. Very much a 'coals to Newcastle' diversion. It was not a particularly memorable holiday other than for the fact that booking in on my return flight my hand luggage was conscientiously weighed by some over-zealous official. It was found that, coupled with my suitcase, I had exceeded my weight allowance by some fifteen pounds. From memory the surcharge was a pound a pound – a not inconsiderable sum in those days. To my embarrassment I then had to search through my dirty laundry in the hope of discarding surplus burdensome items. I eventually pared the excess down to a fiver which, despite my protestations, I still had to pay. This I did, much to the relief of the passengers who up till then had been patiently queuing behind but were fast becoming rebellious.

Aden, particularly during the winter months, was idyllic, it had none of the banality associated with the great international trading centres of the world. Greenery apart, there was no better place to be in the late afternoon of a delicious, cool, sunny winter's day. On leaving the Bank one had first to navigate the swarming tourist area of Steamer Point bustling with shirt-sleeved passengers, just ashore by launch to visit the mainly Indian and Jewish shops of the Crescent area in search of Japanese transistor radios, cameras, etc. which provided remarkable bargains owing to Aden's duty-free status. Departing the port one then set off for the bathing beach at Gold Mohur on a narrow cliff road with the azure sea breaking on the rocks below, golden beaches and, across the causeway, the black volcanic rocks of Little Aden etched on the horizon. Setting off in the opposite direction one travelled along the Ma'alla straight with its solid phalanx of six-storied multi-coloured apartment blocks to zigzag up the volcanic mountainside, through the main pass and down into the old city of Crater, situated, as its name implies, in the heart of the main, fortunately extinct, volcano. This was the hub of the Indian and Arab commercial life, populated by coffee traders, carpet merchants and all the usual emporia as well as many of the Government buildings. Here, as an alternative to the official currency, many of the traders used the silver Maria Theresa dollars which were readily acceptable, as paper notes in the hinterland were viewed with suspicion. Arabs in government service tended to dress formally, while their Bedouin cousins straight from the desert

69

wore flowing robes, with a coloured sash around the waist from which protruded the hilt of a traditional curved dagger. Over the far lip of the Crater one could see the beaches and blue sea stretching out to the wider air of the Protectorate beyond.

There was at the time no place in the world where the gap between reputation and reality was so wide as in Aden. Travellers on their sea journey eastwards invariably gave it a bad name, with memories of the hot, smelly streets of the Crescent with no interesting sights and nothing to do except spend money in the shops. Sandy Gall in his memoirs recounts: 'Aden is the hottest and dreariest place I have ever visited. The heat and the humidity were both intense and the physical structure of the place – a narrow strip of foreshore surrounded by bare, tortured volcanic mountains – intensified the feeling of being shut in.'

If one was stationed there and took full advantage of the social and sporting facilities, and with the sea being just the right temperature, life was more than bearable throughout the year. During the winter months Aden has one of the best climates in the world, and one could comfortably wear full evening dress dining and sitting out under the brilliant Arabian stars. The months of May to September were testing in the extreme, but with modern air-conditioning life proceeded unhindered and Kipling's 'unlit barrack stove' a dated misnomer.

With the Yemen now being strictly off limits to most travellers the following extract from a trip report compiled some years later is relevant in the context of my time spent in Aden.

'Arabia Felix, now known as North Yemen, was fabled through folklore, and history speaks of its fertile soil and progressive civilisations. Among its many dynasties it housed that of Sheba, whose legendary Queen Bilquis struck up a relationship with King Solomon chronicled not only in the Bible, but on the silver screen.

Sitting firmly in the middle of this diverse land is the capital – the medieval city of Sanaa – located in a scenically stunning valley at an altitude of approximately 8,000 ft. It was here that I arrived, togged out in tropical suiting, to be confronted, on leaving the airport, with the worst floods in living memory aggravated by a complete absence of any drainage.

I was already feeling the worse for wear as, on leaving Jeddah, I had succumbed to the plea of a not unattractive American female for assistance with her baggage. Having willingly assented, it was then discovered that the task involved humping through customs some 50 boxes of medical supplies destined for a hospital in Sa'ada on the Saudi border. RLS was correct. 'It is better to travel hopefully than to arrive'.

I had pitched up in Sanaa in the quest for deposits and was well introduced as quite a few of the more prosperous merchants had filtered up from Aden following the communist coup and thus knew Grindlays well. First impressions, if one ignored the cacophony of motor horns (mainly Japanese), was that history had stood still.

Virtually all the buildings were constructed of clay and, apparently, with a few minor repairs, had stood the test of centuries. A rather ominous projection a few storeys up signalled the presence of the master bedroom with en suite toilet; it was always worthwhile having an umbrella handy in case of emergency – the firm message was never look up.

On the Friday, mine hosts kindly arranged a picnic in the valley of Shamlan where the Iman's old palace is sited. This was a most agreeable sortie, meandering through rugged mountain passes to the green oasis below. Closer investigation revealed that these lush pastures had been totally turned over to the cultivation of qat, a mildly narcotic plant which when chewed induces a feeling of well being and produces evocative images, one gathers, of 'celestial bunfights'.

The Northern Yemen was then the recipient of vast amounts of aid from the oil rich States, particularly Saudi Arabia, designed to maintain a friendly buffer zone between the capitalist North and the communist South. As a result, virtually all incentives to grow commercial crops such as the aromatic 'mocca' coffee have disappeared, and the whole land at first sight seems to have been turned over to the cultivation of qat.

Having chosen a suitable spot for the picnic, the main course was then negotiated with a nearby shepherd. Along with the 'guest of honour' tag went the appointment of chairman of the selection committee. This subsequently proved to be a disadvantage as one's choice, a bleating ewe, was promptly dismembered on the spot.

71

A barbecue was then prepared and qat featured as the hors d'oeuvre along with niblets of a small dove-like bird. Although not recorded in the Bible, it was probably on a similar occasion many years ago that the Good Queen Bilquis whispered in her King's ear, 'Why do we not put the qat among the pigeons?' From such simple beginnings legends grow!

After lunch, in the shade of a fig tree, the conversation revolved around such topical subjects as the downfall of Sir Freddie Laker (our Arab friends seem to view him as a modern version of Robin Hood) and the 1956 crisis. Although mostly in Arabic, one managed to cotton on to the drift of the conversation dealing mainly with the mistakes or otherwise of Anthony Eden. The names of the participants tended, however, to get fudged as Balfour featured prominently. Obviously the teachings of the Aden Elementary School had been well learned as, coupled with the effect of qat, the conversation switched from Cromwell to Wolfe and then on to Prince Albert. No doubt such talk was aimed at making the outsider from overseas feel at home, but one wonders how they entertain Japanese businessmen. All was concluded by the loosening of a few rounds of ammo into the air. This produced an unexpected bonus with more titbits for the pot. Virtually all Yemenis not only carry the traditional curved dagger but also the latest Russian weaponry.

Thence back to base. In case one erroneously gains the impression of a totally primitive existence, base in this case proved to be the very comfortable Sheba Hotel efficiently managed by the Taj Hotel Group of Bombay.'

Just prior to the end of my tour I received an invitation from one of the Aden beauties to a party at her flat in London. While sending a note that I would be unable to attend I mentioned in passing that Hugh Freeland was in the UK having taken delivery of a new duty-free Mercedes and that he would probably be happy to put in an appearance. This he did and with his image enhanced by his flash new 'tart trap' swept one of the attendees off her feet, proposed marriage and shortly thereafter brought his new 'bride to be' back to Aden. This caused considerable confusion as previous partners had to be discarded and Sally had to venture into a tightly knit somewhat jaded inner circle. This she successfully did, bringing a freshness and vitality that was needed. The marriage was duly arranged with myself elected as best man. Other than the all important speech my primary duty centred on escorting the bride and the maid of honour to a ladies' hairdressing salon on the morning of the big day – while the groom and ushers enjoyed a few hours water-skiing.

The service went off without a hitch and the reception was arranged at the flat of the general manager of Spinneys who fortuitously was out of station at the time. The plan was that towards the end of the reception the happy couple would leave for an undisclosed destination. Hugh had already taken his holiday entitlement – the undisclosed destination was a romantic two hour drive around the barren rocks of Aden with only the wind and the sea for company.

It was my secondary responsibility to ensure that the flat be vacated prior to their return. Unfortunately the reception got slightly out of hand and two hours after the scheduled finish the party, despite my best efforts, was still in full swing. The happy couple, full of expectation, returned on schedule envisaging a quiet, amorous conclusion to their day. Instead they were rapturously greeted by a heaving mass of humanity 'twisting the night away'. Hugh and Sally, with nowhere else to go, wisely decided to join the merry throng and some hours later I was able to shepherd the last drunken guests on their way. By then it was well past the witching hour and the newlyweds were sufficiently inebriated to suggest that we finish off the few remaining bottles of champagne. Not being privy to the last rites I assumed that all went well – if there were further hitches I was not aware as by then I had lost track of the proceedings. Several days later we agreed that a good time was had by one and all.

As my contract drew to a close I was so enamoured with the lifestyle I actually requested that I be allowed another tour of duty. We were however, expected to have a basic proficiency in Urdu and Arabic. In terms of passing our Urdu we had received lessons from an authorised munshi (teacher) who dressed himself in a flowing dhoti and obligatory pair of steel-rimmed spectacles, which provided the necessary gravitas. I suspect he was a highly intelligent individual as he professed fluency in about six different Indian dialects. We were never able to put him to the test as his English was pretty fractured. This, coupled with the fact that our Urdu was non-existent, meant that while we had some amazing linguistic jousts our skills in learning the language never progressed beyond the elementary. However, by contributing three bottles of whisky to the cause we were provided with the requisite diploma. I thought a further case of whisky would provide me with a certificate confirming that my Arabic was up to scratch. The Bank, however, saw it differently and decided my talents, such as they were, would be better employed back in Kenya.

It was with a heavy heart and decimated bank balance that I embarked on the SS *Canberra* (on its return maiden voyage from Australia) for the UK. I was flattered that about forty people took the trouble to see me off but, in retrospect, I suspect that, apart from having a party on board at my expense, the attraction was to inspect the latest, and one of the largest, luxury passenger liners in commission at the time.

Travel by ship in those days was somewhat different from modern cruises. It was always eventful as most passengers were kindred spirits full of anticipation of home leave ahead. Traditional customs were rigidly observed: white dinner jackets East of Suez and black once through the Canal. With the advent of air-conditioning, no longer did seasoned travellers have their passages booked on the port side going out and the starboard side returning home. By so doing the cabins escaped the worst of the baking sun and this practice was said to be the derivation of the word POSH.

This particular voyage was stimulated by an entertaining but somewhat bellicose bunch of tea planters and their families who had embarked at Colombo. The tea plantations had just been nationalised and many of the now jobless planters were returning to the UK, where their prospects were bleak. The majority were making merry in the duty-free bars of the *Canberra* before returning with a bump to reality. One was swept along on this false sense of jollity and camaraderie; with secure employment it made for me a most enjoyable voyage.

Gibraltar was our first port of call. A fellow passenger had remarked, on good authority, that the 'Rock of Gibraltar looks like an enormous lion, crouched between the Atlantic and the Mediterranean, and set there to guard the passage of its British

74

Mistress.' As such we all scrutinised the rock with care. I saw little resemblance but the more romantic amongst us gave it the nod of approval. The passengers were ferried ashore by tender but after the exotic visual images of the East I found 'Gib' disappointing. It seemed rather like an English seaside town with pubs, fish and chip shops and 'English' policemen on duty. The saving grace was the sunshine and relatively cheap goods, Dunhill pipes and tobacco being a favourite purchase. Someone suggested a visit to the cemetery which proved surprisingly interesting with headstones commemorating a number of men who fell at Trafalgar.

We sailed late that evening with a cold wind blowing from the shore; the following night we came into the Bay of Biscay. Despite the *Canberra* being equipped with the most modern stabilisers the ship pitched around causing considerable discomfort, the normally noisy and cheerful dining rooms notable for the empty places at mealtimes. However, on rounding Cape Finisterre the sea calmed down and spirits quickly revived, with the help of liberal doses of champagne.

The return to one's own country is in its way an emotional experience, sailing up the English Channel with familiar landmarks adding poignancy to the occasion. I had left some three years earlier when the grey, pervading wet swathed the countryside and was coming back to late spring when it is brought home that England is still a lovely country.

IV

Home Leave and Kenya (re-visited)

After going through the formalities of seeing the 'powers that be' at head office and being reunited with family and friends I set about planning how to spend my 'hard earned' six months furlough. A flat in Hove in the proximity of Sussex County Cricket ground was purchased and my TR3 polished and serviced. Quite a few of the Aden contingent had returned and the resultant parties and reunions threw up new relationships. One of the girls, Veronica Delderfield, had married a subaltern in 4/5 Commando and the wedding and reception were held in Sidmouth where the bride's parents lived. Her father was the well-known author of such books as *God is an Englishman.*

'Low Goal' Polo at Cowdray Park featured and one of the Aden 'belles', having completed a spell at finishing school in Switzerland, threw a cocktail party at the Hyde Park Hotel. This transformed the rest of my leave as after the reception a crowd of us went on to Quaglino's where I took a shine to a girl who had all the attributes of good looks, intelligence and a great sense of fun. Anthea Legge was, alas, just eighteen and I an ageing twenty-nine, which seemed quite an age gap at the time. She lived in rather splendid digs in Pelham Crescent. We got on swimmingly and I was invited down to meet her grandparents in West Sussex – her parents, coincidentally, were in Kenya.

The estate in West Sussex certainly impressed a humble bank employee; it was in fact, a bit of an eye-opener. A splendid house where the sun rose on the East Wing and set on the West – I seem to remember a Canaletto in the drawing room. What took me aback was the string of racehorses (trained by Noel Murless, ridden by Lester Piggott) with *Casabianca* one of the favourites for that year's Derby. Another horse, *Goldendale*, had just won the Gold Cup at Ascot. Apparently, the family wealth was founded on sugar – grown in Mozambique and shipped to Portugal. The shares were listed in London and were the continental equivalent of Tate & Lyle. Our relationship blossomed to the extent that, to capture our last moments together, I forewent one of the highlights of my leave and returned to Kenya not by the desired means of sea travel but by air.

A.L.'s father had just been seconded to the High Commission in Nairobi as the military attaché and I was destined for Fort Portal in Uganda. Fortuitously, the Bank's General Manager for East Africa was Eric Williamson (ex Aden) and he, without any prompting, had changed the line-up and seconded me to his staff. Thus, to our shared delight, we both found ourselves in Nairobi, although I didn't go down too well with the parents who, I believe, thought Mark Vestey, of meat fame (in Kenya with the Scots Guards), was a more desirable and eligible hand for their beloved daughter. However, with the support of friends we managed to sustain the relationship – despite A.L. hopping back and forwards to the UK where she was studying fashion design.

As one gets older some trifling incidents are recalled with remarkable clarity. More momentous happenings are lost in the mist of time. The following illustrates this perfectly.

Shortly after arriving back in Kenya I was waiting to meet A.L. at the Thorn Tree coffee shop when an old golfing friend from Kisumu, Fergus McCartney, sat down at the same table and, after a perfunctory 'hello', carried on reading his paper. It transpired he had not realised that I had been away for over three years and presumed I had been posted 'up country'. Fergus, with Kenya gaining its independence, had ceased working for the Colonial Office as a district officer and taken over the running of a coffee farm at Kiambu just outside Nairobi. He recommended that I join the Kiambu Club as, apart from a challenging golf course, it had a particularly friendly membership. On the back of his introduction I took A.L. to play tennis there. When we arrived the courts were empty and, whether or not it was the altitude or our ineptitude, our tennis, which was normally passable, proved distinctly substandard. To boost our confidence we lowered the net by six inches and thundering serves and decent rallies suddenly materialised with the ball sizzling over the net where previously it had dropped limply on the wrong side. Other players arrived and having watched our apparent competence with undisguised admiration, challenges were issued. We pleaded fatigue and, before leaving, surreptitiously raised the net back to its correct height. While I duly joined the club and participated in a number of golf competitions, when I was invited to play in the tennis team I modestly pleaded non-availability owing to prior commitments.

Sadly, our mixed doubles 'partnership' never materialised. With A.L. back in London and Nairobi full of counter attractions absence in this case did not make the heart grow fonder and we went our separate ways with, I hope, mutual regret.

The General Manager's office in Nairobi was certainly, in banking terms, the place to be. It was staffed by some splendid colleagues, Sandy Phimister, a scratch golfer, and George Cook (ex Gulu) becoming staunch friends. I actually took over from an old chum, Fraser McKenzie, who in later years went on to augment his pension in some style when he took over the reins as General Manager of the National Bank of Dubai. Coincidentally, his predecessor in Dubai was Sandy Phimister – in those day I am not sure if any of us knew where Dubai was!

All of the Bank's business in East Africa was directed and controlled from Nairobi, whether it was loans and advances or the refurbishment of bank houses and premises and the transfer of staff. Being at the hub I could at least keep a tab on my future movements, if any, and for once was able to plan my life accordingly. All correspondence was directed to the General Manager. He, in turn, distributed it to his minions to write a suitable response which he then signed off. This put us in a position of considerable power as we could thus disdainfully criticise our superiors in print knowing that they had no recourse to us personally.

George Cook and myself had the responsibility for investigating and reporting on the feasibility of opening new branches and new centres where the mobile banks could operate. At the time there was great competition with Barclays and the Standard Bank for having the widest representation. Needless to say, we took the most scientific approach. Equipped with a large-scale map of East Africa and a blowpipe we fired darts at random.

Should they stick at a populated junction quite often in the middle of nowhere, we would send off an unsuspecting junior officer to report on the potential. Amazingly, this approach occasionally bore dividends, with previously unexplored territory deemed ripe for banking services.

In those days the Banks worked Saturday mornings. My established routine was polo Saturday afternoon, followed by a party in the evening. Quite often we finished up at the Equator night club where we danced to the haunting melody Malaika, the great Swahili song which became a worldwide hit. On Sundays polo in the morning, then swim and lunch at the Nairobi Club and if still fit, golf in the afternoon and, quite often, the cinema in the evening. All in all, the perfect life.

Since my previous tour, with the advent of independence Nairobi had changed radically. With the influx of vast amounts of aid skyscrapers and new modern hotels were springing up all over the place. With its new-found prosperity came the inevitable traffic congestion and since the climate was reasonably predictable, I added a scooter to the TR3; the former enabled me to glide free as a spirit, a Vespa Valkyrie, through the steaming traffic jams and zip around Nairobi without hindrance.

When I arrived, the polo club was going through a period of metamorphosis, heavily reliant on polo-playing regiments like the Scots Guards, and the Kenya army for support. The former being transient, it was either feast or famine, so I along with some new recruits from Benson's Advertising Agency – Chris Knocker (later captain of Sunningdale Golf Club) and Guy Elkins – were made most welcome. The old stagers – namely Sir Derek Erskine (the galloping grocer), Peter Johnson, Bill Rawson-Shaw, etc. – provided the continuity. Conversely, polo as a game flourished 'up country' with teams based in Kinyatta (Gil Gil), Molo, Timau, Machakos, Nanyuki, Kikabus and Kitale producing a reasonably high standard. All these centres had their individual tournaments spread over three days with the locals providing abundant hospitality and accommodation, normally in rambling old farmhouses.

The houses of the settlers were mainly in that style of architecture which results from intermittent prosperity. Depending on a good crop, a chance windfall, the original domicile had been expanded to accommodate additional bedrooms, bathrooms,

79

etc. The birth of children, an influx of guests from overseas, often prompted a further burst of optimism. Most were built with local labour, utilising local stone; the roofs were either tin or thatch. With the addition of a veranda, covered with climbing bougainvillaea, they presented, despite their hotch-potch construction, a surprisingly welcome and attractive appearance. Normally, we were obliged to drive great distances along rough tracks. To find our hosts we followed signposts in the middle of nowhere which simply bore the names of the settlers in the surrounding area. The compensations were, however, many, as we navigated through countryside pleasing to the eye and of considerable interest.

As mentioned previously, being at the centre of power, I was able to cadge Saturday mornings off and play in most of these tournaments. Not only was it a memorable way of seeing Kenya in all its past colonial glory but I met and became friendly with many of the old established land-owning families. We also entertained on a grand scale and, on a regular basis, hosted teams from the various Cavalry Regiments based in Aden. Visits from the 10th Hussars and Inniskillen Dragoon Guards were particularly memorable. Geoffrey Kent, at that time serving with I.D.G.s, went on to establish the now well-known travel firm of Abercrombie & Kent. (His parents were old Kenya hands.)

By practising on a regular basis Nairobi could field two or three sides. The pinnacle of our achievement was winning Kenya's top handicap tournament, normally the preserve of the better-mounted sides of farmers and 'white' hunters from up-country. Our team consisted of a farm manager from Machakos, Peter Hannath, a racehorse trainer, Denis Lathbury, an actor/producer, Robert Young, and myself. Robert, who has subsequently achieved prominence as a film director of world repute was at that time married to Petal, the daughter of Sir Derek Erskine. Petal has since been subjected to some notoriety in the British Press by living with her current husband, the hunter David Allen, and ex-husband, Lee Harragin – a practice deemed acceptable in Kenya but convention-flouting in the staid suburbs of Bath. If the press headlines are to be believed Petal is part of a very unusual ménage à trois, the result of an astonishing life of infidelity, excess and ultimately redemption that had its roots in Kenya's hedonistic Happy Valley set.

Robert's influence in the film world ensured that any visiting stars of the silver screen normally finished up at the Polo Club. Our only non-European member in those days was 'Gabby' Sheikh, a smooth, debonair operator whose family fortune was based on a number of second tier hotels and some reasonably profitable property developments. 'Gabby' was at the time a confirmed bachelor and had all the accoutrements of a successful playboy – a large apartment in the centre of Nairobi (furnished in somewhat garish style with leopard skin sofas and subdued lighting), a hospitality box next to Lord and Lady Delamere at the race course and a large, flashy, yellow convertible Cadillac. Although he himself did not drink (in keeping with his Muslim faith) Gabby's parties were legendary and, by dint of keeping friendly with the Donovan Maules (who ran the local theatre), he kept tabs on the recruitment of any young budding actresses. To ensure he had first choice he quite often arranged to meet them at the airport on their arrival in Kenya; the Cadillac invariably came up trumps.

Sir Charles Markham, Bt. used to patronise the club and, when not selling wines and spirits, did a reasonable impression of Raymond Glendenning, commentating at the races. Beryl Markham looked in occasionally. Her book, *West with the Night*, has received much critical acclaim, recounting, amongst other adventures, the first solo trans-Atlantic flight from east to west. At one time she was a legendary beauty with many famous paramours, but in the '60s she was a rather frumpish, albeit successful, trainer and breeder of racehorses.

I recount the following incident as, while in itself of little significance, it demonstrates how times were 'a-changing' in the new Kenya.

Dr Nkrumah, President of Ghana, had recently been overthrown and in the retribution which followed his recognised No. 1 mistress, Genevieve Marais, was in danger of her life. Apart from her relationship with the good doctor Miss Marais fronted the Ghanaian TV news programme and, being cape coloured, was immediately recognisable. One of the Gilbey gin family had gallantly rescued her and flown her in his private aircraft to the comparative safety of Nairobi.

Predictably, on arrival in Kenya she was allocated to 'Gabby' to look after, much to his chagrin, and with my having a couple of spare bedrooms he tried to palm the responsibility for her welfare on to me.

Avril Harriman, the Nigerian High Commissioner in Nairobi (if I am not mistaken, I believe his son played rugby for England; how he qualified I am not quite sure) threw a party to which we were all invited. After more than a few glasses of champagne I was chasséing round the dance floor with Miss Marais when I felt a tap on my shoulder and an African gentleman enquired if I had a valid work permit. On responding in the affirmative I was told that it could be easily cancelled and Dr Mungai – the then Minister for Foreign Affairs – was of the opinion that I should take my leave, alone. Not fancying the predicament I was in, or for that matter Miss Marais, I took the advice and left. I can only presume Dr Mungai looked after Miss Marais' welfare thereafter.

The polo club regularly hosted parties and its reputation for pleasurable activities combined with plenty of booze ensured a full turn out. Robert Young, Bobby Knight and his sister-in-law, Trish 'hollow legs' Edwards, provided the cabaret and did more than a passable imitation of Peter, Paul and Mary. *Puff the Magic Dragon* and *Leaving on a Jet Plane* being particular favourites. A regular attendee was Errol Trzebinski whose novel, *Silence will Speak*, was subsequently used as the basis for the film, *Out of Africa*.

At one party the lovely Julie Felix, on a visit from London, captivated us with her beauty and voice, and had us all spellbound with her renderings of Bob Dylan's most popular numbers. We all thought her much better than Joan Baez and dashed out and bought her records.

Lunch parties regularly got out of hand. It was standard practice to throw in a couple of bottles of gin to add zest to an already potent brew of Pimms. With a large water tank adjacent to the clubhouse, as the effects of the alcohol took hold, partially dressed guests invariably decided to cool off and take the plunge for an impromptu dip – the resultant photographs were in much demand and offers to destroy the negatives subject of prolonged negotiation.

I was privileged to include in my group of friends the French Cultural Attaché, the grandly named Isabelle Costa de Beauregard. She was the ultimate diplomat, cultivating a wide circle of admirers. Not only did Isabelle host the most elegant dinner parties but she managed to attract to her table an impressive array of famous personalities as they passed through Kenya on business or holiday. To the delight of her female friends, Yves Montand pitched up at one function and, to the delight of her male friends, Candice Bergen put in an appearance at another. Miss Bergen was still relatively unknown and was making a 'B' movie in Tanzania, so she was not averse to being chatted up by the hoi polloi.

Away from the office most expatriates working for reputable international companies enjoyed a cossetted life style. This was not always the case for the offspring of the local settler community. Quite a few of the land-owning families were well-heeled but others, while being asset rich, were distinctly cash poor. I was particularly friendly with one such family – it would be embarrassing to mention their name, as at various times the Bank was obliged to take 'remedial' action.

One of the sons, a cheerful extrovert, occasionally sought 'a bed for the night' when in Nairobi. He had found work, in some-what unlikely circumstances, as a loss adjuster. Being of a hospitable, if impecunious, disposition, as a reciprocal gesture he organised parties at the family ranch, sited at the base of the escarpment as it dropped down to the Rift Valley. While it was the most idyllic location it was not the most productive or profitable of farms. For the 'bright young things' that received invitations the great attraction was a spectacular natural pool of unplumbed depths – fortunately free from the dreaded bilharzia.

It was a wonderful feeling, floating on one's back under a cloudless sky, with eagles and other birds of prey using the thermals to glide and swoop overhead. A quick reassessment of the situation was made when menacing vultures joined the circling throng; otherwise it was the most tranquil of settings. Having dived in off one of the surrounding high rocks, I found the caressing mud at the bottom of the pool provided a source of comfort and heightened the sense of well-being. This was quickly dispelled if something strange and unexplained was encountered in the murky depths. Although this was normally nothing more hostile than a submerged log, it promoted a momentary feeling of panic and quickly brought one shooting upwards to burst with a sense of relief into the reassuring sunlight.

After the frolics in and around the pool a barbecue was served. A return to Nairobi in the scented evening – replete and sun-tanned – rounded off the most pleasant of excursions.

At Christmas most of the 'social action' shifted down to Mombasa and Malindi. I was recently reminded that in 1965 Gerald Cubitt, Clive Oak-Rhind and myself called in some 'markers' and bummed our way along the coast, cadging festive fare and accommodation from generous and, at times, unsuspecting hosts. We were invited to spend Christmas Day itself with the Larice family. Mr Larice was the boss of a major Italian construction company and the family were famed for their ostentatious lifestyle, boasting a gold-plated dinner service amongst many other extravagances. The decision was taken to have lunch on board their luxurious motor launch, which seemed a good idea at the time. Along with their daughter, Fiametta, they had invited Gill (née Trayner) and Bridget Nye to keep us company.

After a splendid repast anchored just off the reef at Nyali, the rocking of the boat brought on a distinctly queasy feeling. While Mama Larice lay groaning on the bunk calling for 'just another peach' (she consumed everything in sight, despite professing to be critically ill) Bridget, myself and Gerald plunged overboard to escape the heaving boat and restore our heaving stomachs. We then disconsolately paddled around in the sea, keeping a sharp look out for sharks for the next half hour waiting for the return trip to the safety of the shore. Gill, unaffected, remained on board, getting burned and cross, and Papa Larice, a seasoned sailor, apparently unaware of our plight, contently tossed a line overboard seeking to hook anything that trawled by. On eventually returning to shore we profusely thanked the Larices for their hospitality, confided amongst ourselves that it had been the most fraught Christmas ever and headed up the coast to the less taxing delights of Malindi.

On another trip to Mombasa early in 1966 I was invited, along with some friends, to a party hosted by Anne Aitchinson and June Durrant, held at the spacious villa of the French Consul, which they were currently 'house sitting' in the Consul's absence. I was put up in the guest suite and, delving around in the medicine cabinet, came across some tubes of Retardex. According to the label this product had stimulating properties, pharmaceutically well ahead of its time. Presuming, optimistically, that it had been placed there for the benefit of guests I somewhat guiltily purloined a tube, thinking that I would find a time in the not too distant future when I could put it to good use. Some weeks later the occasion did, in fact, arise when I was due to meet up with an old flame flying into Nairobi with Aden Airways. Having taken the precaution of carefully following the instructions and anointing myself well in advance I duly repaired to the airport with an expectant expression, raring to go, to greet the lady in question. The intention was to whisk her off to my bachelor pad. Unfortunately, much to my consternation, the aircraft was delayed for over an hour and I had the considerable mortification of having to skulk around the reception area, in priapic discomfort with a newspaper held firmly in place to hide my embarrassment. The plane did eventually pitch up but the ensuing liaison would not have been a good advertisement for the product in question.

Kenya in those days seemingly endeavoured to maintain its suspect reputation for wife swapping and loose morals. The combination of bored housewives, armies of servants, perpetual sunshine and husbands quite often out of station on business, proved a potent formula. As a bachelor one was quickly drawn into this sybaritic lifestyle and at one stage I formed a meaningful relationship which went beyond 'beer and skittles'. Fortunately for both of us, the lady in question, who had a young family to whom she was devoted, had sufficient feelings for her absentee husband not to seek a divorce.

Kenya also provided the opportunity for uninhibited challenges. Some friends on the spur of the moment hired a helicopter and attempted to scale the twin peaks of Kilimanjaro and Mt Kenya the same weekend – needless to say, they failed. It was quite common for the up-country farmers, after a polo match, to fly their light aircraft down to Kilifi, north of Mombasa, for some deep sea game fishing, where blue marlin regularly featured on the menu.

Lunchtimes during the week were spent round the swimming pools of the Nairobi and Muthaiga Clubs where a regular crowd of sun-worshippers gathered. The legendary 'Grogs' Grogan, by then in his late eighties, a frail but handsome man, sometimes could be spotted at the Muthaiga Club reclining in the shade, sipping a pink gin. Other than to his rapidly declining circle of immediate friends, he was a rather remote figure but always had a kindly word for a pretty girl. He was, of course, famous for walking from the Cape to Cairo. (Previously I had always assumed he had walked from Cairo to the Cape – on a map it looks so much easier going downhill than the reverse!) Popular rumour had it that this prodigious feat was apparently accomplished to win the hand of a girl in marriage. Once achieved, no doubt distracted en route, he no longer wished to marry the maid in question. Another story that went the rounds was that he was in the employ of the British Secret Service and the walk was designed as a cover as he sniffed out intelligence along the way.

As one of the early settlers, Grogan had acquired an expansive property portfolio with his flagship the Torrs hotel, a favourite haunt of the older settlers. Occupying a prime position in the centre of Nairobi, opposite the New Stanley hotel, this was latterly purchased and converted into suitable premises by the Ottoman Bank (subsequently Grindlays) when they opened a branch in Nairobi in the late '50s.

If the weather was inclement we would pop into the Muthaiga Club, evocative of chintz and smelling of flowers and furniture polish, where an extremely good meal could be had for a very reasonable price. One friend, Gerald Cubitt, decided to throw in his routine office job and become a wildlife photographer. He became so successful he is now one of the top photographers based in Cape Town and accepts commissions from all over the world.

With old girlfriends from Aden Airways still flying to Nairobi and the polo groupies one was never short of female company. Following an introduction at one of Gabby's parties I was lucky enough to strike up a relationship with Malcolm MacDonald's stepdaughter, Jane Rowley, who had arrived from Ottawa. She was an extremely attractive girl in whom every prospect pleased – the flash of her ready smile enhanced her considerable charms. Malcolm was Britain's 'roving ambassador' to Africa, based in Nairobi. The MacDonalds lived in some splendour at Flagstaff House in Karen and with its own tennis court I was obliged to play some competitive tennis with the net at regulation height! I did, however, gain some kudos by recognising, without prompting, that two of Malcolm's collection of oil paintings were by the legendary equine artist, George Stubbs.

Malcolm's father was, of course, Ramsey MacDonald, the first labour prime minister. M.M. was the most extraordinary man and his unconventional attitude had earned him the title of the 'shirt sleeved' diplomat. He used to recount how, when Commissioner-General in South East Asia, he played 'blindman's buff' with Dyak maidens. He achieved high office in many and diverse countries: amongst other elevated posts he was High Commissioner to Canada in the early '50s; thereafter to India and Kenya in 1964. In 1965 he was promoted to a new post of special representative to the commonwealth countries in East and Central Africa. Along the way he spurned many honours, much, I suspect, to the chagrin of Jane's mother, but was awarded the Order of Merit in 1969. Despite his exalted rank he was remarkably unstuffy with ornithology, in the strictest sense of the word, featuring as his main recreation. Altogether a remarkable career and a remarkable man.

Jane and I really hit it off from the start and spent an idyllic weekend up in Molo staying with David and Anne Dicker (née Aitchison). En route I was given the responsibility of looking after the Bank's stand and dispensing hospitality at the Nakuru Show – this proved slightly more than I bargained for with a regular stream of polo-playing farmers popping in for a free drink and many staying on. It all slightly cramped my style, with Jane revelling in the attention of an admiring if inebriated throng, augmented by a Nairobi team of 'tent peggers' – a sport still practised and one of the highlights of the show. Just as the relationship was beginning to take root Jane had to return to Canada to further her studies. While we carried on corresponding the fickle hand of fate intervened, of which more later.

One of my jobs at the Bank was looking after visiting dignitaries and their wives – quite often taking them round the game reserves. I am now a strong believer that our destinies are determined by the cards we are dealt. By being heavily involved in putting together a non-banking programme for Lord and Lady Aldington's first visit to Kenya, I got to know both of them reasonably well. Thus, when certain plum jobs in Grindlays came up in the future, my name somehow crept to the top of the pile.

I was also secretary to the Bank's local Board of Directors – a not particularly demanding job, which mainly involved taking the minutes at some pretty unproductive meetings. Lord Delamere, very much looking the part, spent most of the time putting in fresh eye-drops and Lord Twining, whenever given the chance, regaled us with amusing tales of when he was Governor of Tanganyika. Lord Twining was consideration itself and, although in retirement a heavy drinker, he was the most affable of men. His wife, however, strongly disapproved of his tippling. At cocktail parties we had a coded system in force that if he requested a small gin he actually wanted a large one; stipulation of a tonic water with lemon meant a small gin.

The board meetings were rounded off by a sumptuous lunch to which the General Manager invited important clients – existing and potential. On the odd occasion I was called to make up the numbers. At such times I was positioned firmly below the salt.

About this time we recruited our first African executive, Lee Ngugi (needless to say, the nephew of the Finance Minister). Despite spending many years in Kenya I regret to say he was my first and only black African friend. Having lived some time in the UK, Lee had a thick skin and a great sense of humour. Predictably, he didn't stay long in the Bank and when last we met he was one of Kenya's most successful entrepreneurs. I was privileged when he sent his daughter to Malvern Girls' College to be made an 'honorary uncle'.

At the end of 1966, not being able to get time off to go down to the coast a group of us decided to stay in Nairobi to see in the New Year. While there were attractions of mooching along to the Muthaiga Club some friends in the wine trade, Nick White and Tim Hazell, had by circumstance found the ideal alternative venue. Without benefit of company accommodation and to eke out their meagre housing allowance they proffered their services to look after properties for non-resident owners. Being deemed 'respectable and reliable' they were able to work the system on a regular and mutually satisfactory basis. Over the festive season they had installed themselves in Armand and Michaela Denis's house at Langata on the outskirts of Nairobi. As was to be expected this was a spacious property, spectacularly sited and an ideal location for giving a party. For me it was particularly nostalgic as it was the Denis's TV series, 'Filming Wild Animals', produced some fifteen years previously, which had drawn me into seeking employment in Kenya.

The house, what we saw of it, was full of interesting relics and souvenirs of their ground breaking wildlife programmes which in turn spawned David Attenborough's award winning series.

Armand and Michaela were still very much celebrities in their own right and it was a privilege to be introduced to them, albeit fleetingly. They had amassed a substantial fortune having augmented their income from filming by investing wisely in property in New York, Florida and Antwerp. When in London they normally stayed at Claridges. Although in her early fifties Michaela was still a strikingly beautiful woman. It was only afterwards I learned she had had her faced remodelled by cosmetic surgery following a bad car crash some years previously.

The party went with a swing and was very much a gathering of kindred spirits. Nick and Tim, anxious to preserve their reputation as responsible tenants, kept a firm hand on the proceedings and, with the majority of the bedrooms firmly out of bounds, there was none of the uninhibited carousing of previous years. Nevertheless, it proved a most enjoyable way of celebrating the New Year.

Life at the time seemed so comfortable I could have happily spent the rest of my time in Kenya but towards the end of my tour fate intervened and I met, yet again, the girl of my dreams.

Elizabeth Masson, the daughter of an executive with Caltex, had just returned to Kenya from London where she had completed a secretarial course. A friend of Liz Block (daughter of the hotelier Jack Block) they shared a flat together and suddenly injected fresh spice into the Nairobi social scene. At a charity ball I was fortunate enough to grab a dance with E.M. and managed to elicit a telephone number. In those days when not gyrating to the *Swinging Safari* one could canoodle on the dance floor and actually hold a conversation with one's partner. Not the present terpsichorean jumping up and down three yards apart with 'music' blasting one's eardrums. I was looking for someone to take to a dance at the Nairobi Club and Elizabeth agreed to come along looking ravishing in a white ball-gown. I subsequently discovered she looked even better in a bikini. The rest, as they say, is history.

With a view to furthering my cause I suggested a trip to the Mount Kenya Safari Club at Nanyuki which, at the time, was owned by William Holden. Apart from providing immaculate grounds, pool and dining facilities it offered stunning views of Mount Kenya. Many years before I had spent a week-end there in its previous guise as the Mawingo Hotel. It had been so built that from every window there are magnificent panoramas of the mountain with its snow-capped craggy peaks – sometimes wreathed in wisps of cloud, sometimes with its glaciers icy blue in the moonlight. Most beautiful at dawn with the rising sun turning its eternal snows to ethereal shades of pink. If this did not work nothing would.

The drive back to Nairobi was a smooth continuity of contentment with the last golden rays of the sun dropping behind as we drove over the escarpment. And then darkness with a vast canopy of stars above. I was marvelling at the beauty of life and nature when Elizabeth brought me back to earth with a bump when she mentioned she was just about to fly the coop and seek pastures new in South Africa. Spurred into action I proposed there and then and, after some hesitation, to my relief, was accepted. The Massons were somewhat taken aback and even though Elizabeth was not yet twenty-one, provisionally agreed (I was by then thirty-two). There followed a round of congratulatory parties and we were fortunate enough to be invited by the Earl of Portsmouth (Gerard Wallop) to spend a few halcyon days at his farm at Kitale. Gerard Wallop loved Kenya and he was one of the pioneers who successfully established and farmed estates, mainly tea and coffee, on the slopes of Mount Elgon, a stand-alone volcanic mountain which straddles the Kenya-Uganda border. His pride and joy, however, was his garden where he cultivated tree- and ground-orchids. Given the rich dark volcanic soil, provided there was water, virtually everything could be grown with umpteen varieties of fruit trees ranging from peach to plum augmented by many flowering trees from the purple Jacaranda to the scarlet of the Nandi Flame Tree. With an expansive rose garden surrounding

90

a lily pond birds of every description were attracted to bathe. A man-made paradise, which brings back poignant memories, escaped now like a white kite, as though time has cut the string.

The only fly in the ointment was that somebody back in head office thought that I had had it far too good far too long and decreed that my next posting be Chittagong in East Pakistan. Despite being described in a tourist brochure as a 'sleeping beauty emerging out of misty water' Chittagong was depicted in less flattering terms by my more experienced colleagues as the 'arsehole of the Empire'. On hearing of this posting I had discussions with Jack Block regarding taking a job as General Manager of Kerr & Downey – a leading safari firm – of which he was the main shareholder. Not the most obvious career change but I hasten to point out the job involved meeting clients at the airport, finance and administration – the actual looking after clients on 'safari' was left to the experts. Tom Sutton, a member of the polo fraternity, was one of their many skilled specialists. While the job sounded glamorous, the prospect of marriage dictated that I seek a greater measure of financial security and thus, rather boringly at the time, I opted to stay with the Bank. Fortunately, with a bit of moaning and groaning in the right ears, the posting was subsequently changed to Karachi.

The plan was then cobbled together that I would sail home on the SS *Kenya* (I plaintively held out that it was too late to change my schedule) and Elizabeth would join me in the UK when we would meet respective parents, relations, etc. To cut the requisite dash involved hiring an MGB, proceeding to Islay, Argyll and all points north and then down to the south of France where we all met up again. Along the way a friend who was spending a fortnight's holiday on the Continent bravely entrusted me with his spanking new 'E' type Jaguar on the condition that I drove him to, and collected him from, Gatwick. For a couple of weeks we swanned around in the ultimate automobile, much to the envy of all we met. These journeys in themselves are worthy of a chapter but do not form part of this particular journal.

The wedding was in Nairobi – the service in the Cathedral with the reception at the Muthaiga Club, George Cook being my best man and Liz Block one of the bridesmaids. It was a typical Kenya wedding with a good cross-section of society, just about everybody knowing everybody else. The polo club presented me with a mounting block and Jack Block, having found out that we were spending the first night at the Norfolk Hotel, equipped the suite with a number of marital aids and a congratulatory bottle of champagne. George, a dab hand with a cine-camera, had imaginatively produced a film of the activities prior to the wedding, the ceremony itself and our departure after the reception. The end result was worthy of David Lean – however, in those pioneering days of homemade movies he had, alas, at a crucial moment forgotten to change the film so instead of the happy couple coming down the aisle we had an oil tanker with waving palms in the background.

Fitted out with flippers and masks, for all the right reasons, the honeymoon was spent at the Sinbad Hotel in Malindi, north of Mombasa. In those days Malindi was the prime resort on the coast, with surfing and a variety of aquatic sports making for a perfect holiday. It brings back memories of white sand, the white line of the coral reef, pounding breakers emerging from far out in the Indian Ocean, the sky a hazy blue with heat and midday sunlight, and palm trees rustling in the sea breeze.

Today, with the river silting up the beach, Malindi has fallen into disrepair – all the previously first class hotels have closed. The Government, in an effort to bring it back to past glories, without any proper research, opened a casino. This too has failed and is mainly frequented by the flotsam and jetsam of society – prostitutes and sad Greeks who retired to the coast and do not have the money to leave.

While we were closeted at the Sinbad Hotel the coast was subjected to unseasonable rains and the murram road back to Mombasa was flooded and in some places said to be impassable. Adhering to a strict schedule we decided to make a break for it in Elizabeth's Hillman and slithered our way back. In places the water was so deep I persuaded my new bride to roll up her skirts and wade in front of the car charting the most acceptable route. Until then Elizabeth had not fully realised my chauvinistic tendencies, but she gamely did as instructed and after a few mishaps we made the Mombasa Club, famous for its char-grilled lobsters, in time for dinner – the original intention had been lunch.

I to some degree placated her by recounting the story of an old friend, Captain Jimmy Butts. Jimmy was at one time ADC to the Governor in Uganda, stayed on in Kenya and got a job with Caltex as a salesman. While his patch was down in Mombasa he was a great supporter of the Limuru Hunt, Nairobi, and drove back every weekend to participate. While thought to be a confirmed bachelor, in his early forties he met a kindred spirit and they duly got married. It was a rousing Kenya wedding with everybody getting tight, including Jimmy. Somewhat belatedly the couple eventually set off from Nairobi for Mombasa in Jimmy's Volkswagen Beetle. Just after Athi River, where the tarmac ended, the heavens opened and the VW spun off the road. Jimmy, never being short of ideas, persuaded his naïve new bride to get out, stand on the back bumper (which had hoops) clasp the roof rack and with the redistribution of weight the wheels had sufficient purchase to get the car back on the road. It was only when he reached the next stretch of tarmac some three hours later that a thumping on the roof got through to his sozzled mind that his new bride must still be clinging to the back of the car, as indeed she was. His feeble explanation that he had not heard anything earlier owing to the rattling of the car on the corrugated murram road was not well received. Amazingly, unlike most Kenya marriages, theirs, at last count, had still survived. Presumably everything got better after their first three hours together – or should that be apart?

Thirty years later I returned to Kenya on another trip. Apart from the profusion of flowers, the smell of dust after the rains and the great expanse of East African sky Nairobi had changed dramatically. Every street had a story, every building a recollection. Those blessed with wonderful experiences can drive down memory lane and happily roll back the years. Unfortunately, the reality of change erases the good and in the end we were happy to leave. While we knew Africa would be there for ever it would not ever again be quite as we remembered it.

The continued infusion of aid had built a new conference centre, more new skyscrapers and modern hotels. However, without the infrastructure, poverty was just round the corner with shanty towns on the outskirts, beggars in the streets and crime and corruption rife. The Thorn Tree coffee shop at the New Stanley Hotel had, in the old days, been a civilised meeting spot for farmers' wives, after a day's shopping, or the business community grabbing a quick snack. Now it was inhabited by back-packers nursing cups of coffee, hoping to hitch a lift, and prostitutes hoping to attract a client. While in the old colonial days it was frowned upon to consort with the local African girls, times had changed and despite the advent of AIDS the 'skin trade' flourished and was an accepted, if not welcome, part of the Nairobi scene.

Moving out to the more salubrious suburbs the grand houses were still there, but barbed wire and armed security guards were now very much in evidence. The saving grace was the Windsor Golf and Country Club at Kiambu, where we stayed. First rate accommodation and food and possibly the best golf course in Kenya after Karen. Apparently it had cost a bomb and was losing money fast – at the time the owners were looking to sell. One of the African principals behind the original deal was an ex-banker – where he found the millions of dollars to complete the project one can only guess. Presumably, aid funds from donor countries had been diverted on some pretext or another.

One could not but help feel a romantic wave of nostalgia for the 'good old days'. In an antiquated notebook I had scribbled down the following:

> Do you ever dream my sweet-
> heart, of a twilight long ago
> of a park in old Nairobi
> where the bougainvillaea grow
> – Years have flown since then,
> my sweetheart, fleet as orchid
> blooms in May
> but the hour that fills my
> dreaming, was it only
> yesterday?

94

V

Pakistan

The flight to Karachi with my new bride was not particularly memorable although I remember we were inconvenienced by having to lug along as hand luggage some unlikely items such as a table-lamp and foot-stool. Last minute wedding presents handed over just prior to our departure from Nairobi, by well-meaning friends.

We arrived late at night to be confronted as the aircraft doors were opened by a warm blast of humid air and the befuddling smells of the East. On reaching the airport buildings all was chaos, swarming with travellers of every description. In the ensuing clamour it would appear that luggage had gone missing and the customs ofifcials were being particularly difficult in clearing the incoming passengers. Our landing had coincided with a flight arriving from the Middle East filled with returning migrant workers, most of them loaded down with transistor radios and other electrical goods not readily obtainable locally. Fortunately, we were able to extricate ourselves relatively unscathed and were met by some old bank friends, Leslie and Doris Price, and whisked off in the Bank's minibus to our designated quarters.

From what we could see of Karachi at night the prospect did not please, with a general air of decay evident as we passed through the outer suburbs. At first glance neither did our accommodation. It was far from distinguished and I was taking over from a bachelor who had spent most of his leisure time at the Yacht Club and allowed the apartment to fall into a state of disrepair. More was the pity as within a fortnight of our arrival we had visitors from Kenya seeking a 'bed for the night'. Nick White (now Sir Nicholas) was travelling back to the UK by a somewhat circuitous route and Zuul Kassim Lakha was over in Pakistan keeping an eye on the family business interests. The Lakha's were 'big in jute' in East Pakistan, which was still linked to the West and plans for an independent Bangladesh had not as yet reached the drawing board.

Shortly thereafter I was thankfully put in charge of one of our branches and provided with my first ever Bank car – a Ford Cortina, a bit of a come down after revelling in the 'E' type Jaguar but, nevertheless, very acceptable. More importantly, our accommodation was upgraded accordingly. We were allocated a spacious top-floor flat in a modern block in the upmarket suburb of Clifton. It was not until the humid summer months that we realised the disadvantages of being on the fourth floor without a lift. In fact, apart from the banks and hotels, very few buildings in Karachi had elevators in those days. When the Habib Bank built the first skyscraper the lift shaft had imperceptibly narrowed the higher it went. During a trial run just prior to the grand opening ceremony the lift shot up to become firmly wedged near the top. An expensive mistake.

Christmas coincided with my taking charge of the Garden Road branch (in the heart of the industrial area) and I was surprised but gratified as messengers arrived at the apartment bearing gifts of beautifully packed baskets of fruits from grateful clients. After accepting the initial wave, we thought we had enough fruit to last us the rest of our tour and redirected the gifts to other, less fortunate, colleagues. Never have I been more popular – unbeknown to us it was the tradition to camouflage the contents and hidden under the mangos, pineapples, plums, grapes, etc were bottles of Dimple Haig, brandy and other illicit items. Apparently, we were permitted to accept consumables as they were not considered 'undue influence' in a banking context. I did not make the same mistake the following year when I dug deep before passing on similar gifts.

Elizabeth led an interesting life. When not wrapping bandages for the local hospital she was honorary secretary to the English-Speaking Union and a model much in demand at the various charitable fashion shows. On reading my morning paper, *The Dawn*, I was quite often pleasantly surprised to see the visage of my lovely wife beaming from the social pages. Most expatriate wives seemed to enjoy Karachi and it was no bad life with many friendships forged round sunlit swimming pools. A regular attendee at the Sind Club pool was the very young Benazir Bhutto who was a near neighbour of ours at Clifton. Her father, Zulfikar Ali Bhutto, was rumoured at the time to be conducting an affair with President Suharto's wife. Whether there was any substance in the gossip I know not but she was certainly a frequent visitor to Karachi.

While we lived in a perfectly pleasant residential suburb it was a bit of a shock after Nairobi for it lacked the orderliness, greenery and, in summer months, the flowers. However, our environment was not without interest.

Sir Charles Napier, Governor of the Province of Sind, recounted in 1847, 'You will yet be the glory of the East, would that I come again to see you, Karachi, in your grandeur.' If he came back today, he would see many modern skyscrapers, some attractive, some ugly, that have sprung up in the urban sprawl. With independence Karachi took on increasing importance as an international port and flourishing industrial and commercial centre. Apart from the local banks our main competition came from the Chartered Bank, Eastern Bank, Mercantile Bank (now HSBC) and Citibank.

The road system had not, alas, kept pace. On the streets taxis, buses, streetcars and modern automobiles mingled with camel- and donkey-carts with jingling bells, scooters and horse-drawn vehicles. One of my favourite headlines in the local press was 'Local man injured by hit and run camel cart'. Occasionally one witnessed the President's bodyguard, resplendent in their scarlet and gold tunics on beautifully groomed horses, canter by. Even the lorries were a colourful spectacle with the drivers' cabs decorated with hand-painted images of snow-capped mountains, rivers and, somewhat incongruously, modern aircraft.

Out of town the 'highways' quickly deteriorated and merged into a single lane of tarmac with a steep fall off on either side. Predictably, this resulted in those drivers travelling in opposite directions holding their pole position to the last minute – giving way meant an uncomfortable detour to the dusty red tracks which ran alongside. The winner normally was drugged by qat and impervious to the dangers – a large overloaded lorry helped sway the conflict. When two equally matched contestants met, this invariably resulted in a fatality with the skeletons of wrecked and burnt out vehicles lining the route at regular intervals proving the point. Needless to say, when venturing out of Karachi we carefully weighed up the odds and generally took evasive action. Overtaking was also a gamble fraught with difficulty and here again discretion was the better part of valour and we spurned the local technique of 'he who dares wins'.

In the crowded bazaars one could buy a vast assortment of articles and foodstuffs. The saris of the women coloured the streets with all the hues of the rainbow. Massive mosques and delicate minarets tangled with the smart hotels and clubs. At weekends we were able to watch the craftsmen making intricate designs in fine silverware and witness young children weaving oriental carpets. Once finished, these were often left out on the road, where a mixture of dust, camel dung and the midday sun gave them a semblance of authenticity to enable them to be sold to the unwary as antique 'Persian' carpets.

Cricket was the national sport with games in progress on every conceivable piece of wasteland, often with improvised equipment. It was no wonder that a burgeoning sports equipment business had been established at Sialkot, north of Karachi, producing good quality cricket bats and balls, hockey sticks and squash racquets. While today the goods are acceptable under their own label, in those days to obtain market share they used names approximating to better known brands, so equipment which at first glance was made by Slazenger actually was inscribed with Slashunder. As everything was produced at half the equivalent price in England the sports gear was in fact exceptionally good value, unlike Bangkok where the counterfeit watches, although cheap, are nevertheless suspect.

Compared to Peshawar and Lahore, whose origins are lost in time, Karachi boasts no ancient lineage and its beginnings are traced without difficulty to some three hundred years ago when the navigable channels of the Indus silted up and became unsuitable for shipping. In the late 19th century Karachi took on a newfound prosperity, when the American Civil War created an enormous demand for Indian cotton as the Northerners had blockaded the Confederate ports.

Karachi has more in common with the Middle East than any other Indian or Pakistani city. Rain falls, on average, only once or twice a year and the hinterland is basically desert where very little grows except bush cactus and the occasional palm tree. The population of Karachi is, of course, related to the Middle East by religion and when we were there the majority of women seen in the streets wore burkas, as purdah was still strictly observed by most families.

In the evening the city underwent a transformation when the noise and bustle abated and the setting sun stained the deep blue Arabian sea a burnished rose.

Karachi was a city of contrasts. At weekends we used to pack picnic lunches and go out to Hawks Bay where the Bank owned a number of beach bungalows. There you could browse or sunbathe to your heart's content. However, to get there one had to traverse some of the most decrepit slums in the world – a stinking cesspit of squalor with poverty and disease sitting on the edge of a mosquito ridden swamp.

Where we lived at Clifton was probably the most popular beach for the local populace. However, we very rarely went there as one was continuously being accosted by hawkers seeking to sell cheap, locally made trinkets. The compensation was watching burka-clad ladies, heavily veiled, paddling their feet in the surf – an extraordinary sight.

One of the Bank's clients, the Minwalla family, who owned the Hotel Metropole, also owned the Grand Hotel at Malir. This provided an ideal weekend retreat with a sparkling swimming pool and 'Polynesian' night club. The intention was to produce a south sea island effect under a starlit sky although one was quickly brought back to reality by the male vocalist's rendition of *The Green Green Grass of Home*. Another welcome relaxation at weekends was to take out one of the yachts and, with plenty of booze on board, go crabbing. The T-shirt emblazoned 'I caught crabs in Karachi' was worn with pride.

As was usual the Clubs provided the requisite quality of life for the expatriate community. Being by the sea the yacht club featured prominently with at least eighteen dinghies competing most weekends painting a kaleidoscope of colour in the harbour. The Boat Club, a black and white timbered building, was situated on the banks of the Chinnah Creek, an extension of the harbour, from which it is separated by a large expanse of low, dark-green mangroves. This was a popular venue, where the Bank's oarsmen competed on a regular basis. There were also facilities for rugby, cricket, golf and polo.

The hub of the social scene was, however, the Sind Club, steeped in tradition and with residential quarters. The gardens in the winter months were brought to perfection with a blaze of contrasting colours. Apart from tennis there were four squash courts under the supervision of the ex-world champion, Roshan Khan whose pinguid frame disguised an unexpected slickness around the court. For a few rupees he would give instruction on the finer arts of the game and for substantially more rupees he would take on anybody for one game starting with a minus sixty handicap. This gave rise to a rather offbeat wager. Surrey/Middlesex young cricketers were touring Pakistan and in the team was a certain Stuart Courtney who had made the national squash team back in the UK. We duly piled in with our bets, with Roshan unaware of the calibre of his opponent. After an amazing two hours of squash Roshan, despite being in his fifties, triumphed 9–7. Regardless of losing our wagers, in the end the whole gallery was rooting for a home win.

Lunch, alfresco, at the Sind Club could, for the uninitiated, be a nerve-wracking experience with dive-bombing kite-hawks depriving unsuspecting sunworshippers of their club sandwiches and other snacks. These omnipresent scavengers would perch on the surrounding buildings waiting to swoop down and scoop up the dish of the day – chips being a particular favourite. A simple calorie-free salad didn't hold the same attraction and was a safer choice.

Interestingly, another institution, the Gymkhana club, existed with facilities every bit as good as the Sind Club. In the '30s the Gymkhana was the hub of the social life of the newly arrived expatriates – the Sind Club was deemed more exclusive and was very much a meeting place for the burra-sahibs (senior executives). Behind its high hedges was a full size cricket ground, tennis and squash courts and a couple of swimming pools. In the '60s the membership ran into thousands and the cost of joining ran into thousands (of rupees) but even in its heyday during the Raj it never had the same social cachet of the more exclusive Sind Club. Remarkably the club's presidents from the year of its foundation in the 19th century until shortly before our arrival were strictly British names but thereafter it became a haven for 'new money' and few, if any, expatriates were members in 1967.

There was quite a lot of activity on the banking front with Citibank taking a major stake in Grindlays who, in turn, had acquired the overseas branches of Lloyds Bank – their very young General Manager in Karachi was George Vojte who eventually went on to reach the top of the banking tree back in America. I again met up with him later in Japan – I always found him most helpful and friendly in what, after all, was a highly competitive environment. Another Citibanker, Steve Spalding, won an inhouse competition for a suitable phrase to be used in their advertising. He came up with 'My pulse is the heartbeat of the Bank' which was sadly discarded for the more apt 'The City Never Sleeps'.

The majority of my prime clients were of Parsee extraction. Apart from owning most of the top hotels they also operated one of the few car and lorry assembly plants in Pakistan. Another client owned a major cosmetic plant producing every toiletry from shaving cream to toothpaste. Their workforce was not the most attentive and on one memorable occasion they mislabelled the products. Sales of toothpaste sold as shaving cream shot up but, alas, the reverse was not the case!

On another notable occasion a history professor at the local university produced as a potential customer an old crone chewing betel nut. I paid little attention until she filled in the account opening form stating she was Miss Ali Jinnah, sister of the 'founder' of Pakistan. This had everybody leaping around, including the Pakistan Government, who, despite the professor producing certain credentials, were not sure whether she was an impostor. Reluctantly, the authorities afforded Miss Jinnah a suite of rooms in the somewhat rundown Pink Palace where we were invited to take tea and phan with her. Fortunately for the Pakistan Government she died shortly thereafter without a rupee to her name. This saved them considerable embarrassment as at no time could they vouchsafe her kinship.

In terms of relaxation Elizabeth and I normally met up at the Sind Club for lunch and a swim. We quite often entertained, and were entertained, there in the evening. As mentioned previously, it was very much a traditional colonial institution of big-bladed fans, potted palms and passageways that smelt of floor wax, lavatory bleach and stale tobacco. In the Deep End Bar, which was for men only, at lunchtime elderly bores in cravats, voluble with too many G & Ts bemoaned how standards were falling. The house rules were rigidly applied with lady guests confined to the Shallow End. Formal suiting was a prerequisite for dinner as I found out to my cost when I pitched up in a blazer and tie and was politely refused entry.

Although a strictly Muslim country there seemed to be no shortage of alcohol and our Pakistani friends regularly threw cocktail parties where the drink flowed freely. At one such gathering, hosted by P.I.A., the national airline, we were engaged in a lively, if frivolous, conversation with the chairman, a distinguished retired air marshal. He suggested that we repaired with him to a local nightclub. When we demurred he said another drink would change my mind. This he courteously went off and got for me – after a couple of swigs I felt distinctly queasy and the room started spinning round. Our host said not to worry, his driver would take me safely home and he would accompany Elizabeth to the nightclub. Sensing something 'fishy' and being a loyal wife she sensibly spurned the invitation and drove me back to our apartment where I was violently ill. On reflection we decided my last drink had been 'spiked' and our 'courteous' host had arrogantly assumed that he could take advantage of the situation. We allowed the matter to rest as the air marshal was far too powerful a figure to tangle with and we consoled ourselves that at least Elizabeth had been saved from 'white slavery'!

This incident apart, the social scene was great fun. We were particularly friendly with Happy Minwalla and his wife, leading members of the local 'jet set' and owners of the Hotel Metropole. This was an enormous, if somewhat run down, hostelry which suffered by comparison with its neighbour, the luxurious, recently built Inter-Continental Hotel.

Happy's rather curious moniker resulted from the fact that primogeniture was of prime importance to his father; he had, however, bred in quick succession four daughters. Fortunately for all concerned his fifth progeny was a boy and Minwalla senior was so relieved and delighted that he named his son 'Happy'.

To stimulate trade the Metropole opened a new nightclub with all the latest gimmicks: strobe lighting, piped music when the band stopped playing, etc. The opening coincided with the Khan of Kalat winning the jackpot at the local races, by any yardstick a not inconsiderable sum. Flushed with his good fortune he decreed that the nightclub remain open morning, noon and night with drinks on the house – with guests restricted to Happy and his friends – until his winnings ran out. This was duly achieved in double quick time, whereupon the Khan returned to his ancestral estates in Quetta leaving a dishevelled and hung-over bunch of revellers in his wake. We popped in occasionally to check out the action but it was all a bit too much and over the top, to put it mildly.

The Khan was an interesting cove. During colonial rule the British had recognised the strategic importance of Baluchistan, at the time governed by the Khan of Kalat. To gain his co-operation and compliance he was extended the flattery of a nineteen gun salute by British troops on all ceremonial occasions. At the time only five other native rulers in the whole of India were granted a more resounding tribute. Although independence had extinguished this honorarium the family was still relatively well-off and the Khan himself was a respected and influential figure around Quetta. Presumably his followers were kept in the dark as to his escapades when his retinue 'hit' Karachi.

Apart from a regular game of squash I spent Wednesday evenings and most weekends playing polo. I was generously supplied with ponies by Rolf Hegge, a Norwegian shipowner, and played for a team sponsored by the Inter-Continental Hotel Group. They were to some extent parsimonious in their sponsorship and restricted their generosity to providing shirts with their logo, polo sticks and, somewhat ironically, free membership of their swimming pool. As a side we were reasonably successful and reached the finals of quite a few tournaments. Having got that far we were invariably thrashed by the President's Bodyguard team, who had the advantage of a string of high quality ponies and practising together on a daily basis. Brigadier Hesky Baig, who had played alongside Prince Philip, was the doyen of the polo scene and became a firm friend. A very young protégé, Podjer Effendi, went on to become a top class, high-goal professional in the USA.

During one match, playing a rather ambitious 'under the tail' shot, I slipped a disc and was carried off on a stretcher to the local hospital. The next morning I met Mr Ronald Simcox, FRCS, who gripped me firmly by my hand as he looked into my wife's eyes. He said I was just like an Aston Martin that needed fine tuning as he stuck in a needle that plunged me to oblivion. On coming around some hours later I was informed I had undergone traction but did not see Mr Simcox again. Apparently, his qualifications were bogus and in fact he was a Fellow of the Royal Geographical Society. These initials were conveniently smudged on his letterhead. To be fair, Simcox, who had served in the medical corps during the Burma campaign, rank unknown, had seemingly amassed considerable experience in treating the wounded and was probably as skilled as most surgeons. What happened to him I know not but I duly recuperated and despite a recurring twinge and a slight deformity I am none the worse for wear.

About this time Elizabeth's father came to see us from Kenya. Unfortunately, his visit coincided with Uganda expelling the Asian Community and Pakistan, along with India, decreed that anyone from East Africa be inadmissible on the grounds they were Britain's responsibility. Applying some formula which defied logic the immigration authorities prevented my father-in-law from entering. We duly sought help from Hesky Baig at the Sind Club where he was downing his evening tipple and he immediately commandeered an army jeep and brought my father-in-law back to our flat. Pakistan was very much a country where having the right contacts invariably oiled the 'decision making' wheels.

Local leave proved a welcome break, particularly as Elizabeth, much to our joy, was pregnant. Having planned a fairly relaxing trip to explore North Pakistan it proved to be anything but. We initially flew to Lahore, and stayed at the luxurious Inter-Continental Hotel. As a devotee of Kipling I was delighted to see in the middle of the City, Zamzamah, the canon straddled by Kim 'in defiance of municipal orders.' The authorities have recognised its significance as a tourist attraction and it is now sited on a marble plinth protected by a small fence and surrounded by a little moat. These precautions were presumably in place to discourage the locals and tourists seeking photo

104

opportunities from replicating Kim's actions. Even viewed at a respectable distance it is still a very impressive piece of heavy artillery with a barrel over fourteen feet long and capable of firing ten-inch cannon balls. Lahore, now known as the 'City of Gardens', is a gallery of past civilisations and a prodigy of modern times and far removed from Kipling's 'City of Dreadful Night'.

The old times were recalled purely by strolling down the narrow dark streets of the walled city. Emerging on the Mall, wide-paved avenues and modern structures quickly brought us back to the present. For the next few days we were royally entertained by the polo playing community. An interesting trip was arranged to Aitchison College – the Eton of Pakistan. The college consisted of quadrangles of boarding-houses built in traditional style – the most striking aspect was the beautifully maintained cricket ground surrounded by splendid trees with a pavilion complete with white picket fence.

Another highlight was a visit to the exquisite Shalimar Gardens of Shah Jahan, the great romantic who tended to wear his heart on his sleeve – the Taj Mahal being his greatest tribute to everlasting love. The gardens come a close second.

They were enclosed by substantial sandstone walls and mainly given over to sweeping lawns, rose beds and magnificent shade trees said to stem from when the gardens were designed early in the 17th century. An oasis of calm compared to the frenzied chaos outside. The main feature, however, was the hundreds of fountains which were serviced by water flowing down a network of canals leading to fine edifices built of white marble. An amazing engineering feat, even though some no longer functioned properly – those that did sparkled in the radiant sunlight. A most relaxing break – as it also appeared to be for the numerous birds that had found sanctuary on the trees and chirruped contentedly in the background.

As someone who tends to restrict tangible gifts of affection to birthdays, anniversaries and Christmas, Elizabeth predictably looked at me askance when our guide recounted the tale of Shah Jahan's lavish and apparently spontaneous tribute to his wife, Mumtaz Mahal. She was far from placated by what I thought was a generous offer of some sweetmeats saturated in syrup purchased from a stall holder on our way back to the hotel. It was suggested in no uncertain terms that I needed to raise my game.

We took delivery of an air-conditioned car (Japanese) and drove up to Rawalpindi, the headquarters of the Pakistan Army and where the President's Bodyguard were based, a most pleasant town with tree-lined avenues within easy reach of the Himalayan foothills. It was a typical cantonment town with whitewashed bungalows, barracks, churches and hospitals and a sprawling bazaar on the outskirts. Troops were being drilled on the parade ground, ponies schooled on the polo ground and prospective Imran Khans were going through their paces in the cricket nets. An outward impression of ordered calm, which we knew from experience was, if anything, deceptive. The capital, Islamabad, was still in the process of being built.

We stayed with a madcap bank colleague, John Winning. John had, with a couple of sherpas attempted to climb K2, the world's second highest mountain and, while, unsuccessful, the Russian Ambassador had been so impressed with his courage and initiative he transferred all the Embassy accounts to Grindlays. Shortly thereafter John decided to utilise his six months home leave by travelling overland back to the UK by Land Rover and camel. He apparently got waylaid in Saudi Arabia and the whole expedition eventually took over a year during which time he became a fluent Arabist. Not having kept the Bank informed of his progress he was predictably sacked on pitching up at head office. John, nothing daunted, went back to the Middle East where he used his contacts to good effect.

During our time in Rawalpindi we took the opportunity to visit the hill station at Murree situated at about 7,500 feet; here the serious scenery began. While a spectacular drive, it was not without its hazards. Often we were confronted with lorries propelled by sleep-deprived and qat-chewing drivers thundering down in the opposite direction oblivious of the highway code and assuming the right of way on all corners. These were augmented by buses, invariably full to bursting point with the excess load of passengers clinging precariously to the back plus a few chickens flapping around on top. Not the restful introduction to the tranquillity of Murree that we had expected, but arrive we did with our faithful Datsun car virtually intact.

The 'town' was very much a relic of the Raj with old fashioned hotels situated in secluded, heavily-scented pine woods carpeted with flowers. The basic crops were cultivated on steeply terraced hillsides. The English Church was of particular interest and the older gravestones, now covered in lichen, depicted an era where the expectancy of life in foreign climes was remarkably short. Many of the headstones bore regimental crests and it seemed ironical that so many servants of the Raj were buried in the warm silence of the graveyard under the grass and flowers in this most healthy of climes. Presumably, many had contracted some life-threatening disease in the plains and had, as a last resort, been sent to Murree in the hope of recuperating. While we were there, suddenly the weather changed and we experienced a cold, grey afternoon of lowering skies and a bitter wind and the surrounding snow-capped mountains were momentarily obliterated in the squall of driving rain. With the thin air starting to chill one's lungs, maybe it wasn't quite so healthy after all!

From Rawalpindi onwards to Peshawar. This stretch was not without interest as we drove through the Margalla Pass just north of 'Pindi' and crossed the great bridge at Attock – here the rust-red waters of the Kabul River (tainted with blood from a tribal skirmish upstream?) merge with the glacial blue of the Indus and form a mighty torrent. At the time the Attock Oil Company were one of our major customers – I would be interested to know if they still exist. Beside the road near Margalla a commanding obelisk was erected by the British in honour of General John Nicholson recording his many conquests and the inscription: 'Mourned by the two races with equal grief'. In fact, Nicholson was much admired by the 'natives' and developed a cult-following which kept the Punjab loyal during the Indian Mutiny. He also played a major rôle in the capture of Delhi. His various achievements were awesomely listed on the obelisk and we were even more awestruck when we noted that he died at the relatively young age of 36. He must have started campaigning at a very early age, judging by all the decorations bestowed upon him, and thereafter risen quickly through the ranks.

As we progressed along the Grand Trunk Road we passed through Nowshera and came across an enormous complex of

107

barracks built in the early 20th century by the British. Then it was an important garrison town in terms of providing supplies and reinforcements for the various wars waged to the north. The Pakistan army had decided this encampment was still of strategic importance with everything looking spick-and-span. The old maxim, 'If it doesn't move, whitewash it', obviously still applied.

We eventually reached Peshawar, which still preserves some of the colour and feel of Omar Khayyam and the Arabian Nights. The magic and mystery of the Orient was quickly dispelled when we booked into Dean's Hotel for dinner where the recommended items on the menu were Brown Windsor Soup and Spotted Dick. For the main course we were served by an ancient waiter frightful helpings of the ubiquitous mutton, predictably the 'dish of the week'. This was doused in the local version of HP sauce – with tomato ketchup on hand to add extra piquancy if needed.

While the interior was shambolic and gloomy and in need of a lick of paint, fortunately our suite of rooms was cheered up by a wood-burning fire in the sitting room. Conversely, outside the gardens and flower beds were still immaculately cared for. It was a delight after a dusty drive to be served drinks on the tonsured lawns and recline in 'planters' chairs which, although frayed, still served their purpose of providing a resting place for a tired body and rejuvenating glass. It was easy to let the mind slip back into the past, if one ignored the parasols with obtrusive logos advertising a popular brand of drinks.

Peshawar itself was a town of two parts. The British had constructed a cantonment with all the accoutrements of a garrison town. Spacious bungalows for the Indian Civil Service and quarters for the officers, barrack blocks for the lesser breeds, a cathedral full of memorials to soldiers – many of them pitifully young – and the obligatory cemetery full of gravestones and evocative memories. A grandiose memorial hall had been built for civic functions and, no doubt, hunt balls – the Peshawar Vale Hunt was active in the days prior to partition. The well-appointed club replete with lawn tennis courts was full of relics of Winston Churchill when he campaigned in these parts. There was also a very pretty, tree surrounded, cricket ground.

The old city, if one could negotiate the heaving traffic and bullock carts loaded with sugar cane, was redolent of the timeless East.

In the bazaar the coppersmiths mingled with the sandal makers and gunsmiths. At the end of narrow alleys one could espy sculptured minarets. The goldsmiths were hard at work making elaborate headpieces and earrings for brides and veiled women who are never seen. But like so many other old towns this ancient heritage was despoiled by ugly new concrete buildings which were beginning to blot out the charm of the past.

Peshawar offers two experiences with the ancient clutter of the bazaar relieved by looking in other directions towards the distant line of mountains. The feeling of space could not have been more different.

Virtually all the locals carried a fearsome array of weapons, their sun-hardened faces bearing the stamp of a mixture of ancestors. Some, however, were pale of skin with ginger hair and blue eyes, no doubt descendants from the time when Alexander the Great and his armies had exercised their 'influence' in these parts. They now carry modern rifles and not-so-modern Lee Enfields in place of the old jezails and no youngster worth his salt is seen without some form of weaponry forming an integral part of his dress. The old traditions of hospitality, chivalry and sanctuary are nevertheless still apparent.

'Dizzy with Kipling and diesel fumes' Peshawar is very much a centre of intrigue where the Machiavellian realities of Central Asian politics are evident. Here, in dark alleys, Pathans – a proud, independent, handsome and murderous race – mixed with their Pakistani 'brothers' to hatch business deals, which quite often in those relatively peaceful days related to the smuggling of opium.

Peshawar is, of course, the gateway to the Khyber Pass which we ventured up as far as Landi Kotal, approximately halfway en route to Kabul. Landi Kotal was a rather strange centre in no man's land where just about everything under the sun was traded at market prices and a variety of currencies defined by the laws of supply and demand. Marks & Spencer underwear, Japanese electrical goods, Chinese silks, Players cigarettes and blocks of opium all seemed sought after. In those days it was permitted to exist by both the Pakistan and Afghan authorities

109

to barter in goods both legal and illicit. Lorries and pickup vans loaded to the 'gills' sallied back and forth in both directions. Presumably overall control was exercised by some tribal mafia as the laws of Pakistan did not extend to the Tribal Areas. When in possession of illicit goods, any guilt of 'smuggling' only attaches to the customer if one tries to get the purchases back to Peshawar.

The Pass itself begins with dramatic suddenness with a series of ancient circling roads with obscure villages, each one a fortress in itself, dotted on the barren mountainside. Following the road for much of the way is a single track railway, built at enormous expense for military purposes – winding through tunnels, over rickety bridges to the top of the Pass and down into the valley on the Afghan side. I cannot believe it still exists today. Since time immemorial the Pass has been woven with stories of courage and tragedy. Carved into the rocks were the Regimental Crests of British, Sikh and Punjabi Regiments who fought side by side and were involved in the various tribal wars which had been fought over this inhospitable landscape ever since it was part of the 'Great Game' with Russia.

The Khyber is not the most dramatic of the passes out of Peshawar but it is undoubtedly the most romantic and historic. Nevertheless, it was still evocative of camel-trains and creaking gun carriages with steam trains laboriously conveying troops back and forward. In the late '60s it was a changing scenario. Where armies had marched, hippies now meandered and it was possible to take cars and buses overland from London, Paris, etc to Iran and through to Delhi.

Having survived the rather tortuous and, at times, menacing experience of traversing the Khyber we thought a little more relaxation was called for. On our return it was a clear day with the sun having burned off the early morning mist and we were able to drink in the great vale of Peshawar ringed by hills with the glittering snow-topped range of the Hindu Khush as a backcloth. Another horizon beckoned and we headed our faithful Datsun towards the many splendoured valley of Swat approached by 100-odd miles of motorable road from Peshawar. If my memory serves me right we were obliged to drive through the Malakand Pass where, many years before, a young Winston Churchill, then a war correspondent with the *Allahabad Pioneer*,

110

had distinguished himself in some clash of arms with local tribesmen. There he wrote his first book, *The Malakand Field Force*, which was published in 1898 and is now widely recognised as a military classic.

The fertile valley of Swat was a marked contrast after the parched landscape and rocky terrain of Afghanistan. To attract tourists a basic golf course had been constructed, the main attraction being that the fairways were lined by every conceivable type of fruit tree. It was a captivating sight catching glimpses of the snow-capped peaks through the lattice work of spring blossom of every description, the pink of the almond trees predominating. With an abundance of early fruit available, lunch very rarely featured on the agenda.

Presumably in a vote-winning exercise President Ayub Khan had built numerous educational establishments – most of which appeared devoid of pupils.

There was one acceptable hotel at Saidu Sharif memorable for the en suite deep concrete baths. A strange experience as although the water came steaming out of the taps by the time it reached the bottom of the bath it felt distinctly chilly. The only entertainment on offer was a game of table tennis against the local champion who had mastered the tilt at one end and a drooping net. These were but small discomforts as we were more than adequately compensated by incomparable scenery which unfolded as we drove higher into the surrounding mountains. Emerald green lakes at 9,000 feet and, as we ventured higher by car along some near inaccessible roads, trout streams were left behind as we hit snow-clad passes with glaciers trundling below. Having reached the last designated dâk-bungalow, a remote cabin buried in a wood of pine trees, which was closed, before turning back we were able to drink in amazing views with the mighty Himalayas providing an unforgettable panorama.

Back at our hotel we rose early to watch the dawn and see another beautiful day unfold revelling in the cloudless sky as the sun touched the surrounding mountains which changed colour in the variable light. At day's end the sun's rays faded – a brief twilight before the reddened sky gave way to blackness. Occasionally, a shooting star or it might have been an aircraft, flashed across the sky reminding one of a more urgent world.

111

On returning, five months later, to the UK I sold some of my 'happy snaps' of Swat and the Khyber Pass to a geographical magazine for the then not inconsiderable sum of £100. I duly put my photographer friend, Gerald Cubitt, in touch with the parent organisation and he sent off a splendid wildlife portfolio for consideration. Not only were they not published but he never got the photographs back. Still a sore point which is invariably raised 30 years later when we meet up in Cape Town.

Exhausted but rejuvenated we returned to the more ordered life of Karachi where Elizabeth joined a jolly class of 'mothers to be'. One notable social event was a stag party hosted by a polo friend, Sayed Chinoy, for Prince Hassan of Jordan (King Hussein's brother) who had come over to claim the lovely hand of a beautiful Pakistani girl, Savarth. The marriage has proved a durable success, although there was ultimately some controversy when King Hussein died and was succeeded by his son, Prince Abdullah, and not Prince Hassan who had been the longstanding Prince Regent.

Welcome visitors in the winter months were various international cricket teams – official and unofficial – from the UK. Away from the confines of their hotels they always welcomed hospitality from the expatriate community. We normally took them out to the Bank's beach bungalows at Hawkes Bay where, liberally supplied with locally brewed beer and distilled gin, cricket matches were arranged. For me the highlight was carting Derek Underwood into the sea and bowling Dennis Amiss with a ball which skidded along the sand. In exchange complimentary tickets were provided for the Test Match which led to a highly embarrassing moment. It was customary to wear 'whites' to the office and after a quick lunch of sandwiches and a couple of beers I sped along to the Stadium. Before taking my seat, a need to relieve myself was paramount and I joined a queue of approximately 30 locals at the men's urinal. Unfortunately, in my whites I was mistaken for one of the players and ushered up to the front of the line. With a massed audience holding their collective breath to hear the 'steady stream on tin' I was unable to perform. For the next half hour, in dire straits, and pursued by a horde of misguided autograph hunters, I was seeking an alternative receptacle when an unexpected diversion

112

arose which enabled me to escape the attention of prying eyes. With Alan Knott just about to score, I believe, his first Test century and inflict on Pakistan a heavy defeat the crowd, to my relief, decided to burn down the stands. I thought it a rather unsporting step to resolve my 'small' problem.

One weekend we were invited to a client's country retreat some forty miles outside Karachi in the Sind Desert. As we drove on a rutted road across miles of wasteland knowing not what to expect we came across an oasis in the midst of which was built a 'Beau Geste' type fort with turbaned followers manning the battlements. On being admitted we were confronted by a bejewelled host and even more heavily bejewelled statuesque blonde lady, introduced as his wife. Behind them, within the confines of the 'fort' was a kaleidoscope of colour – immaculate lawns and carefully tended flowerbeds in the shade of ancient mango trees.

As we wended our way to the main house legions of gardeners carefully averted their eyes; apparently it was unwise, for fear of punishment, to gaze at females not heavily veiled. After lunch the wife, who was German, mentioned to me as we walked some distance from our host that before meeting her husband she had been on a grand tour to Djibouti and Hargeisha. When I raised a quizzical eyebrow at her travelling to such outlandish places she admitted having been a showgirl-cum-stripper. Life, apparently, had not been kind to her. Having begun in the more 'cultured' environment of the Rieperbahn, her 'career' went into decline and she was obliged to perform in front of the remote and less lucrative audiences of Hargeisha and finally descend to the Tartarean abyss of the Djibouti dockside flea-pits. Here she was now in a paradoxical situation where no man could look at her other than her husband. The irony was not lost on her and she feared that once out of favour she would be relegated to a compound, admittedly comfortable, at the other end of the estate to see out her days with the seraglio of discarded wives. She gave me a sealed letter for delivery to the German Consul in Karachi. Presumably this outlined her plight but we never knew what happened to her. I left not only with the letter but clasping a sack of mangos and a wife, counting her lucky stars that she was not in a similar predicament.

On the return trip the rugged terrain which on the outward

113

journey had been lustreless and unattractive took on a different hue with the dull browns replaced by a palette of ochre, red and purple as the sun went down.

One evening we were gathered together at Mike and Judith Jackson's house (Mike was the Bank's general manager for Pakistan) to meet Lord Aldington on a brief stopover during a whirlwind tour of his banking empire. In giving his usual pep talk he announced that Grindlays had recently purchased the Ottoman Bank's business outside Turkey. This added France and the Middle East to our range of branches. Not thinking much more of this, life carried on as usual until out of the blue, shortly after, I received a phone call to say that I had been selected to be the Bank's Middle East representative based in Beirut. I was also instructed to brush up on my French and Arabic, essential prerequisites. Ignoring the fact that my French was of the schoolboy variety and my Arabic non-existent I accepted with alacrity.

A flurry of parties followed, including a Bignell Farewell Tournament at the Polo Club. Inter-Continental Hotels at last came good and produced the silverware for the winning side of which I was a carefully selected member.

The polo fraternity also gave us, as a memento of our stay in Pakistan, an antique stone frieze of Ghandhara art, approximately 2 ft x 1 ft. This particular piece was an historical relic of an old Buddhist dynasty, excavated at Taxila, an ancient city of carved stones. Taxila, once the seat of oriental culture, was discovered in the latter half of the 19th century and has been described as a 'Metropolis of seven successive civilisations.' Apart from its considerable weight I thought it wise to get clearance from the National Museum of Pakistan to export the piece back to the UK. I duly took it round to the Director-General of Archaeology for inspection and in response received a note saying the museum would like to acquire it and compensate me to the extent of the price I paid. Alternatively, I was at leave to pass it on to a friend, presumably on the basis that the item stayed in Pakistan although this caveat was not specifically stated. The letter, which I still have, was signed by Mr S.A. Naqvi, TI, MA, LLB, FRAS, AMA (London). While I never discovered what his qualifications actually were, he seemed a man not to be argued with.

To my everlasting shame – and this book is a useful tool for purging one's conscience – I loosely interpreted the content of the letter and contacted a friend in the United Nations who without hesitation said he would ship the piece back to the UK with his personal effects. Apparently he enjoyed some form of diplomatic immunity and his luggage, on leaving Pakistan, was not subject to the usual scrutiny.

In due course we took delivery and, not having a suitable alcove, or for that matter a spotlight, in our small flat in Hove we lugged it along to Spinks for valuation. They were prepared to fork out £300 on the spot, a not inconsiderable sum in 1969, and with a mortgage to be paid we took the money and ran. It would be interesting to know what an item of this nature would be worth today. We were also given as a farewell gift a hand-woven bedspread, which we still have.

The boss of Burmah Shell, Sandy Smith, hosted a roulette evening in our honour and in an effort to get rid of my surplus rupees, as strict exchange control was in force, I gambled extravagantly. Needless to say, I kept winning the jackpot and finished up donating great piles of chips to the 'House'. All enormous fun, though less so for Elizabeth who was heavily pregnant. It was decided that she would return to her parents in Nairobi to have the baby and I would proceed to London for instructions and a crash course in languages.

Having packed up I left two days prior to her departure and, as I travelled courtesy of Middle East Airlines (I was stopping off briefly in Beirut to reconnoitre), the plane actually flew low over the flat roof of our apartment. Poignantly, I could see Elizabeth waving and my underpants, which I had forgotten to pack, fluttering on the washing-line in domestic harmony.

As though in salute the plane banked slowly to the right giving me one last lingering look at Karachi. Out of the window I could see Defence Colony (a suburb for retired army officers) and in the distance the hotel at Malir where we had spent so many happy weekends. Closer was the baked earth of the racetrack with the polo ground etched out in the middle. Other landmarks were picked out in the bright sunlight. The Sind Club like an oasis of green with the pool a sparkling blue against the beige of the surrounding buildings. And then off across the Arabian Sea, leaving behind a flurry of white sails as boats tacked back to the yacht club. Many happy memories encapsulated in a fleeting snapshot before the plane rose above the clouds.

VI

Addis Ababa and Beirut

Despite the infinite patience of my tutors, and considerable work on my part, my efforts at gaining any fluency in the French language proved fruitless. This was particularly galling for my new masters (ex-Ottoman Bank) who had tended to recruit graduates for their linguistic skills in the hope that their ability to master the fundamentals of their trade would quickly follow. It was even more galling for their managers in the field who had always viewed a posting to Beirut as the ultimate place to finish their banking career – now pipped at the post by some upstart with little understanding of the region.

To bring me up to speed it was considered that a week with our merchant banking representative in Geneva would prove beneficial and broaden my horizons. It certainly did, as our then Rep. saw me as a good excuse to bolster his expense account by entertaining me at all the best nightclubs in town. Despite my 'strong' objections I was nevertheless subjected to this indoctrination and carried on my way somewhat bewildered as to what my rôle in Beirut would entail. However, the future looked auspicious.*

My next port of call was Nairobi to view my newly born son. Cossetted in the midst of her family Elizabeth was in remarkably good heart, as too, judging by the noise, was my son Guy. Plans were made for them to follow me to Beirut as soon as suitable accommodation was acquired.

---

*To keep the record straight I hasten to add that this was just prior to Charles von Westenholz taking over the rôle as the group's representative in Geneva.

Addis Ababa

In the interim I was required to stop over in Addis Ababa, since Grindlays in their new expansionary rôle had recently acquired a significant stake in a local Ethiopian Bank – the Addis Ababa Bank SC, the largest private bank in the country. With a feisty Scotsman, Jimmy McDonald, in charge of the purse strings, a tightly controlled operation was ensured and he made sure my waking hours were profitably employed in promoting the Bank's business.

Ethiopia operates its own calendar containing 13 months, which proved somewhat confusing when trying to fill appointments in advance. I suspect our Chairman would have found this calendar a convenient compromise. With his constant world-wide travel through different time zones his contention that he was the only bank executive to work an eight day week would have slotted in neatly.

I was informed by Jimmy that the surrounding countryside was very beautiful with good trout fishing readily available, but my itinerary did not permit time to indulge in such 'frivolity'.

Addis, in those days under the despotic rule of Haile Selassie, was a reasonably stable place with an expanding economy. Altitude-wise it was very similar to Nairobi and possessed one of the finest and healthiest climates in the world. One tends to forget that as early as the fourth century Ethiopia adopted Christianity by following the beliefs and practices of the Coptic Church based on the doctrines of St Mark.

I was impressed by the educated Ethiopians I met. They were handsome to look at, most with slender, rather than negroid, features no doubt stemming from historical links with the Arab world and latterly with Italy. They also had an air of confident superiority, not found elsewhere amongst the native population in Africa. The beauty of the women was dazzling, carrying themselves with grace, with golden-brown skins and features of the utmost fineness.

In the 1930s Italy, using rather unsporting tactics such as phosgene gas, which contravened accepted protocol, had managed under Mussolini to colonise the country. Prior to that Abyssinia, as it then was, had retained a powerful understanding of its past glories. Not only, as mentioned earlier, did they claim to

118

be among the earliest Christians but had invented their own calendar – incomprehensible to an outsider – and churned out documents in their own script. Ethiopian Airlines in those days was one of the best in Africa with able pilots seconded from Pan Am and beautiful air hostesses cultivated locally. Coffee and tourism were major earners of foreign exchange. At the time of my visit the country thrived under the firm rule of Haile Selassie, Lion of Judah and, somewhat surprisingly, the head honcho of the Rastafarian movement. Bob Marley, a latter-day Rastafarian, made dreadlocks fashionable, which were said to represent the 'Lion of Judah' – 'Don't remove the kinks from your hair, remove them from your brain,' was the message.

The Emperor's rule was not without incident and he had survived a number of attempted coups d'état in the past. Some years previously 'Sonny' Bumpus, an old Kenya hand, had regaled us with a story of the days when he was the polo coach to the Emperor's Bodyguard. The senior officers during one of Haile Selassie's many absences overseas had foolishly plotted to assume power. There were, however, sufficient elements of the army loyal to the Emperor and the plot failed. 'Sonny', who was on leave in Kenya at the time, returned, not having kept abreast of affairs, and as he drove from the airport into Addis Ababa glanced up at the lamp-posts and noticed they were festooned with what, on second glance, were some recognisable scalps. Apparently, the remains of the miscreants, after 'sensitive' interrogation, had been draped on the lamp-posts to remind the populace of the folly of questioning the ruler's authority. 'Sonny' sensibly turned round and caught the next plane back to Nairobi. Whether he had embellished his tale under the influence of a few whiskies I know not, but on balance and having witnessed the brutality of subsequent events in Ethiopia, it smacks of the truth.

Sonny had achieved some notoriety in his youth in the '20s when as a young inexperienced jockey he had ridden a young inexperienced filly, 'Wild Child', to secure a first against all the odds for a young inexperienced trainer, Beryl Markham, in the Leger, Kenya's top classic at the time. The race is described in vivid and exciting detail in *West with the Night* with Sonny portrayed as a 'lean dark-haired boy – a grand horseman, honest as daylight'. Surprisingly, this was one tale I didn't hear

119

him recount. Possibly by the '60s he had narrated the circumstances of the epic race so many times that he assumed everybody by then had been bored by his 'when I won the Leger in the 1920s ... etc.' He was nevertheless a remarkable character, even though he was no longer lean and dark-haired, with the jury probably out on 'honest as daylight'.

Incidentally, where his bodyguard had previously failed Haile Selassie was deposed in the Marxist revolution of 1974 and died in prison the next year. The true cause of death was never established, but it was believed he had been suffocated on the orders of the country's new rulers.

His replacement, Mengistu Haile Mariam, following a misguided doctrine, set about massacring the ruling élite and professional classes. In the process he destroyed the economy, ruthlessly wiped out the opposition and did nothing to help alleviate the famine in 1984 when millions perished. But that is another story.

I stayed at the Ghion hotel which was unique in my experience having a thermal swimming pool fed by underground mineral springs. While it was said to possess therapeutic qualities it was not particularly pleasant for somebody adept in my style of swimming, i.e. breathing in water and spouting out air. Even if I had been able to reverse the process, the stench of sulphur – a smell normally associated with the social discomfort felt after a generous helping of baked beans – was not an attractive alternative. Certainly any health-giving properties were not immediately apparent.

I wasn't particularly enamoured of the cuisine either. The national dish of a rubber-like bread sandwich with a filling of curried stew liberally seasoned with hot red peppers soon brought the colour back to one's cheeks in every sense. This was washed down with Tej, a drink made of honey and water and fermented with a local leaf, the name of which escapes me. Initially innocuous but of disconcerting potency. Being entertained by our local partners was a strange experience. As was customary, the host made little wads of the local delicacy and then passed these round with the booze in horn drinking-pots. Thereafter, the dancing girls were brought on – or so I imagined.

At the time of my visit the United Nations Economic

120

Commission for Africa was headquartered in Addis, housed in a building which was modelled on the United Nations headquarters in New York. With palaces, churches, modern bank buildings and a splendid new university located in a well laid out campus of evergreen and flowering trees, Addis had all the ingredients of a prosperous capital forging firmly ahead. What it is like today I have no idea but as a country torn by war and famine I cannot believe these promising prospects have been realised. In keeping with his image Haile Selassie had brought together the world's biggest collection of well-fed lions in captivity – these were housed in a specially constructed zoo, a major tourist attraction. I hope this facility still exists as, otherwise, there must be an awful lot of hungry lions roaming the countryside looking for a square meal. Possibly for this reason Ethiopia is now best known for its long distance runners. Addis itself is the centre of the conveyor-belt of Ethiopia's running revolution. Here athletes, hardened by a childhood of bare existence, whose only advantage is their country's high altitude, are honed as future Olympic champions in an attempt to escape from its grinding poverty.

Beirut

With the oil rich states of the Gulf coming on stream Lebanon was quickly establishing itself as the Switzerland of the Middle East and Beirut as the financial centre was all that it was cracked up to be. Beirut as seen from the sea was an unforgettable sight, with a skyline of modern skyscrapers and old red-tiled stone houses, against a backdrop of steep green-sided mountains the summits of which were covered with snow.

Following the influx of oil money scores of banks, both international and local, had set up shop along with the already long established financial institutions. 'Face' was everything, so the new office blocks vied with each other for the ultimate in air-conditioned luxury. Somewhat incongruously the souks presented a pleasant blend of the ancient with the modern. These were situated on narrow picturesque lanes in the heart of the city and offered a variety of spices, fruits, vegetables, footwear and all kinds of local handicraft. With the new-found wealth many of the shops concentrated on expensive jewellery and gold embellishments of every conceivable kind. In the evening, as the sun set on the darkening Mediterranean, local families came out in force to promenade along the palm-fringed corniche.

The Lebanon has an extraordinary history. At the beginning of the 14th century the Phoenicians arrived from the Persian Gulf and in the 20th century the Palestinians arrived in force following the creation of the State of Israel. In between times the land was fought over many times with Turkish domination being the most recent until after the end of the first world war when the Ottoman Empire collapsed and France re-established the Lebanon's natural boundaries. The resultant mixture of highly successful traders, French culture and the survival instincts of the Palestinians made for a potent mix of professionalism and opportunism. A dangerous potential flashpoint was the clash of Christians and Muslims vying for dominance.

At the time of my arrival I wrote a paper for the Bank's chairman that 'the Lebanese had successfully walked a tightrope for many centuries; if they ever fell off they would never get back on'. Regrettably, some of the apocalyptic prophecies of ethnic warfare have come to pass but in those days everything in the garden looked rosy.

Along with the oil money came the gambling clubs and nightspots, affluent shops, high-rise luxury apartments and enormous powerboats in the harbour at Jounieh. Snappily dressed conmen escorted and showed off showgirls who looked and dressed like Bridget Bardot. Driving around in flashy new sports cars they competed for attention as they cruised the corniche, a marked contrast to the traditionally clad Arabs. Apart from the deprived Palestinians, in their camps, everybody seemed to luxuriate in the warm Mediterranean climate. The bronzed and the beautiful frequented the beaches, elderly men indulged in endless games of backgammon, fortunes were made, palm trees swayed and, on the surface, all seemed at peace with the world.

After the restrictions of Karachi one of the pleasures of living in Beirut was that, in addition to the top hotels and nightclubs, there was a host of very fine restaurants offering every conceivable type of cuisine, with the French influence predictably dominating. This extended to the wines, although again there were some very acceptable local offerings. They were produced in the mode of the classic Bordeaux varieties at well-kept vineyards in the Bekaa valley. Regardless, it was very much the fad to serve Mateus Rose. While very much derided now – then it was the popular 'cool' drink to complement the relaxed Mediterranean ambience.

Coincidentally, we purchased our present house from Richard Rawlings whose family flouted the gloomy forebodings of the wine buffs and introduced Mateus Rose to the UK. The experts pointed out that the peculiar shape of the bottle meant that it could never be effectively stored on a wine rack. They had not factored into the equation that the attractive bottle would become a fashion statement and was in great demand as a lamp base/candle holder. Princess Margaret gave it the ultimate seal of approval by stating that it was her favourite tipple. While it can still be obtained today the strength of sales achieved in the '50s and '60s has never been repeated.

As previously mentioned it was of prime importance in Beirut to keep up appearances. The directors of the Bank (ex-Ottoman), knowing this, had booked me in at the top hotel, the Saint George – the ultimate in traditional luxury, with its own beach club and moorings. It was sited directly opposite the equally luxurious but modern Phoenicia Inter-Continental Hotel. While the latter did not have the same prime position it benefited from a viewing platform in a bar beneath the surface of the swimming pool. This was a popular spot for voyeurs checking out the talent – one didn't have to go to such extremes at the St George where the showgirls were readily on view, lying on their sun-beds with their attendant sugar daddies.

After the day's work was done I kept my hand in at water-skiing and my skills improved dramatically. While the azure waters of the bay looked inviting enough, over the centuries the town fathers had not addressed the problem of how to dispose of the city's sewerage so one took a nose-dive at one's peril.

My arrival coincided with the collapse of the Lebanon's largest local bank, the Intra Bank. Kidder Peabody, the American Investment Bank, were sent in to sort out the resultant mess. Colin Allen, my boss in London, came out to check on progress and we paid a courtesy call on Kidder. William Ladd, their Managing Director, had taken over for his personal use the penthouse formerly occupied by Intra Bank's chairman, and was looking for new tenants. To my surprise Colin Allen said Grindlays would be interested and, having viewed the most expensively appointed and tastefully furnished apartment in Beirut, the deeds were signed and I moved in. Colin knew what he was doing as below me in the same block were a plethora of multi-millionaires. Dr Pharaon, King Saud's personal adviser, had an apartment. Ministers of the Government and local bank chairmen also resided. In flying the British Flag I had purchased the latest model Rover (car of the year) but this now looked incongruous parked in the basement garage alongside the Ferraris and Lamborghinis. No matter – I had acquired the most sought-after apartment in Beirut.

It had spectacular, all-encompassing views. A panorama of snow-capped mountains and the sweep of St George's Bay. It was so breathtaking I took a series of photographs depicting the different mood swings throughout the day. It was not the scarlet claw of sunset or the rosy-fingered dawn of the African plains. At early dawn, with the mist over the sea, empty of clouds, the cool grey-blue of the sky turned to yellow then, as the sun climbed, to aquamarine. Before dusk one could feast, in the golden light of evening, on the snow of the mountains as they turned from pink to arctic blue. A perfect setting for the evening sundowner on the terrace.

Most of our Lebanese friends lived in houses/apartments fitted out in the French style with plush curtains, gilt furniture, numerous ornaments and invariably over decorated to provide evidence of their prosperity.

Lord Aldington had decreed that the Bank's representative office should rival in opulence the finest the competition could offer. Accordingly, architects and interior designers were briefed and builders and decorators drafted in to meet their criteria. Grindlays had inherited from the Ottoman Bank a substantial share in the Société Nouvelle de Banque du Syrie et du Liban. Accordingly, a floor in their head office was set aside to be suitably renovated – when finished to the most exacting standards, I took up occupancy. A far cry from my last office in dusty Karachi – fake veneers and plastic had been replaced by

124

mahogany, modern works of art and mind-bogglingly expensive Barcelona chairs.

Not only had I arrived but also my family, who were comfortably ensconced in their new, somewhat daunting, apartment. What more could a man want for other than a fluency in French, which was proving hard to come by. In retrospect one of my major achievements in Beirut was persuading the French management of the SNBSL to hold their board meetings in English.

One of my early contacts was with Albert Abela who ran the Casino of the Lebanon and whose company provided the inflight catering for Middle East Airlines. The casino was one of the Lebanon's main attractions about half an hour's drive from Beirut. Apart from the elegantly furnished gambling rooms, according to the blurb it was ... 'the world's most spectacular pleasure palace with an ultra modern theatre providing the best international floor shows'. Albert had married one of his star performers, an ex-Miss Germany. Driving back late at night the curve of the bay lit by a myriad lights was like a diamond necklace.

The Abela contact came in useful as, again on a flying visit, Lord Aldington had a brief stop-over at Beirut airport and required an update as to the office's progress. Albert duly togged me out in the uniform of one of his catering staff and much to Lord A.'s surprise, within the restricted confines of the airport, I pitched up at his elbow offering a soft drink with the query, 'Are you being served?' More brownie points for the future, I thought.

Alas, these were nullified as on his return he actually took time to stop over in Beirut and an appointment was arranged with the Prime Minister. Lord A. opened his spiel by remarking that he had breakfasted that morning on the terrace of the Bank apartment gazing at one of the most spectacular views – the cerulean Mediterranean, snow-capped mountains, etc. The PM politely enquired in French where I lived and, having recently moved in, I had no idea of the address. After fifteen minutes poring over street maps – and liberal use of the interpreter – we located the Yamama Building, by which time the PM had excused himself and dashed off to his next appointment leaving a bewildered Lord A. in his wake. Fortunately,

125

a successful opening reception for the representative office was widely covered in the national press and Lord A, departed suitably mollified.

The Beirut social scene was liberally studded with cocktail parties and formal dinners – in fact, we were invited out more or less continuously. At first this was exciting but after a while it grew somewhat tedious and we became more choosy. At one rather grand dinner party we were sitting at a table with the Lebanon's most glamorous couple, Danny Chamoun and his wife. Apart from being notorious sybarites the Chamouns controlled the far right Christian militia (the Phalange). Finding myself on the dance floor with Mrs Chamoun I complimented her on her beauty (first having established that she had once been Miss Australia) and to further impress I executed what I thought to be a rather complicated double reverse whisk only to find that she was smoothly in control. It transpired that she had previously been married to Victor Sylvester junior.

Danny's father, Kamille Chamoun, was President of the Lebanon in the mid '50s. Under his stewardship the Lebanon became a haven of freedom and security and a last bastion of liberalism in the Arabic-speaking world, all of which contributed to the country's subsequent prosperity. Despite the support of the business class he was resented, however, by the less well off Lebanese Muslims – a downtrodden majority in a Christian dominated State. With the establishment of the United Arab Republic the internal situation of the Lebanon deteriorated further with Muslims in open rebellion. Chamoun called in the assistance of the American fleet. This quelled the revolt and the Lebanon returned to some normality with the slogan, 'no victor, no vanquished' becoming the formula for peace. Unfortunately for Chamoun the perceived political alliance with the USA was not popular and cost him his job. I have mentioned all of this as it illustrates that discontent between the Christians and Muslims was always festering just below the surface. The Phalange had been formed about this time as a Christian para-military group to counteract a similar organisation set up to protect Muslim interests.

Danny Chamoun was later brutally murdered during the internecine strife that followed some years later when the Lebanon erupted into carnage.

126

We became quite friendly with Roger Tamraz (ex-Kidder Peabody) and his wife. Roger, an Egyptian by birth, subsequently went on to take control over most of the local banks at the height of the Palestinian/Israeli conflict in Beirut. I wonder if he is still such a powerful influence in the financial affairs of the new Lebanon.

While on the subject of the social scene it was considerably enlivened by the comings and goings at the British Embassy. Although we were only in Beirut for just over two years during this time we paid our respects to no fewer than three British Ambassadors. Cecil King was on the point of retiring when we arrived and his successor, Sir Paul Wright, took his place but briefly, when he in turn was replaced by Alan Edden. We were not privy to the reasons for the quick changeovers but nevertheless enjoyed the hospitality meted out as a result. Lady Wright (Babs) was remarkable having given up a promising future as a politician to support the consular career of her second husband. Previously married to John Rathbone she had the distinction of entering the House of Commons as the second American-born woman, after Viscountess Astor, to become an MP. At the time she was considered to have the making of a Prime Minister – shades of Margaret Thatcher! All this was to change when she married Paul Wright and followed the diplomatic flag. Coincidentally, her son, Tim Rathbone, was our local MP until he died recently. Alan Edden did not last long in the post and, again coincidentally, I met up with him for lunch some twenty years later in Pietermaritzburg. His replacement, Sir Peter Wakefield, we got to know on our next posting when we were transferred to Tokyo, where he was the Commercial Minister at the Embassy. I had always assumed that the Bank was unsurpassed for switching its staff from pillar to post at short notice but this convoluted tale would suggest that the Foreign Office were serious rivals in the 'upheaval' stakes.

The foreign banking community, while being overtly competitive, could not have been more helpful and entertaining and many worthwhile relationships were established. Peter Wodtke (Citibank) and his charming wife, Carol, became lasting friends and our paths crossed again in Japan and the USA.

Grindlays Bank had now come to the conclusion, no doubt

prompted by my shortcomings, that to be successful in the Middle East a fluency in Arabic was advantageous. We accordingly sent our graduate trainees to MECAS (Middle East College for Arabic Studies) at Shemlan, the infamous spy school of Kim Philby notoriety. This was a costly exercise as, once they passed the exam most, but fortunately not all, of our staff were lured away to competitive financial institutions at twice the salary. Nothing ventured nothing gained.

VII

Wandering Around the Middle East

While in Beirut the main thrust of my energies was to solicit deposits, promote trade related activities with the local banks and cultivate international clients and persuade them to utilise the services of the Grindlays branch network. I was also called upon to resolve situations where branches had problems in the region.

Syria

On one such occasion I found myself on the Road to Damascus. The panorama as far as the Syrian border was quite dramatic with snow-capped mountains, pine-clad hills and fruit orchards strung along the Bekaa valley. Syria – the cradle of ancient civilizations – was a different kettle of fish and, while in parts the scenery is attractively varied, the lasting impression was of endless deserts and extensive plains. Damascus was a grave disappointment; it had obviously seen better times. A grid of claustrophobic, charmless streets that seemed to suck the life from the struggling palm trees that lined the main thoroughfare. I was informed, but found it difficult to believe, that the prophet Mohammed never wanted to revisit Damascus as he did not wish to enter heaven twice.

Apart from the odd attractive mosque I saw nothing of note and my task of finding the 23rd People's Bank (all the banks had been nationalised) nearly proved mission impossible.

I eventually located the bank down some side street, having been misdirected umpteen times. The interior was shabby in the extreme. Furnished in plastic with intimidating portraits of the ruling junta glowering down. Having sought out the manager, no-one would have in any way connected him with a bank. He was very fat, very dirty, and unshaven, with a straggling moustache offset by a lugubrious expression. Not a promising start and, having outlined the problem, I was met with a typical shrug of the shoulders and fobbed off with the vague promise that the matter would be investigated. If anything his approaching siesta seemed an issue of greater importance. Predictably, I heard no more and, like the prophet Mohammed, but for very different reasons, did not return to Damascus.

Tripoli

My next trip was to Libya where Colonel Gadaffi was wreaking havoc. Grindlays had inherited from the Ottoman Bank, along with Lebanese partners, a small stake in a Libyan bank. Following the recent revolution the Bank in question had been nationalised and, as far as I could gather, the local directors executed.

On arrival in Tripoli I had been instructed to carry out 'the legwork' and meet up with our Lebanese partner – an influential lady by the name of Nadia Khoury – in the evening. To add to the general air of confusion Gaddafi had decreed that all signs, including advertisements, be painted over in Arabic. Knowing that Barclays Bank had a major presence in Tripoli and thinking they would be the best source of unbiased information I made my way to what I thought was their head office. Once inside, having wasted a futile 30 minutes, I suddenly realised I was in the Post Office. The mistake rectified I linked up with Barclays and subsequently met the boss of Shell Co. They both advised that there was little to be achieved in resuscitating the Bank's fortunes and suggested a quick cultural tour of the city with its many museums.

I was rather impressed with Tripoli and could well understand why so many Italians (now disconsolate) had made it their home. It was a city of contrasts, comprising an old town characterised by a network of ancient narrow streets counterbalanced by modern broad walks lined by cafés with colourful umbrellas providing shade – and the blue Mediterranean beyond.

Cairo

I had a number of reasons for visiting Cairo. Firstly, it was within my parish but, primarily, I was sent to assess what chance the Bank had of re-establishing a presence in Egypt. It was rumoured that the authorities were relaxing the regulations and permitting foreign banks to operate there with a restrictive licence. Also, of course, part of my responsibilities was to promote reciprocal business with correspondent banks, in this case the nationalised Egyptian banks.

Cairo was then, and probably still is, the largest city in Africa. Steeped in history, at one time it was famed for its modern architecture, luxurious hotels, restaurants and gracious boulevards intersected by the mighty Nile. On my arrival none of this was evident as a pall of smog overhung the city. My visit got off to a bad start. The humidity was like steam from a hot bath, the luggage trolleys didn't work, the porters didn't look inclined to work and to get access to a taxi I had to fight off a rabble of competing cabbies jostling for business. The taxis were mostly antiquated American Chevrolets. In my case, according to the driver, who wore a singularly vile expression, his meter was not working. I was thus wrongfooted in having to haggle for a fare for which I had no basis for comparison. On leaving the airport I was immediately caught up in a massive traffic jam – my feeling of discomfort was not helped by gusts of heavily polluted air blowing through the car's ventilation system. Having accepted the inevitable snarl up, the journey thereafter proved remarkably interesting as I had time to absorb a passing kaleidoscope of old and new with the commercial centre apparently humming with activity. As I was to find out the next day nothing in Cairo hummed with activity. Eventually, we reached my designated hotel, the Nile Hilton, which, as its name suggests, was located on the banks of the river.

From my bedroom balcony at night the city was transformed. As the traffic evaporated, so too did the smog, and the dark corridor of the Nile, lit up by the odd pleasure boat and bordered either side by the brilliant lights and neon signs of the city presented an unforgettable sight. The 'mysteries of the East' were encapsulated in a mélange of fragrances: smoke

131

from cooking fires, open sewers, orange blossom. The sounds of unfamiliar birds filled the night. It was only the sporadic hooting of familiar traffic which brought one back to normality.

Alas, the rest of my visit was pretty forgettable and, apart from the odd snippet of business and a splendid lunch at the famed Shepheards Hotel, I wasn't sad to depart the 'City of Minarets and Belly Dancers'.

In fact my abiding memory is of a city sweating, stinking and crumbling under a stifling, baking sun; of being stuck in traffic with the poisonous fumes of exhausts constricting my lungs; and of a threadbare infrastructure cracking under the strain. It has been remarked that no sound made by mankind is quite so strident as two Neapolitan washerwomen in full flow. Obviously Cairo had not been factored into the equation as the voices of two Arab women at loggerheads is every bit as dire. This ululation seemed to be the norm rather than the exception as I wandered about my business. At times the discordant blare of traffic horns was hard-pressed to compete.

President Nasser's subsequent assassination put on hold the granting of restrictive banking licences, although I believe Lloyds Bank eventually established a presence there, but I don't think they ever made a profit.

Dubai

Although the bank did not have a branch in Dubai we had a meaningful stake, in those days, in the National Bank of Dubai which also had the considerable backing of the ruler. The management staff had been recruited from Grindlays and for many the generous terms of service made a welcome top-up to their pension. The General Manager, David Mack, was no slouch in making himself comfortable and had constructed a splendid apartment covering the whole of the top floor of the head office. An interesting feature was that he had the only 'sunray' lamps in the Middle East; these were trained on tropical plants festooned round some of the reception areas. A splendid beach house was an added perk.

At the time of my visit Dubai had but two hotels, the Carlton in the centre of the city and the Al Bustan at the airport.

132

Although Dubai was not directly involved, the 'oil rush' was on and such was the demand for rooms one was invariably obliged to share with a not particularly couth rigger from Texas. Fortunately, the Al Bustan was owned by Laura Bustani, a Beirut client, so I was given favoured treatment in the form of my own bedroom with en suite bathroom to boot.

Between the airport and the National Bank in the town centre, was a great expanse of sandy wasteland where one could see, early in the morning, numerous games of cricket in progress with players from India and Pakistan. With the Gulf States booming there was a considerable demand for construction workers from the sub-continent.

Dubai, unlike its neighbours, didn't have any worthwhile oil reserves and depended on its trading links, chiefly in gold, spices and pearls. It was also, rather strangely, the largest importer of Swiss watches, particularly Rolex, in the world. The gold was in the main illegally exported to India, where traditionally the populace have a distrust for the local currency and like to see their wealth in some tangible form. The importation also was subject to prohibitive taxes. As such the gold was shipped in dhows which in addition to their quota of sails had, below decks, powerful engines.

Apparently the ploy was to stand off the Indian coastline until nightfall and then, under cover of darkness, step on the accelerator pedal, beat the patrolling customs launches and deposit the gold ashore. This was a highly risky business – the rewards were great but, if caught, the gold and the dhow would be confiscated. This trade was financed by wealthy syndicates in Dubai who took the profits and underwrote the losses (shades of Lloyds of London). One such syndicate was operated by some of the expatriate management of the National Bank of Dubai. If the voyage was successful the initial investment, I was told, would produce a very tidy profit – a run of bad luck could just as quickly wipe out any gain. All good fun if you could afford it.

Then the most dominant architectural features were the traditional wind towers and I vividly remember the spice souk where you could find sacks brimming with frankincense, dried lemons, ginger root – the aromas which wafted around were intoxicating. Dubai is divided by a creek and a regular service

133

of small wooden boats shuttled between the two shores – this gave a close-up view of the boat life: a mix of traditional dhows, cargo ships and a smattering of luxurious yachts.

Dubai today, of course, is one of the most vibrant and successful cities in the world with spectacular hotels, first class golf and race courses, luxury shopping malls and the famous gold souk (now air-conditioned) to tempt both businessmen and tourists alike. If it is a party you are after Dubai offers a huge range of nightclubs offering every form of entertainment. At the time of my first visit I recollect but one venue, where, after a few beers, the Johnny Cash impersonator's rendition of *I Walk the Line* got one's feet tapping.

In terms of a profitable return, my trip was reasonably successful. Other than the National Bank of Dubai, numerous local banks had sprung up and many were managed by ex-Grindlays staff. They, in turn, were looking for agency arrangements to promote financing their export/import trade through an internationally recognised bank in London – such as Grindlays.

Oman

In the late 1960s it was extremely difficult to obtain a visa to visit Oman which was still very much a feudal state with the old ruler, Sultan Said, exercising restrictive powers through his right hand man, the British Resident. Accordingly, even to pay a routine visit to our newly opened branch I required the trumped up excuse of a need to inspect the books for any discrepancies.

The capital, Muscat, was then enclosed within city walls. There were no hotels, and I was accommodated in the Manager's flat above the bank situated just outside the main gate to the old town. Taxis were never allowed inside. Three hours after sunset a gun was fired, the main gate was closed and all pedestrians within the walls had to carry a lighted paraffin lamp. On being invited out to dinner by an old friend from Aden we trooped through the narrow streets carrying lanterns which threw shadows against the beautifully carved doors of the old Arab homes. All very atmospheric. In the days of the old ruler all the local people had to wear a regulation dress of an ankle length white shirt, similar to a nightgown, topped by a skull cap, fortunately without a tassel.

While Grindlays had a fair slice of the business on offer, having opened in 1969, the British Bank of the Middle East (now HSBC), had set up shop as early as 1948. It thus managed the bulk of the Government's finances and with oil production coming on stream this was a lucrative business. Out of town Shell Co. had a large expatriate presence with their own makeshift golf course carved out of the desert. Their catering requirements were met by my old friend, Albert Abela.

In my meetings with customers, existing and potential, I was received with particular courtesy when I mentioned the time I had spent in Zanzibar. Prior to Zanzibar's independence, in addition to the Sultan, all the ruling class had Omani backgrounds and there were strong trade links.

I was privileged to be invited to tea by the British Resident who lived in an imposing, if somewhat ramshackle, villa built on a prime position at the entrance to the harbour.

To my embarrassment during my visit the normally relatively clear waters of the harbour were stained a murky brown. At this time trade agreements were in force which imposed strict coffee quotas. Apparently these could be sidetracked by exporting coffee to the Middle East. One of my customers in Beirut, Hassan Moledina, had spotted this loophole and arranged for a large shipment of coffee beans from Uganda to Oman. While en route the regulations had been relaxed and Moledina stood to suffer a substantial loss. As was customary in these dealings the ship in question sank in mysterious circumstances just off shore and an insurance claim was duly lodged.

On the day of my departure my flight was indefinitely delayed, the airport announcement giving the rather advanced technical reason that the rheostat was not working. My host, Des Hardman, suggested a swim off a beach near the airport, reassuring me that we would see the aircraft approaching and have plenty of time to change. It was during this dip that I realised that as a drink coffee and salt water was not a pleasant brew. The aircraft, a Fokker Friendship, eventually hove into view three hours late. When I enquired from the pilot if the rheostat had been satisfactorily repaired he looked puzzled and said the problem had been with the rear steps!

At one time Oman was a maritime force to be reckoned with, having a power base encompassing Mogadishu, Mombasa and Zanzibar and, latterly, Baluchistan. However, with the development of the steamship and the opening of the Suez Canal a lengthy period of stagnation resulted. This was all to change with the discovery of oil in commercial quantities in 1964.

Oman, under the enlightened leadership of Sultan Quaboos, after the death of his father in 1970 is now probably the most attractive of the Gulf States scenically, offering unexpected delights for the more adventurous tourist. First class hotels, lovely beaches and well constructed motorways giving access to the mountainous hinterland provide major attractions. The country's wealth has been wisely utilised and an abundance of banks, local and international, have sprung up to service the broad spectrum of financial needs. Sadly, the old town of Muscat is now unrecognisable, having been swamped by the surrounding developments. Fortunately, the old airport with its runway ending abruptly in front of a sheer cliff face, has been re-sited and replaced with an ultra-modern facility catering for every type of aircraft imaginable.

Gulf States

At times, during my travels, I fondly imagined that I was following in the footsteps of the great explorer, Wilfred Thesiger, whose fascinating crossings of the 'Empty Quarter' are recounted in his book *Arabian Sands*. Despite BOAC's reputation – 'Better On A Camel' – I nevertheless flew where Thesiger had trekked.

On arrival I was greeted with a blast of hot desert air and found a luminous landscape, half sea half sky, divided by low horizons of deserted beaches and seascapes running all the way across to the Indian sub-continent, dotted by dhows with giant single sails harnessed to the trade winds. The new-found wealth of the region was evident, with giant oil tankers cluttering the sea lanes.

It was only appropriate that I should visit the Bank's branches in the region: Abu Dhabi, Sharjah, Qatar and Bahrain (where we had an interest in a local bank).

We were still in the process of getting permission to have a presence in Ras al Khaymah, a small state bordering the mountainous region of Oman. It had nothing to commend it beyond the fact that the 'visionary' Albert Abela was building an hotel there in the hope that he would get a licence to operate a casino and also, of course, the prospect that oil might be discovered within its boundaries.

I had arranged to meet the ruler, assisted in my task by his Palestinian advisor who was seeking to get his brother a job with the Bank. I arrived bearing a gift of an ancient map of the Gulf discovered in Beirut, at no small cost, emphasising the existence of Persia, Ras al Khaymah and Oman but making no mention of Kuwait, Bahrain, Dubai, etc. The ruler was tickled pink that his 'insignificant' state had been given such prominence. As far as meetings go it was not the most stimulating. After exchanging a few introductory civilities we sat in silence for about twenty minutes contemplating our coffee. I was then seen out by the ruler's interpreter when I endeavoured to seize the moment and submit our case for a banking licence. We conversed in a laborious mixture of French and English. Having announced that he spoke English this was clearly an exaggeration as his English was as bad as my French. While he had a flair for the narrative the ensuing discussion was fairly incomprehensible so I was more than slightly surprised when the requisite banking licence was subsequently granted. Possibly the present of the map swung the decision in our favour.

While on the subject of gifts, one of our managers, who will remain nameless, came up with the cunning plan to have the ruler's portrait painted in oils. He secured the official photograph, sent it back to London, had the portrait expertly reproduced and lavishly framed at the Bank's expense and personally presented it to the ruler on his birthday. The gesture was much appreciated and on her birthday the manager's wife received a magnificent emerald ring in return. The couple in question shortly after moved on to pastures new.

With so much wealth sloshing around, for some it became a rather bizarre and artificial existence. One of our managers built a grand villa with all mod cons and sizeable swimming pool, an unheard of luxury in those far off days when there were no desalination plants and fresh water was in short supply.

137

An unpredictable water level was an added distraction and could cause problems if one plunged in at the shallow end. That said, life was never other than interesting. Abu Dhabi and Doha were rising phoenix-like out of the desert, with building contractors making and losing fortunes. The only persons secure in their wealth were the Palestinian middle men, who took a commission at every turn.

Bahrain conversely, with very little oil to speak of, had successfully built up a commercial infrastructure which flourished as the oil wealth of its neighbours spilled over – it had a gold souk to rival that of Dubai. One of our customers from Beirut had a successful business there and drove me round the island in his Buick Riviera – air-conditioned luxury only matched by that of the most expensive Cadillac. The causeway to Dharan in Saudi Arabia was still on the drawing-board. Bahrain took on added importance as many of the major airlines used it as a staging post for their international routes. It has, of course, since been superseded by the magnificent airport built in Dubai, one of the finest in the world.

Sharjah

En route to Abu Dhabi I stopped over in Sharjah where we had recently opened a branch. Although it is the third largest of the seven states which comprised the United Arab Emirates in the late '60s the 'town' was but one main street and little more than a fishing village. There were, however, signs of a considerable amount of construction work in progress. In the late '50s Thesiger called it 'as drab and tumble down as Abu Dhabi but infinitely more squalid for it was littered with discarded rubbish which had been mass-produced elsewhere'. Even in the late '60s it still had not really got its act together.

As an employer, Grindlays was reasonably generous in many ways but I found the first clash of cultures with the newly joined Ottoman Bank staff. The appointed manager – a relatively young ex-graduate – had as his first priority purchased a top of the range Land Rover to enable him to explore the hinterland with his family at weekends. Until then the rule was that Bank cars should be used primarily on bank business and, depending

138

on status, must fall within a certain price range. This seemingly went by the board at the time of integration and a Mercedes, certainly in the Gulf, became the norm rather than the exception.

Without the benefit of oil, the town's main attractions then lay in tourism. It offered a fine beach and traditional native markets with a wide range of local craftwork – daggers, copperware, 'antiques', etc. The ambition was to turn Sharjah into a flourishing commercial centre. However, Sharjah's fortunes changed dramatically with the discovery of off-shore oil in 1972, although the oil price crash of 1985 left the state heavily in debt. In 1992 major new natural gas discoveries improved the economy to the extent that the city's motto, 'Smile you are now in Sharjah', seems more appropriate. I still have reason to visit Dubai and next time it will be worth travelling further 'up the road' to see if Sharjah has kept pace with the other states in the region, but I somehow doubt it.

Abu Dhabi

Abu Dhabi is the largest of the Trucial States with the town itself built on a sandbank. Even in those far off days it was beginning to resemble a huge building site. At the time of my visit the highway to Al'Ain, the only other town of any note, was in the process of being completed. A French contractor was installing an irrigation system to provide water for the newly planted palm trees and flowering shrubs destined to line the route. At the time I thought this an extraordinary extravagance. I was recently informed that a six lane highway now provides the 100-odd mile link between Abu Dhabi and Al'Ain. It is divided by a constantly watered grassed reservation, planted with palm trees, bougainvillaea, oleanders and other flowering plants. A thick belt of trees on either side keeps the desert at bay. It is a far cry from the original sandy track that existed before oil came on stream. Abu Dhabi also now boasts its own championship golf course. Such is the power of the extraordinary wealth created by the discovery of enormous oil reserves during the late 1960s.

Apparently the previous ruler, Sheikh Shakhbut, had kept most of his money in a mattress under his bed until persuaded by the manager of the Ottoman Bank to do otherwise. I believe the manager's name was Gillespie, a fluent Arabist who finished up running a bank in Kuwait. Thus Grindlays (in the form of Ottoman Bank) had a head start, particularly when John Butter who was well known to Grindlays in Nairobi where he had been financial advisor to the Treasury, had been transferred to undertake a senior rôle in administering the state's finances.

In those days the expatriate community was a friendly and closely knit group and during my short visit I was quickly swept up in the local social life, where Captain Jimmy Butts (who featured in an earlier escapade) was still happily married and in charge of the ruler's stables – a rewarding and well paid position. Brian Constant was the manager and had recently acquired for the Bank a well-equipped high-powered speedboat. Thus, with swimming, sailing and water skiing on the agenda the expatriate staff seemed reasonably content with their lot. Despite the extremes of heat – air-conditioning was the norm and with most afternoons off it wasn't a bad life.

Just prior to leaving Karachi we had the privilege of meeting the ruler, Sheikh Zayed, at a reception hosted in his honour. In fact, Elizabeth's photograph had appeared in the local paper shaking his hand. He and his entourage had been invited to Pakistan by the United Bank, who then rather cleverly had arranged a hawking trip, a favourite sport throughout Arabia (our spies informed us that other, less sporting, pastimes had been laid on but the least said about these the better). Apparently, the Pakistani falcons were much in demand and, once trained, they were ideal for hunting birds and rabbits. A Citibanker in Jeddah had come up with the cunning ploy of importing from the USA a tracker device which could be fitted to a falcon. With well-trained birds hard to come by and, if side tracked, difficult to locate, this proved a much sought after gadget. Accordingly, the banker in question found marketing opportunities opening up in areas which had previously been difficult to penetrate.

Re-reading my Thesiger it would seem that as recently as 1948 he described Abu Dhabi as a small dilapidated town along the sea-shore surrounded by empty desert – a far cry from the building site at the time of my visit and the thriving city it is today with its striking modern architecture and every conceivable amenity.

Qatar

Larger than most Gulf States, Qatar is 'a teardrop peninsula attached to Saudi Arabia almost as a divine afterthought'. About 80 per cent of the population live in Doha. The indigenous population is swollen dramatically by the large numbers of expatriate workers. Originally, and before the discovery of oil, Qatar was famous for its pearls but the advent of the artificial variety severely damaged this trade. Rather surprisingly oil was first discovered in 1940 and the Ottoman Bank, realising its potential, established their first Gulf branch there in 1956.

Although in the '60s the advent of oil had transformed Doha from a small pearling and fishing community into what was fast becoming a modern city, the Bank's business was still mainly centred on the financing of imports and looking after the needs of the merchants in the Bazaar. At the time of my visit the main branch was located in the somewhat down-at-heel original premises in Suq Wakef. New office blocks had been built alongside, blocking out any natural light, so this was known as the 'Black Hole'. However, I was shown plans drawn up by our architect in Beirut for a spacious new centrally air-conditioned office and the foundations had already been laid, albeit in what was then one of the outer suburbs. I understand that following the 'oil hike' in 1974 and with the expansion of business it was soon back in the heart of the action. In the 1960s the development of Doha was somewhat ahead of the Emirate States – there was already a modern comfortable hotel in place with its own beach club.

Architecturally Doha was a bit of a hotch-potch although an attractive 'corniche' was nearing completion and the main mosque, ruler's palace and clock tower were not without their attractions. But, along with its neighbours, Qatar was going through a metamorphosis and obviously there have been dramatic improvements since my fleeting visit in the '60s. I was amazed the other day to witness on TV the splendid new golf course with verdant fairways and greens to rival the splendid, well-established courses in Dubai. An amazing transformation compared to the gravelly terrain and bleak hinterland of distant memory. Also, of course, Qatar now has the world's largest natural gas reserves, a resource which is bankrolling the State's rapid development.

141

Saudi Arabia

Saudi Arabia was one of the first countries in the Middle East to become a major player in the oil game, when the 'black gold' was first discovered in the late 1930s. Prior to that time it was better known for the exploits of Lawrence of Arabia, Wilfred Thesiger and other notable worthies. With the discovery of oil came all the benefits, and disadvantages, of modern society. Although to outsiders it appears an unnecessarily strict and at times cruel régime, it seems to work: there is very little crime and an abundance of good manners. The Saudis are justifiably famous for their boundless hospitality, the taking of coffee being an important part of any introduction. Most meals were enjoyed at modern hotels and I was not subjected to the ordeal of having to chew the dreaded sheep's eye. I'm still not sure if this is fact or fiction.

Saudi Arabia was a natural target for any self-respecting banking representative. In doing the ground work I chatted up my contacts in Beirut and came up with some interesting letters of introduction. One of my neighbours, Kamal Khoury, suggested I visited friends who ran the Bin Laden Construction Co. in Jeddah – a multi-million pound conglomerate. Albert Abela recommended I look up Prince Turki (now the Saudi Ambassador in London) his Patron who took care of his various interests in Saudi, ranging from Kent cigarettes to luxury cars. Armed with these, and a few others to lesser mortals, I set off initially to Riyadh, the administrative capital. Here I joined up with Philip Brewer from our Karachi office, who wisely followed up the contacts he had made and subsequently took early retirement and became General Manager of the Riyadh Bank Ltd.

After making the statutory business calls I met up for dinner with friends from Aden, Hugh and Sally Freeland. Hugh ran the major supermarket which operated under the Spinneys franchise. They seemed to enjoy the lifestyle, being heavily involved with the equine scene. Their social life revolved round the numerous expatriates who had set up shop in Saudi to install and service the many defence projects resulting from contracts won by the British government.

After Riyadh we flew non-stop to Jeddah – or so we thought. Being an evening flight we had just finished dinner when we

142

landed and our fellow passengers in first class disembarked. Like sheep we followed into the pitch darkness of the night to a small hut lit by a single lantern at the end of the runway. Apart from being colder than we expected we were further mystified when a waiting European grabbed one of the awaiting cars and shot off into the Stygian gloom. On enquiring about customs formalities we were told there were none at Taif! We then realised our mistake. Fortunately, so too had the pilot and the departing aircraft shimmied to a halt at the end of the runway.

We dashed back in some confusion and, once settled in our seats, it was explained to us that members of the ruling family had diverted the aircraft to their summer palace in the mountainous region of Taif. An announcement had been made to this effect in Arabic. On reflection we assumed that the fast disappearing European had thought that we were unannounced inspectors coming to investigate the local oil company's books. The error of our ways and the naivety of our mistake threw into question our image as international bankers when we arrived at the vast airport in Jeddah packed with thousands of pilgrims en route to Mecca.

Jeddah, while being a bustling metropolis, was then but a shadow of its present self. All the banks that could get a licence, had gathered like vultures round the honeypot. The manager of the Dutch Algemene Bank said it was the ultimate pre-retirement posting as he was paid a bonus related to profits generated. As one of the original banks, Algemene had enormous deposits on which they paid no interest, in line with Sharia law. Accordingly, it was one of their most profitable branches.

Citibank had managed to establish a joint venture and we had dinner with one of their managers. They had their own housing complex boasting every amenity with a full-size swimming pool, tennis courts, etc. A friend, seconded from Morgan Guaranty, worked for the Saudi Arabian Monetary Authority and, being Friday, which is a holiday, we spent a pleasant day at his beach house and water-skied along the Creek. All in all, taking into account their bulging pay packets, most expatriates considered it to be a life to be recommended on a short term basis.

I was duly invited out to dinner by executives of the Bin Laden Group at the company villa – the hugely wealthy founder had come up from the Yemen. After a convivial meal, attendants brought hookahs which were passed round for a communal smoke. I had previously been warned that if I sucked one of these I was bound to catch some frightful disease; I did so, however, without any lasting ill effect. Having passed the test I left with some worthwhile Euro Dollar deposits which were placed in the name of family members. Today, presumably, they would be subjected to the ultimate scrutiny.

With the consumption of alcohol strictly banned one tended to drink copious amounts of coffee, quite often washed down with apple juice. While helping one's colonic irrigation it was no substitute for the real thing. Accordingly, most expatriates I met, despite dire threats of punishment, had rigged up Heath Robinson style stills producing a surprisingly drinkable 'gin'.

Iran

I made two trips to Teheran in 1971, both times in the winter. I have never felt quite so cold. Despite the splendour of the surrounding snow-capped mountains, Teheran is not the most attractive of cities. There seems to have been no concept of central planning, with ugly concrete buildings overpowering what was good of the traditional architecture. The saving grace was the Bazaar – a virtual treasure trove of antiquities as Russian Jews, fleeing persecution, had cashed in family heirlooms as they made their tortuous way to the 'promised land'. For the tourist, old Persian miniatures painted on ivory were beguiling. Regrettably, to the untutored eye, it was well nigh impossible to spot the imitations from the genuine article. I contented myself by purchasing an old hookah embellished with a filigree of silver and semi-precious stones.

The first visit was to follow up an introduction from the Kettaneh family in Beirut – a cousin looked after a number of lucrative agencies ranging from Sikorsky helicopters to General Electric refrigerators. This produced a number of worthwhile leads. I was also present at the signing of a Euro Dollar loan to Pars Paper Factory, a deal originated by our merchant bank in London. This in turn lead to another proposal which would probably have gelled if the political scene had not changed.

On my first visit, being new to Teheran I booked in at the most central hotel in the commercial district so that I could walk to most of my appointments. This was a mistake as this particular hostelry had certainly seen better days – the saving grace was a red-hot stove in the bedroom. Adequate compensation for any discomfort arrived the next day when I was entertained to lunch by Bank Melli. Lashings of Beluga caviar and blinis washed down by 'copious' amounts of ice-cold vodka followed by grilled salmon steaks certainly promoted a feeling of well-being. By the time I was conducted on a prolonged tour to see the closely guarded Peacock Throne surrounded by buckets of precious and semi-precious stones and other treasures I was also feeling distinctly queasy and the buckets looked positively inviting. The offer of a chauffeur driven car back to my billet was accepted with alacrity. The next day when I was confronted with the same menu at a lunch hosted by the BP representative I knew how to pace myself. Cooper Bros, for a change of scenery, entertained me to lunch at the Teheran Golf and Country Club – I wonder if it still exists.

On the second visit I was joined by one of the Bank's General Managers in London, Brian Barr. Our brief was to investigate the feasibility of taking a major stake in one of the local banks. This proved an onerous and time-consuming task: not only were we assessing management and questioning balance sheets but also judging the possible reaction were we to move matters forward. Brian, a senior colleague, could not have been a more amiable companion and his fluency in French made up for my own inadequacies in this regard. Learning from my previous mistake, this time we stayed at the very comfortable Hilton Hotel sited on a hill with the city stretched out below – what one could see of it. With virtually every automobile run on diesel and every household burning some form of fuel that billowed smoke, rather like Cairo, a polluted pall hung over the city.

Shortly after our visit, the Shah was overthrown and, with the collapse of the private banking sector, our research came to nothing. Rather surprisingly, my abiding memory is of the electric shock one often got when one shook hands. The ultra-dry climate, allied to the fact that most fitted carpets were made of a synthetic fibre, seemed to produce this oscillatory discharge. Presumably, when the locals got together in a clinch they utilised the traditional Persian carpet.

Other than the Shah, the most important family at the time was the Farmanfarmayan clan, who seemed to have their fingers in every pie. It was quite a feat arranging meetings with the government ministers concerned; it was an even greater feat pronouncing their names once met.

Jordan

I visited Jordan on a number of occasions, each time under very different circumstances. There is an interesting overland route by car to Amman via Damascus – I went by air.

We had a steady stream of clients from Amman making secretive trips to Beirut to conduct their 'off-shore' financial affairs. As a result, to drum up even more business, I was invited by the General Manager, Maurice Constant, to visit the Bank's various branches in Jordan – Amman and Irbid in particular – which allowed me, in passing, to visit the 'rose red city' of Petra – a great tourist attraction. The only access to Petra is through a narrow, winding defile hemmed in by gigantic cliffs, a defile that in a bygone era a handful of men could hold against a marauding army. In olden times the city lay along the main Arabian-Syrian trade route and the locals amassed a fortune by collecting tolls from the caravans carrying frankincense in exchange for a guarantee of safe conduct. The wealth thus amassed was lavished on building a city out of the red sandstone – a city so magnificent that it retains its beauty and splendour even in the ruins.

Sadly, the Bank's branches situated on the West Bank and now under the control of the Israelis, were 'out of bounds'.

Without the benefit of oil, agriculture, tourism and the generosity of neighbouring states constituted Jordan's main sources of income. Amman is built on seven arid hills and is picturesque rather than attractive.

Maurice Constant had fostered a growing business but his main achievement was coercing King Hussein to turn out for his cricket side, the King having perfected his off drive in the nets at Harrow. I stayed at the Bank House, a very splendid

146

The original Nairobi branch in 1904

The chief Nairobi branch in 1964

Nita Decker - Malindi 1956

The Bank house
- Gulu 1957

The Bank house
- Nairobi

Philip and Vivian Percival - Machakos (Hemingway's 'The finest man I know')

Crossing the Nile en route to Gulu 1957

The 'unrecognisable swing' - Kisumu 1959

Relay racing Aden 1961 - Mark Cato in the 'hot seat'

Water ski-ing - the barren rocks of Aden in the background

Fancy dress Aden 1963 - 'The large Edwardian family'

Anthea Legge - looking glamorous - Nairobi 1964

Lord Aldington meeting local dignitaries - Nairobi 1965 (the author 3rd from left)

High jinks Nairobi Polo Club (Guy
Elkins shaking a cocktail)

Tying the knot - Nairobi 1967

Elizabeth on honeymoon - Malindi 1967

Water ski-ing - Brighton

Lining up against the President's Bodyguard - Karachi 1968

The winners' enclosure Karachi 1969 - syces lined up in the background

Elizabeth modelling at a charity show - Karachi 1969

View from the terrace of the Bank penthouse - Beirut 1970

Lord Gore-Booth, Colin Kerr and
author with secretaries at the
opening of the Tokyo office 1971

'Three Merry Maids' Tokyo 1973

The hazardous drive to Simla - a rocky landslide prior to our arrival on the scene

A remarkable scene outside Kanpur branch - during three days 25,000 cricket enthusiasts unable to get tickets watched the proceedings on the Bank's TV screen

Winter scene - Srinagar, Kashmir

Shikaras at
Srinagar
(Photograph
courtesy Indian
Government
Tourist Office)

Lower Stonehurst Farm

William and Amanda Bond Elliott (at their wedding reception)

Royal Ashdown Forest G.C. outside the Southampton Club, Long Island

Geoffrey Kent (far left) lifting the ultimate polo trophy at Palm Beach

Ashdown House Under Eleven cricket team. Guy and Adrian seated on left (can you spot the budding Soames Forsyte?)

The author and wife in retirement

residence with a retinue of servants under the strict control of the housekeeper, a large, formidable lady with a bristling moustache and a baritone bark any Guards RSM would envy!

According to Maurice life ran smoothly and he led a well-ordered and pleasant existence.

All was to change in September 1970 when the Fedayeen, under the guise of the PLO, took on the might of the Jordanian army. For those not familiar with the background to the uprising a few words in clarification may not come amiss.

As a result of the numerous altercations with Israel and the loss of the West Bank many thousands of refugees had poured into Jordan (a lesser number pitched up in the Lebanon). Somewhere in the region of 50,000 were housed in the main camp at Beka'a on the outskirts of Amman in the most appalling conditions, despite the best efforts of the United Nations to provide makeshift living accommodation and basic facilities. Here they eked out an existence of unrelieved drabness. The only evidence of cheer were the tin huts which glinted in the bright sunlight. Predictably, with discontent rife these camps were the ideal breeding grounds for guerilla groups (some might categorise them terrorist cells) with Israel and the West being seen as the common enemy. Reinforced by Russian weaponry, supplied by Syria, these groups gained in confidence and began to exercise considerable control and influence, not only in their camps, but in the centre of Amman itself. The élite Jordanian army, mainly drawn from the Bedouin faction, found they were in danger of being usurped by this rag-tag Palestinian force who were quickly establishing a state within a state. Despite strong reservations King Hussein finally decided, on the advice of his generals, to exert his authority and suppress what was fast becoming an imminent threat to his régime.

The battle, when it started, proved to be a bloody affair with Jordanian army tanks and ordnance matched against Soviet weaponry. The professionalism of the army, in a relatively short but extremely fierce encounter, eventually won the day. However, with most of the battles fought in and around the refugee camps the Palestinian casualties – many of them civilian – were inordinately high. Apparently it was a close run thing. The promised Syrian air power in support of the PLO failed to materialise and the government, with control of the skies,

147

was able to wipe out the opposition's heavy armour. With what proved to be a decisive victory King Hussein's popularity reached a new high amongst the indigenous population, although, as subsequent events have shown, the Palestinian problem has never been resolved.

As the conflict raged the Bank decided to evacuate the expatriate staff and they were flown to safer climes. While quite a few of the war correspondents were holed up in the Inter-Continental Hotel, which was regularly shelled, a fair percentage of the world's press took refuge in the bar of the St George Hotel, Beirut, where they regularly filed back home imaginative reports of the carnage in Amman. It never ceased to amaze me the extent to which journalists thrived on bogus expense accounts in justification of the bogus and far-fetched reports which they compiled and sent back to base from the comfort of Beirut's luxurious hotels.

When it became apparent that the army would triumph the Bank, having lost touch with our local managers, requested that I take the first flight in to assess the situation. At first sight this was not pleasant and at first smell even worse; the road leading from the airport was lined with open graves filled with festering bodies. Apart from a few walking wounded the Bank staff had fortunately escaped relatively unscathed. I expected the Bank House to have been looted, but apparently the rampaging hordes, bent on rape, pillage and revenge had met their match in the Bank's housekeeper. Rumour had it that when she welcomed the revolutionaries in for a bit of 'slap and tickle' they fled in panic! This time I stayed at the Inter-Continental Hotel which bore the scars of battle and was heavily pockmarked from the shelling.

With the army back in control the city soon recovered a sense of normality and the banking and commercial communities resumed trading, with the added stimulus of foreign aid pouring in to prop up King Hussein's stabilising influence in the Middle East.

I returned several months later with one of our new graduate intake, Tim Ingram (now Chief Executive of the Cayzer Group). We were advised to take two precautions. Firstly, not to wear a short-sleeved shirt with a Parker pen sticking out of the breast pocket; we could be mistaken for Americans and shot. Secondly, with a cholera epidemic raging we were advised to have the requisite preventative jabs. We rigidly observed the first warning and ignored the second, both being anti-needle. We fortuitously survived on both counts.

Since those days Jordan, despite the presence of large Palestinian refugee camps, has managed by good governance to steer a relatively safe course through the Middle East minefield and has deservedly achieved a degree of prosperity.

Turkey

Having purchased the business of the Ottoman Bank outside Turkey it nevertheless made sense to visit that country, and Istanbul in particular. This magic city, so rich in historic and artistic attractions and offering such a magnificent diversity of beautiful scenery, is of course the only city in the world that bestrides two continents. The Bosphorus that connects the Black Sea with the Sea of Marmara separates Europe from Asia. Charming fishing villages, beaches and verdant hills dotted with characteristic wooden houses sloped down to pale-green, opaque waters, icy from the Black Sea – the area was breathtakingly beautiful.

The city itself looks distinctly dilapidated. Nevertheless with its bazaars, museums and myriad mosques and minarets, it makes fascinating viewing if one can forge through the gridlocked traffic. The bazaars were particularly interesting, although one quickly became bored by the need to haggle for even the smallest item and, even by bargaining, it was difficult to establish what was the real value of the goods on offer. However, I did negotiate what I thought was a reasonable price for a bag of pistachios, until, later on, I saw the same bag in a local market at half the price.

I made time to visit the Topkapi Palace Museum, a veritable treasure trove of precious stones, emerald-encrusted thrones and other priceless artefacts. The Chinese porcelain on display in the old kitchens is one of the largest and richest collections in the world, rivalling those of Peking and Berlin. Apparently the result of presents (or, more likely, bribes) given to the sultans by merchants criss-crossing the country as they plied their trade with the Far East, particularly China. The story goes that officials of the Kemalist party, when making a tour of the buildings in the first months of their occupation came upon a room stacked from floor to ceiling with priceless 16th century porcelain, still in the original wrappings in which it had arrived by caravan from China. It had been no one's responsibility to unpack it, and there it had lain through the centuries. There was so much wealth on view that I found it surprising that this amazing hoard had not been raided by the Turkish Government which always seems to be teetering on the brink of insolvency.

I stayed at the Hilton Hotel and was upgraded to the executive floor on the strength of a passing acquaintance with the German general manager when he ran the Ambassador Hotel in Nairobi.

The management of the Ottoman Bank made me most welcome and the highlight of my stay was having dinner with the expatriate manager and his wife at their fine apartment with a terrace leading down to the banks of the Bosphorus. It was quite an unnerving experience having pre-dinner drinks with enormous Russian battleships sliding by, their guns rotating and the officers of the watch peering through their binoculars for any likely trouble. We were close enough to pick out the rank of the officers (assuming their livery was similar to that of the Royal Navy) and the wash from these enormous vessels had all the small craft at anchor bobbing in the wake. I met one of the sons of the manager who went on to become Chief Executive of Cathay Pacific; the other son, Dom Anthony Sutch, became a well-known figure as headmaster of Downside.

The cuisine in the hotels and restaurants was pretty humdrum and the much publicised Turkish Wine (gold medals at Ljubljana 1962/63) even more so. I might just have been unlucky but Turkish delight it was not.

At the Ottoman Bank's insistence I flew to Ankara, the capital, to visit their branch there. This, in banking terms, was a complete waste of time. I was, however, privileged to be taken out to lunch at the newly opened golf club. Although it was midweek the course was crowded with American Army and Airforce officers on active service garnering another chestful of medals as members of NATO. Other than seeing these service personnel on 'combat duty' the most memorable sight was the Mausoleum of Kemal Ataturk situated on a hill dominating Ankara. As everybody knows, or should know, K.A.'s far reaching reforms placed Turkey firmly on the path of westernisation.

Kuwait

The Ottoman Bank should have been the first bank to operate in Kuwait. Having, after much negotiation, obtained the necessary permissions, they then somehow managed to upset the ruler who decreed that they should never be given the opportunity again. In terms of missed chances it must rank alongside that of Stuart Pearce's in the World Cup and the National Bank of India's decision to close their branch in Hong Kong in 1869.

Kuwait was one of the first of the Gulf States to exploit its vast oil reserves and even in the '60s had a sophisticated infrastructure as evidenced by the modern government buildings, office blocks and luxury hotels which dominated the skyline.

On arrival, I was surprised by the total indifference of the taxi-drivers as they lounged smoking and chatting round their Cadillacs – so different from their counterparts in other capital cities. Apparently, all genuine native Kuwaitis were paid a not inconsiderable 'subsidy' by the Government, so for this privileged group there was no great incentive to work. Owning and driving a smart car for profit at their convenience seemed a not unattractive sideline.

Most of the manual and clerical jobs were carried out by imported labour, mainly Palestinian or from the Indian sub-continent.

In terms of business Kuwait was a worthwhile port of call. There were five local banks bursting with liquidity and these were regularly trawled by reps out of Beirut seeking surplus funds for placement in London and New York. Most of these banks were managed by ex-employees of the Ottoman Bank and Eastern Bank where experience of the region was an important qualification. The Gulf Bank was managed by a former Grindlays employee, Bob Sinclair, who had been my predecessor in Karachi. I was able to trade Bank gossip for deposits over dinner at my hotel. Although alcohol was officially

151

banned Bob had brought with him a couple of bottles of wine in his briefcase. The waiters did not seem at all surprised when these were uncorked. How different from Saudi Arabia where such a flaunting of convention would have had serious repercussions.

With all the expatriates earning good money in not particularly demanding jobs and living in comfortable, air-conditioned villas, a spell in Kuwait was not without its attractions.

Cyprus

Cyprus was but a short hop from Beirut and, as part of my Middle East responsibilities, it was suggested that I pay a fleeting visit to the Bank's branches there, particularly as Beirut was increasingly being used as an off-shore banking centre for wealthy Cypriots.

Not having kept any notes I remember very little of the trip, particularly as it coincided with the Nicosia wine festival. An old friend from Kampala, Len Hendry, took me under his wing and with the wine flowing freely (as a promotional gimmick most of it was, in fact, free) it is small wonder that most of that period remains a blank. I do have memories, however, of numerous drunken United Nations troops being rounded up by the Military Police.

During my visit the Graeco-Turkish conflict was festering. The strong United Nations contingent was commanded, coincidentally, by an Indian general. On being introduced at a cocktail party he voiced his admiration for Grindlays Bank. Experience suggests this is normally a build-up to seeking a loan or employment for a close relative and this proved to be the case.

Fortunately, the no-go zone which now divides the island – a Mediterranean Berlin wall – had yet to be erected and I was invited to lunch at the old coastal town of Kyrenia. The chosen restaurant was justly famed for its seafood, stuffed vine leaves and kebabs. It overlooked the beautiful horseshoe-shaped harbour. Equally famous was Kyrenia castle which loomed above the harbour, its towering walls virtually dipping into the green-blue sea. This vast fortress was built to defend the town from invading Arabs. Sad to relate, these splendid forts, constructed to repulse attacks by sea, proved redundant as this magical island was subsequently torn apart by internal fighting. An uneasy truce now exists, the Turkish Cypriots living in the North and the Greek Cypriots in the South. Not far from Kyrenia is the house where Lawrence Durrell wrote *Bitter Lemons* during the years he spent in Cyprus in the 1950s.

As part of my work schedule, I met a few of the Bank's more influential clients, but as I was shortly to be on the move from Beirut I have no idea if these contacts subsequently proved valuable to the Bank.

Beirut

After living out of a suitcase it was always a relief to get back to the more ordered existence of my family in Beirut. Much to our delight Elizabeth was pregnant again – there must after all be something in the saying 'absence makes the heart grow fonder' – and Adrian duly entered the unsuspecting world at a fighting weight of 7½ lbs. In retrospect, and much to my shame, it was customary in those far off days for the father to arrive for a doting hour's viewing *after* the childbirth and then disappear with his closest chums to celebrate in not inconsiderable style, and at no little cost to his pocket and constitution. Such behaviour does not seem 'politically correct' today.

After a few alarms and excursions with Adrian's innards, he quickly developed into a fine physical specimen and joined the other water babies at the club, where most could swim before they could walk.

Although Elizabeth had reservations about our rather sybaritic lifestyle, Beirut was an extremely civilised place to live. We were members of the Delhamyeh Country Club, thirty minutes drive south of Beirut. It had been financed by the Kettaneh family and was, in their eyes, the ultimate country club. They had, at great expense, hacked out a championship golf course from solid rock – lush fairways and immaculate greens, but no rough. If one strayed off course the ball was likely to ricochet among rocks and boulders, rarely to be seen again. To soothe the ruffled nerves the Kettanehs had installed piped music at some of the tees, but Bing Crosby's rendition of *Straight Down the Middle* didn't always have the desired effect. An Olympic size swimming pool with a vertigo inducing high-diving board (on a misty day you could not see the top), squash and tennis courts, a five star restaurant and holiday cottages completed the package. Mike Spencer, the Dunlop representative, brought out Roberto de Vincenzo to play in an exhibition match. To give him some incentive we all confidently contributed to a fund that he wouldn't break the course record, safe in the knowledge that one visit to the rocks would destroy his card. Not once did he stray from the fairway and went round in a new record of 68. We all willingly coughed up, scarcely believing such a feat was possible. In one knockout tournament I managed to beat Colin Duncan of the British Bank of the Middle East 10 and 8. He is now a member of a local club, Piltdown, and has since got his revenge.

For those not interested in the ramifications of the rules of golf the next paragraph could well be skipped.

I experienced one curious, if not unique, experience when playing the first round of one of the more prestigious golf tournaments in the Lebanon. My partner, Peter Johansen (later to become financial director of the Swire Group of companies), hit an immaculate drive off the first tee, to all intents and purposes straight down the fairway. He then 'feathered' his second about 180 yards to the heart of the green. As he was about to putt he noticed he had played the wrong ball – easily done as, being one of the early starters, we had driven directly into the sun. On returning to play his original ball it could not be found so eventually, after five minutes of frantic searching, Peter was obliged to return to the first tee to start all over again. There, the official starter rather smugly informed him that he had exceeded the stipulated time to play a hole (rule 33-1) but as it was his first offence he was probably only going to be penalised one stroke, plus the penalty shots for a lost ball and playing the wrong ball. By this time we were all rather flustered and not sure how many penalty shots had been incurred. Our dilemma was heightened by the knowledge that a further penalty and/or possible disqualification would result if we recorded the wrong score (rule 6-6D). Peter said that as far as he was concerned it did not matter and, with remarkable aplomb, played the rest of his round within his handicap. I thought at the time his calmness under duress would stand him in good stead in later life, as indeed it has. For what it is worth I got a five at the first hole – one over par.

A lot of memories come flooding back. President Nasser's assassination caused predictable unrest in Beirut. If one didn't bedeck one's car in black ribbons in sympathy one was liable to be shot. It was similarly hazardous at weddings, funerals and on New Year's Eve. Whether it be in celebration or in mourning the average Lebanese, given any excuse, had sufficient weaponry to fire a fusillade of shots into the air. With such indiscriminate shooting it was amazing there were not more fatalities; certainly the odd family feud was settled at the time of such revelries.

Another comparatively minor incident in life's big picture springs to mind. During the summer one of our wealthier clients had purchased a new 100ft motor cruiser, complete with every amenity and device. He kindly invited us on the maiden voyage. Having been told it was just a case of putting it on auto-pilot and his foot on the accelerator we duly set off from the yacht basin at Jounieh, laden down with hampers of food and booze. Confident that all we had to do was circle the bay, eat, drink and sunbathe, we were somewhat disturbed when fighter aircraft came buzzing overhead. Apparently, we had strayed off course and were heading for Haifa, much to our and the Israelis' consternation. Fortunately, the waving of white bikini tops saved the situation and we were permitted to retrace our steps, with some difficulty, back to Jounieh. The auto-pilot hadn't been programmed for such a crisis.

Needless to say, we were inundated with visits from directors and senior executives from the Bank in London. William Clark took his responsibilities seriously and lectured the Anglo-Lebanese Chamber of Commerce (of which I was a committee member) on the world economy. Lord Lloyd was more interested in the delights of the casino. Others put on a conscientious front, meeting clients and financial institutions. I was strongly supported by Colin Allan and Colin Kerr (senior general managers, ex-Ottoman Bank) who knew the region intimately and never bore a grudge that one of their chosen, better experienced, protégés was not in my job. On a topical note, many of the senior Ottoman Bank managers had 'cut their teeth' in Baghdad prior to nationalisation of the Iraq Petroleum Company and the banks.

One of the more pleasant excursions was to Byblos about 24 miles north of Beirut. Apart from boasting one of the finest fish restaurants, according to 'tradition' it is the oldest, continuously inhabited town in the world, the buildings reputedly dating back to the year 3200 BC. It has the most picturesque harbour with ruins of crusader forts at the entrance. 'Byblos is a history book in which is recorded a story as old as time itself' – I say no more!

One tends to forget that the Mediterranean is subject to the most violent storms and it was a remarkable experience, safe in the comfort of our penthouse, to watch these storms build up to a crescendo of thunder and lightning, the black of the sea matching the colour of the sky – a phenomenon I have not experienced anywhere else. Another amazing sight was seeing the first jumbo jet, Pan Am 1, on its inaugural flight round the world. As it hovered over Beirut waiting to land it appeared stationary and we expected it to drop out of the sky with a mighty plop.

Having at last, after many tutorials and much heartache, gained sufficient proficiency to order a meal in French my masters back in London (no doubt impressed by this feat) decided it was time for the Bignells to move on and I was instructed to fly to Tokyo with a view to opening an office there.

Just prior to this, and in keeping with the Bank's expansionary vision, we had purchased, albeit belatedly, the Dao Heng Bank, one of Hong Kong's leading finance houses. It was thought fitting that one of their directors, Frank Tung, should be given a whirlwind tour of the Gulf States along with a director from our London merchant bank, William Brandts. This proved a profitable and productive introduction to our branch network and was of particular value to me as I was going to be closely involved with the Dao Heng Bank in the near future. Until this trip I had not realised the conceptual gulf that existed within the Grindlays Group. Our merchant banking colleague, when not seeking deals, spent most of the time on the telephone to his gardener back in Hampshire. Black spot on the roses was giving cause for concern.

On leaving we were swept up in the usual whirl of farewell parties and received a regular mention in the gossip columns of the local press. Not too difficult to manage if the contributing social editor was invited to the various functions. I went to considerable lengths to introduce to the Beirut scene my replacement, by name Ascough-Patterson, who was seconded from our merchant bank. He was predictably christened 'Hiccup'-Patterson by the local banking community. Alas, they were proved right and, for various reasons, he lasted only a few months after our departure and was ignominiously despatched back to the UK.

We left with many fond memories of the region, not realising that, shortly thereafter, the Lebanon would collapse, internal strife (helped by the Israelis) tearing the country apart.

VIII

Thailand – Japan – Hong Kong

Bangkok

Prior to taking up my position in Tokyo, it was suggested that I stop over in Thailand and survey the scene – not a particularly challenging assignment!

When first arriving in Bangkok one cannot fail but to be bowled over by its easy grace and grubby charms. Unfortunately, I could never control the timing of my visits which seemed always to coincide with the advent of the rainy season. The consequent heavy atmosphere mixed with the industrial pollution was a potent encouragement to get on the next plane out.

Traffic policemen wearing surgical masks were powerless to sort out the impenetrable traffic jams or silence the cacophony of impatient horns, only partially drowned out in the heavy air, rancid with a thousand smells. However, things did get better. Bangkok at street level is too busy to be beautiful, but the vignettes of suburban life being played out in front of one as the taxi crawled along made for interesting viewing. In the midst of all this activity you may suddenly be privileged to witness the beauty of a Buddhist temple and the bright orange of a monk's garments.

Everything was to change when, leaving the noise and bustle, I eventually reached the tranquillity of the Oriental Hotel. On arrival one was garlanded with flowers in the imposing lobby and led to a suite of rooms befitting the hotel's reputation as one of the finest in the world. The panoramic view from the balcony was equally impressive with the mighty Chao Phraya river flowing past, decorated with numerous boats of all shapes and sizes ferrying everything from vegetables to call girls, a fluidity of changing colour.

158

There is no point in glossing over the sleazier side of Bangkok. A magnet for sexual tourism, particularly with Japanese businessmen, it embraces hedonism in every form. The night life is plentiful and varied catering for all tastes, the possibilities limited only by the imagination. One evening I ventured forth to view what was on offer and was enticed to enter premises with the assurance of a sign declaring them to be 'Very good, very clean'. They did not seem, on closer inspection, to be either very good or very clean, so I left in some haste and returned to the more clinical delights of the hotel. Nevertheless, there are other attractions, particularly the famous floating market. I found Thai food delightful. The food stalls that line the main streets, stacked with enticing local delicacies, still tempt, despite the compellingly pungent pollution. For shoppers Bangkok offers an enormous variety of goods, both fake and genuine; the key in negotiating the price is to be able to spot the difference.

Bangkok is the 'Venice of the East' with numerous waterways criss-crossing the city. The golden spires of the temples glisten in the sunlight and offer a sense of peace and calm in the midst of chaos. The Thais somehow manage to remain serene and composed in their frenetic world.

Bangkok is a useful stop-over point from London to Tokyo for some 'R and R', but in terms of promoting business one needs a permanent representative on the ground to follow up leads, which are otherwise quickly forgotten.

Japan

When the Bank decided to have some form of representation in Tokyo, Japan was known as the 'Land of the Rising Yen' with the economy forging ahead at full throttle. The problems in getting established there were enormous: office accommodation in Maranouchi – the financial centre – was well-nigh unobtainable, the recruitment of staff with but a smattering of English near impossible and the acquisition of a banking licence in less than three years a Herculean task. According to the Finance Ministry there was a queue of twenty applicants ahead of Grindlays.

We were fortunate on many counts – most of my fellow representatives in Beirut had offices in Tokyo so I was given a list of names to call on when I arrived. My two letters of introduction from the Bank's head office were useful but not particularly helpful – the one to the Bank of Tokyo provided an invitation to lunch and the one penned by Lord Gore-Booth (a director) to the British Ambassador (in the process of retiring) accorded me an invitation to tea at the Embassy. But good fortune was on our side. First Boston had just acquired a full banking licence and were in the process of vacating their expensively furnished representative office in Maranouchi. This we acquired, lock stock and barrel, including more Barcelona chairs! My introduction to First Chicago produced the goods in the most attractive form of probably the best bi-lingual secretary in Tokyo. Their manager, fortunate chap, had recently become engaged to his secretary and it was the bank's policy that the two of them couldn't carry on working in the same office. With the marriage planned some six months away Nobuko was looking for alternative employment and agreed to my offer of work at Grindlays.

In my quest for acceptable residential accommodation, a car with driver and all the requisite office equipment, Nobuko proved absolutely invaluable. Japan was the first country (other than Libya, post Gaddafi) I had encountered where all the street signs were in a totally foreign script. With no knowledge of Japanese, written or spoken, it was quite tricky getting around. Having booked in at the world famous Okura Hotel which was reasonably adjacent to the Tokyo Tower – a mammoth steel structure taller than the Eiffel Tower – I then purchased a compass. With this aid and Tokyo Tower looming above the city I was able to home in on the Okura without too much difficulty. As I had reserved my room for three weeks I was placed on the executive floor.

This led to an interesting encounter. Mohammed Ali had flown in with his entourage to defend his world heavyweight title against some 'no hoper' and was duly accommodated on the same floor. The day of the fight I met his manager, Angelo Dundee, at breakfast and he explained there would be some noisy celebrations later that night and, to save my being inconvenienced, I was invited to join in. I accepted with alacrity and had a few cheerful drinks with the entourage. The next day, again at breakfast, I collected all the autographs (which I have to this day). Ali could not have been more charming and mentioned he had recently been to Mecca in keeping with his new-found faith. The Japanese in their studiously polite way didn't intrude on his privacy and I have an abiding memory of Ali showing off his conjuring skills to a little Japanese boy who was totally unaware that he was being given a private show by the world's greatest living sportsman.

After a diligent and time-consuming search I found an apartment, not too expensive, in the upmarket suburb of Shirogane. It was between 20 and 50 minutes' drive to the office, depending on the traffic and situated on the second floor of a three storey block, with a garage. The owner and his family lived on the ground floor (these were the Oshimas who became loyal friends) with an American family above. The most attractive feature was a full length balcony surrounded by various flowering trees rising from a pocket handkerchief size garden below. Land, needless to say, was at a premium and the incredibly wealthy chairman of Seiko Watches who lived opposite was housed in, by British standards, a relatively modest dwelling.

Having got the prerequisites lined up, Elizabeth with Guy and Adrian (still in his nappies) duly arrived to take up residence in this strange but most hospitable land. For all of us our first impression of Tokyo was of an extraordinary blending of East and West. Modern hotels, shopping centres, impressive office blocks reflected western influences while the East was clearly apparent in the delicate cuisine, the fairy-tale gardens and the pervasive oriental music. Entering the main department stores one was greeted by smiling, bowing hostesses.

While it has a number of compensating factors, away from the moated Imperial Palace, Tokyo is basically an ugly city. The air is grey with the pall of automobile exhausts belching smoke and dulling the ferro-concrete buildings. Traffic chokes the streets, tangled telephone wires and ramshackle shopfronts adding to the impression of chaos. However, at night Tokyo metamorphoses into a kaleidoscope of colour – neon signs come ablaze with light and the fact that the Japanese characters which spill forth are indecipherable only enhances the exotic spectacle. This is particularly so in Ginza and Asakusa, areas dominated by nightclubs and bars where the Japanese businessmen lavished their enormous expense accounts (when not on the golf course). At that time it was estimated that more was spent on corporate entertainment than on the country's defence budget.

For a newly arrived young family one of the great comforts was the total absence of crime directed at foreigners.

In terms of integrating into the social scene we quickly found our feet. The Wodtkes (Citibank and PICA) had arrived from Beirut, Iain and Carol Aitchison from Kenya and the Vojtes (Citibank) from Pakistan.

In keeping with tradition, and in line with all the numerous other financial institutions, Grindlays was obliged to host a grand reception to mark the opening of their representative office. Lord Gore Booth (ex-Head of the Diplomatic Service) and his wife, Pat, had come out from London to fly the Grindlays flag. Early in his career Paul Gore Booth had served in Japan and was actually present during the formalities at the Embassy when war was declared. He was subsequently interned under siege conditions from 1941–1942.

He was particularly well qualified for the task as he was also the chairman of the Sherlock Holmes Society which had a remarkably strong following in Japan. PGB instructed me, with a view to getting the reception off to a good start, that I should suitably introduce him to the throng in Japanese and, thereafter, he would expand on the Bank's objectives, also in Japanese. My riposte was that I couldn't speak Japanese and suggested that speeches at such functions went down like lead balloons particularly as the male guests were only interested in eating and drinking and chatting up the attendant Geisha girls. This was not the response an ex-Head of the British Diplomatic Service expected.

To save me acute embarrassment PGB conceded that the recently retired Japanese Ambassador in London could make the introduction but insisted that he be allowed to have his say, which he duly did. Much to my surprise the noisy chatter of our guests subsided and an eerie hush fell over the assembled multitude. At the end there was polite, if surprised, applause and I asked a nearby Japanese banker what had been the gist of the speech – he said he had not the faintest idea! Apparently, PGB on arriving in Tokyo in 1938 had taken lessons in Japanese from a venerable retired army officer of the old school. However, what he had gleaned was the Japanese equivalent of Ancient Greek and just about as comprehensible as Ancient Greek would be in Athens today. Nevertheless, this episode, being a first, gained Grindlays enormous respect amongst the Japanese Banking Community.

Elizabeth, still a young bride and new to Tokyo, had the equally daunting task of entertaining Pat Gore Booth and the British Ambassador's wife, Lady Simone Warner (the GBs were staying at the Embassy), together with a host of other 'senior ladies' to lunch at our rather small flat. Fortunately, all went well and on our return to London the GBs reciprocated at their apartment in Ashley Gardens (an uncalled for gesture but typical of their consideration and generosity). Paul GB, latterly and in his capacity as a Vice President, put my name forward as a 'Pilgrim'.* Membership of the society has given me much pleasure since.

Despite Tokyo's daunting size the expatriate community somehow became a self-contained village within the enormity of the whole. To promote business, fellowship and understanding, large functions were held at the leading hotels; these in turn were broken down to official cocktail and dinner parties in Embassies and private homes and even smaller parties to which one also invited particularly close friends.

At one such reception to celebrate the 5th Anniversary of the second Republic of Uganda I was intrigued to learn from the ambassador that his wife, Mrs Betty Bigombe, hailed from Gulu. It was becoming increasingly evident from my travels that all roads lead to Gulu, with Rome coming but a poor second.

Progressive dinner parties were then very much in vogue. The form was to get together five like-minded couples, decide on five courses with accompanying wines, liqueurs, etc., hire a minibus plus driver and then proceed from residence to residence course by course and consume the fare and booze on offer. This made for a bacchanalian repast. Thereafter, we

---

*The Pilgrims is an august society to promote Anglo-American good-fellowship.

invariably finished up at a 'Greek' nightclub/restaurant in downtown Tokyo which, having been forewarned, had taken on board a supply of disposable china! I am not sure why this form of entertainment went out of fashion – it takes the strain off the hostess and, provided there is a sober driver on hand, there should be no problem with the law.

We had a more or less continuous round of visitors from all corners of the globe, most of them suddenly realising that, business apart, Japan was not without its attractions as a tourist centre. Most of these we were delighted to see, although looking after friends of friends became somewhat stressful. Amongst the former Geoffrey Kent arrived with his new American bride, Jorie Butler. Geoffrey on leaving the army had inherited from his parents a small safari company, Abercrombie & Kent. There was no 'Abercrombie' but it gave the firm a head start in the Yellow Pages – helped by the fact that Abercrombie & Fitch were well-known safari outfitters in America and much respected by the hunting fraternity. There was thus a certain cachet in the Abercrombie name. Jorie brought to the party a substantial Chicago-based fortune. With Geoffrey's flair and entrepreneurial talents and Jorie's backing the firm is probably now the most successful and best known upmarket travel operator in the world.

Hoping to share in Japan's burgeoning prosperity the whole spectrum of world business had descended on Tokyo. In addition to all the embassies and old established British trading companies (Jardines, Swires, Cornes, Dodwells, to name but a few) just about every financial institution, oil company and commercial conglomerate had some form of representation or presence. Not surprisingly, quite a few of the expatriates had become part of the established 'international' set and many old acquaintances were renewed in Tokyo.

The British Banking community was well represented and had a monthly lunch at the Press Club in Maranouchi where we exchanged views, hatched deals and traded gossip. Most of our membership eventually rose to senior executive positions in the financial fraternity. William Purves (Chairman of HSBC) and Winfried Bischoff (Chairman of Schroders) were both subsequently knighted for services to the Banking Industry.

During our time in Tokyo, the Cambridge rugby team

successfully toured Japan. Prior to their match against the national side William Purves (known to all and sundry, within and without earshot, as Willie) hosted a lunch for some of the reserve players to which we were kindly invited. It so happened that on this particular day the Americans decided finally to withdraw from Vietnam. We accordingly watched with horror the harrowing scenes on television as the helicopters circled over the US Embassy picking up the remaining local staff with many fighting for places as they clung to what appeared to be rope ladders and took off for safer climes. Willie who, as a national serviceman, served with considerable distinction and gallantry in Korea had, as I recall, remarked that now was the time for his Bank to (re) open a branch in Vietnam. By so doing it would show confidence in the new régime, thus giving the HSBC a head start over their rivals. I thought with relief that at least my name would not be in the frame for such a posting, but reflected that Willie would not have thought twice about volunteering himself. What transpired I know not but certainly the Hong Kong & Shanghai Bank, under his forthright and visionary leadership, turned itself from a major player in the Far East to a dominant force in world banking.

Club life revolved around the American Club in Tokyo which was more like a luxury hotel with splendid dining facilities and an Olympic size swimming pool – and the Yokohama Sports Club some twenty miles southwest of Tokyo. Yokohama SC fielded a reasonably good standard rugby side which used to play the top Japanese sides and made for patriotic viewing at weekends during the winter. The cricket side, predictably, was pretty sub-standard; we used to play an annual match amongst ourselves – there was no outside opposition.

Yokohama was a pleasant dormitory suburb away from the pollution of Tokyo. It boasted a number of beautiful parks and quite a few expatriates made it their home (including some of the Grindlays management). Yokohama is one of the principal gateways by sea to Japan and its foremost trade port. Having the benefit of a car and driver, we were able to bowl along the national highway back and forwards in some comfort. Not so my staff who every morning used to be shoehorned into trains, normally filled to three times their official capacity. These, fortunately for the incumbents, were frequent and ran on time.

165

Having a driver was absolutely essential as in Tokyo there is no system of street names and house numbers were not sequential, so very few drivers knew their way around the city. Most expatriates (if they were wise) had maps printed in Japanese and English giving the location of their residences.

Among leisure activities, family outings were arranged to the Hakone National Park, an extensive mountainous region blessed with superb scenery about 70 miles from Tokyo. Mount Fuji, the highest and most beautiful mountain in Japan, also featured. It had its charm, whatever the season, and in the winter when there was a 'nip' in the air its upper slopes are entirely cloaked with snow. Despite its great height it is not a difficult peak to climb and thousands make the pilgrimage in July and August when a number of popular trails are officially open.

Come the summer we decamped and spent long weekends with friends at their beach house in Shimoda, which lay on the Izu Peninsular. It was probably the closest resort where one could escape from the madding crowd – although at times it could be nose-to-tail traffic which at least allowed one to take in the magnificent coastal scenery.

While you remember the unforgettable landscape it is a salutary thought that the landscape will not remember you.

Once a year we were invited by the Sumitomo Bank to attend a spectacular, no expense spared, garden party, along with the rest of the foreign banking community, in Kyoto, the former capital of Japan. We invariably took a few extra days off to explore the city rich in historic association and legendary gardens. Japanese gardens are places of exquisite beauty where the eye is led to perfectly pre-arranged views. Disappointment is in store if one is expecting the disciplined confusion of English herbaceous borders and striped lawns as Japanese gardens depend on symbolism and repeated themes and motifs linked to their religious beliefs. Once one has come to terms with the artifice of neatly pruned trees and gravel raked into bizarre furrows one can see waves in the gravel, mountains in the rocks and stone lanterns honouring the souls of departed ancestors. Some of the famous Zen gardens are strangely mesmerising and when one is in contemplative mood they achieve their objective and become tranquil, soothing domains.

At the time of our visit the added lustre of spring blossom

166

had the cameras clicking. A restful break from the hustle and bustle of Tokyo. The trip by the super-fast bullet train was in itself quite an experience. Running like clockwork to the second, it was a monument to modern engineering as it whisked its way through the countryside giving ever changing views of Mount Fuji.

Official business trips were also made to Osaka and Kobe and the various shipbuilding yards in Hiroshima and Kure.

Grindlays merchant bank in London had become a major player in shipping finance and I was quite often called upon to represent their interests at various launchings or deliveries. The most notable of these involved the *Globtik London* and *Globtik Tokyo*, the two largest oil tankers then in existence. These were owned by Ravi Tikkoo, financed and syndicated by Grindlays and leased out on term charters to major oil companies, the income from which was sufficient to service the debt. I, along with the British Ambassador and his wife (Sir Fred and Lady Warner), joined the Tikkoo entourage and proceeded down to Kure for delivery of the *Globtik London* and the ensuing celebratory parties. Its dimensions were vast. When we inspected the engine room I, along with some of the other guests, suffered an attack of vertigo.

Other than myself and the Ambassador the only person not directly involved in the signing formalities was Nicholas (three wives to support) Monsarrat, author of *The Cruel Sea*, who was writing up the historic occasion for *The Sunday Times*. The night before the official handover, and at his prompting, we slid off to sample the local bars; somewhere along the way I seem to recollect encountering the Warners. Needless to say, no mention of this was made the next morning when we lined up for the official photograph. Nicholas and I, somewhat jaded and worse for wear, can be seen trying to hide at the back. Over the years Ravi Tikkoo has remained a good friend and we still meet up for a nostalgic reunion – occasionally attended by Simone Warner.

Sportswise golf and squash regularly featured. The Japanese were golf fanatics and shares in the various golf clubs were traded for enormous premiums on the Tokyo stock exchange. The cost of a round of golf, even when playing with a member, was the equivalent of £100 in 1972. What it is today one

167

dreads to think. The most exclusive golf club in Japan was the '300 Club' with only 300 members, featuring the rich and famous. Amazingly, it enjoyed reciprocity with the Delhamyeh Country Club in Beirut so I hastily renewed my Beirut membership and, as a result, was much in demand as a golf partner. (I still have my golf cap with the famous '300 Crub' logo – the Japanese could never sort out their 'Ls' and 'Rs'!) Apart from playing business golf with senior members of the Japanese banking and business communities, I established a regular four-ball with Ian Aitchison, a member of the slightly more downmarket but extremely expensive 600 Club, Graham McCallum and Michael Miles, both executives of the Swire Group of companies. We were latterly joined by Sir Michael Wilford (who took over from Sir Fred Warner as British Ambassador). Not only was he an extremely competent golfer but his was a particularly useful name to add to my expense sheet when submitting it to London for approval.

Golf in Japan followed an interesting format. The best courses closest to Tokyo invariably involved over an hour's drive and on arrival, after being allocated caddies (female) we normally played 27 holes, with lunch following completion of the first nine. Further refreshments were provided with numerous 'kiosks' dotted around the course dispensing drinks and snacks of every description. This all helped, with Mount Fuji towering in the background, to enhance the relaxed atmosphere and made for at times some unusually cavalier contests.

At the conclusion, on returning to the clubhouse, it was the accepted custom to scrub down in the shower rooms. Thereafter discreetly holding the specially provided small towels in front of our 'private parts' we adjourned to the communal bathing facilities. Here, having removed our protective gear, we gingerly slid into the steaming water. It was then, seeing the only gaijins (foreigners) in their midst, that the famed Japanese inscrutability was put to the test. The cleansing ritual was strictly observed and very much part of the golfing scene. We wondered what the reaction would have been had we invoked rule 14-3 which covers 'Artificial Devices and Unusual Equipment'!

At one stage Maurice Bembridge (I believe he still jointly holds the record for the lowest round at the US Masters) tried his hand on the Japanese tour. Unless one was regularly in the winners' circle it was prohibitively expensive for a foreigner to play so to cut his expenses he stayed with the Aitchisons. We, in turn, benefited as he sometimes made up our four-ball. When I moved on to New Delhi he came over to play in the Indian Open and we renewed our friendship, along with Joe (the pro) Hardwick, a much respected professional from Hong Kong, who had previously held the post at the Royal Calcutta GC. On enquiring from Maurice why he was not married his riposte was, 'Why buy a book when you can join a lending library?'. He has since bought the book.

The American Club and the British Chamber of Commerce ran hugely enjoyable golf tournaments. We were allowed visiting guests and on one occasion I took along a well-introduced old Etonian toy manufacturer, Simon Radcliffe. As a result of this meeting Michael Miles and myself, playing as the 'Nippon Nomads', when next home on leave, took on the might of Royal Ashdown Forest Golf Club, Simon having conscripted their captain, Roger Whitmore, as his partner. So impressed were we by the course and the ambience of the club that we applied to join as overseas members; so too did Graham McCallum. This led to our putting down roots in East Sussex – Graham and I still play regularly as foursomes partners and we have Simon to thank for the initial introduction. Michael Miles appears occasionally but, as a chairman or director of umpteen major companies, he has less time to play than we ordinary mortals. Another regular visitor to Tokyo was Stuart Hills whose company had dealings with Ian Aitchison. Stuart has recently had published a well reviewed book, *By Tank into Normandy*, which recounts in bloody detail his wartime experiences. His initiative in writing his memoirs in turn has encouraged me to put pen to paper.

Regularly at 06.30 hrs on a Wednesday I was picked up by Graham McCallum in his new Nissan sports car to play squash at the British Embassy prior to going into the office. Why so early? Well we were both devotees of the Tooth Fairy (The Molar Marauder) which was a satirical show produced on the American Forces radio. At least we started the day in good humour – and depending on the result of the match proceeded in even greater good humour.

When not playing squash on Wednesday, I normally had the

pleasant duty of ferrying the young Anne Oshima to the Japanese-American Girls School which was en route to the office. It was the era of the miniskirt and there was no more pleasant sight to start the day than that of the Oriental teenage girls in school uniform – long socks pulled up to their knees, tartan skirts of green and blue (pulled up well above their knees!) and white crisp shirts billowing in the breeze. They were always giggling about something and seemed happy with their lot. Adrian attended the infant department of the same school and even at that young age seemed happy with *his* lot.

By buttering up senior officials of the Ministry of Finance on the golf course and playing our trump card – an extensive branch network in the Middle East – we obtained our full banking licence three years ahead of the norm. In fact, Grindlays was granted a licence along with the Bank of London and South America, who had set up shop in Japan three years prior to our arrival. The Middle East connection was particularly pertinent at that time as Japan was experiencing the 'Oil Shock', their oil supplies being in some jeopardy and at inflated prices. At my suggestion, we were also helped in our quest by Lord Aldington who, along with Willie Whitelaw, arranged for the Japanese Prime Minister, who was on an official visit to London, to take time off and play golf at Royal St George's Golf Club, Sandwich. The Prime Minister deemed this a singular honour and presented the golf club with a heavily decorated Japanese doll enclosed in a glass case. This was at first consigned to the cellars to gather dust. Diplomatically, however, the gesture has been re-evaluated and the gift is now displayed on major occasions when Japanese VIPs and professionals visit the clubhouse.

Prior to obtaining a licence it was obligatory to take on board, at no little cost, a senior banking adviser approved by the Ministry of Finance. This normally entailed recruiting a retired executive from the MOF or one of the major Japanese banks, who had been put out to grass and was seeking a boost to his inadequate pension arrangements. The general idea was that the adviser oversaw the bank in question, ensuring it kept to the straight and narrow and did not infringe any of the Central Bank's many complex regulations.

We were allocated a Mr Kumashiro, a venerable executive

from the MOF who had seemed to spend most of his career representing Japanese interests at the various IMF bonanzas around the world. An important figure and not a man to be toyed with. Unfortunately, in terms of productivity he was more of a hindrance than a help. He spent his entire working 'waking' hours investigating the most basic procedures and would, as a matter of protocol, only deal directly with the senior expatriate management. To obtain a brief respite we packed him off to the Bank's head office in London and thence to the current IMF meeting. We realised that this would be an expensive cop out but quite how expensive we had not budgeted for. In addition to first class air fares, hotels, etc the diminutive Mr K seemed to be able to consume at least four meals a day at the most costly restaurants. The final straw was having to pay his laundry bill. He must have taken his entire wardrobe with him as we were obliged to pay for countless suits, shirts, ties and other articles to be cleaned.

Having been cautioned throughout my banking career by a succession of canny Scottish managers 'to mind the pennies' the Japanese lavish and cavalier use of the corporate expense account came as a bit of a cultural shock. However, I must not be too harsh as Mr Kumashiro proved useful at opening doors, as and when the need arose, to discuss trade related matters with the various government ministries.

The granting of the licence put many things in train. The acquisition of new premises was a paramount requirement and in this case we were fortunate to find and be able to take a lease on the second floor of the Palace Hotel annexe, situated in the centre of the financial district. We also put in a successful bid for some near pristine expensive office furniture; the Chase Manhattan Bank were moving to new, specially designed and coordinated premises. Having got the office organised the only thing left prior to opening was a grand reception to launch the new branch. This was held in the Palace Hotel, with Lord and Lady Aldington heading the Grindlays contingent. This time there were no speeches in Japanese, the only minor setback being that the ice carving of the Grindlays elephant logo developed a steady drip in an unfortunate place!

The opening was a great success. The Japanese Banks and trading companies generously directed 'congratulatory' deposits and deals our way which ensured an extremely profitable first year and the future was pregnant with promise. The management team posted from London (Messrs Maitland, McLeod and Monaghan – the 3 Ms) was highly efficient and motivated and the Japanese staff, mostly seconded from Japanese banks, loyal and productive. Lord Aldington thought, quite rightly, that to get matters off to a good start and help encourage the Japanese staff he would give them a 'pep' talk and explain in greater detail the objectives of the Grindlays Group. He was somewhat disconcerted to find half-way through his spiel that all of our senior Japanese staff had apparently fallen asleep. While this brought his address to a premature end I was later able to reassure him that closing one's eyes was a traditional custom in Japan, indicating total concentration and great respect.

The only setback was the loss of my beautiful and efficient secretary who married, as planned, her American banker and returned to Chicago. We acquired an equally efficient, but rather less attractive, replacement in a Miss Yamaguchi – the only girl to my knowledge who took her vacations in Alaska in the hope of meeting 'Mr Right'.

Prior to Lord A's departure there was the inevitable hiccup – a moment of Whitehall farce. Two interconnecting suites had been booked in the Palace Hotel for the Aldingtons, one for their personal use the other for private meetings. A breakfast meeting with the British Ambassador was arranged and a full English breakfast ordered. Unfortunately, this was delivered to Lady A in their personal suite; she denied all knowledge of it and sent it back. Lord A, ensconced in the adjoining suite with Sir Fred Warner, impatiently got through to room service and re-ordered their requirements. Again this was delivered to Lady A who dismissed it without further ado. By this time a distinctly annoyed Lord A vented his frustration on the kitchen staff. To no avail – the comedy of errors repeated itself. It was only when a breakfastless Ambassador took his leave to be met by a phalanx of groaning trolleys chauffeured by a squad of mystified Japanese waiters bearing copious amounts of eggs and bacon, parked further down the corridor, was all revealed.

With the departure of our VIPs life slowly returned to normal. Business boomed and we were able to put together a number

172

of deals with Japanese companies seeking a greater presence in the Middle East. IHI, builders of the *Globtik London* were involved in erecting a number of cement plants in the Gulf Emirates and Grindlays took on a lead rôle in arranging the requisite finance. Such was the success of these projects that we seconded one of our brighter, recently recruited Japanese staff to Abu Dhabi to act as a liaison officer to promote further transactions of this nature.

Resultant on such deals many celebratory dinners were hosted by our Japanese clients in Tokyo. These were relatively formal affairs with entertainment provided by kimono-clad Geisha girls who sang and told apparently amusing stories in Japanese amidst much giggling. With the drinking of many toasts, and under the influence of saki – a potent rice wine regularly passed round in small delicate cups – the evenings passed with a great deal of bonhomie. It was all innocent fun, the Japanese businessmen seeking more serious pleasures tended to patronise the downtown massage parlours in the Ginza. For those wishing to sample life in the 'raw', an excuse to visit one of the local 'sushi' bars always came in handy.

If ladies were involved they were herded off, separately, to enjoy the incomprehensible delights of the Kabuki theatre. Elizabeth's trump card – if a trip to the local bath-house was spurned – was to take the wives of visiting dignitaries to the home of Mr Serizawa. There they could observe and try their hand at stencil dying. Serizawa had been designated a 'Living National Treasure' for his artistic and cultural achievements – the ultimate accolade in Japanese parlance.

More than any other in Asia, Japan is a country of great contrasts, embracing 21st century technology and ancient traditions. Away from the gleaming skyscrapers, bustling streets and nightclubs where we lived, in the suburb of Shirogane, one could find traditional wooden houses with shoji screens, winding alleys, and, not far away, the tranquillity of Zen Gardens at 'Hapoen'. We found the Japanese very polite, well ordered people. When meeting each other the Japanese do not shake hands but bow. How low you bow depends on the status of the other person – if he is more important, your bow is lower than his. This could lead to some amusing encounters where neither party was sure of the status of the other and the

173

resultant grovelling was comical to behold. Whilst foreigners are excused such formalities one inadvertently tended to get into the routine and I am sure my spinal curvature has its origins in this genuflecting. My arthritic knees could also be due to having sat cross-legged for hours on end at traditional functions. If the compensation culture had been in force in those days I might now be a wealthy man.

The domestic round continued. Guy and Adrian (as previously mentioned) attended pre-prep and kindergarten schools designed for the children of the ever-increasing expatriate community. There were very few English language programmes on TV so when they were home, and when not being introduced to the adventures of Tin Tin, they were fed a diet of Muppet shows – which might well explain certain of their characteristics in later life. They were, with my encouragement, allowed to watch the various sporting programmes on TV – mainly golf, sumo wrestling, ice-skating and baseball.

At weekends, when I was not playing golf, we drove off into the country for a family picnic. We had actually found, after much searching, an uncultivated field in the shadow of Mount Fuji. After lunch we conscripted Elizabeth into throwing a tennis ball at a makeshift wicket and tried to instil the rudiments of the laws of cricket at an early age. Having watched baseball on TV, both boys developed a good flat throw which stood them in good stead when they took up the game properly.

A disadvantage of working in Tokyo was that the business community adhered strictly to local custom. Thus, while there was a fair sprinkling of National holidays, offices were open on Saturday mornings. Furthermore, since the department stores and shopping malls recognised the commercial attractions of Christmas we were obliged to keep the office ticking over through the festive period, although the expatriate staff sloped off early to join their families for traditional Christmas lunch.

The comparative calm of dinner parties was frequently disturbed by regular, and quite often serious, earthquake tremors, since Tokyo lies on a major fault. One soon became used to such occurrences and did not panic unduly. However, when hanging light fittings started swinging uncontrollably we all huddled, as advised by the accepted precautionary measures, under the door lintel, a prescribed safe haven. Depending on the size of the dinner party this led to some unusually close encounters. One tended to construct one's guest lists accordingly!

While we both thoroughly enjoyed our time in Tokyo after four years we felt we had had enough. Thus, when the Bank offered me a posting as General Manager, Northern India, a parish encompassing such idyllic and evocative names as Kashmir and Simla, we accepted with alacrity. By this time our terms of service allowed six weeks home leave on an annual basis and we were anxious to get closer to base. With the time difference it normally took at least two days to recover from the Tokyo/London flight.

I was given a foretaste of my new territory when the Bank held a conference in Kashmir for all of its country managers and senior executives from London. This was a useful exercise as I stopped over in Delhi en route to Srinagar and the then general manager, a delightful Irishman, Paddy O'Gorman, who had spent all his working life in India, introduced me to the senior committee members of the New Delhi Golf Club, on the basis of getting one's priorities right. Apparently, there was a long waiting list, which could be circumvented with support from the correct quarter.

Returning from India I had a most remarkable journey. In those far off days it was considered the norm for Bank executives to travel first class. Accordingly, when I pitched up at Delhi airport I discovered the British Airways flight was running an hour late so, noticing that Singapore Airlines was just about to depart I, with very little fuss, switched flights. A first class ticket worked wonders in getting prompt attention. Both flights were due to proceed via Hong Kong, but when we were about to land a typhoon sprang up and the aircraft was diverted to Taiwan. On landing there I noticed a Cathay Pacific flight was due to take off for Tokyo so, after a little persuasion, I got my luggage offloaded and transferred to the Cathay flight. I was about to board when an alert official decreed that as I hadn't gone through immigration procedures I couldn't leave without a permit. The upshot was, after considerable hassle, I was put back on the Singapore Airlines flight to Hong Kong where, by now, the typhoon had abated. Knowing that Elizabeth would be waiting at Haneda Airport to meet the BA flight I then persuaded the pilot, once airborne, to radio his office, presumably

175

in Tokyo, and alert her to the change of plan. This procedure apparently broke various international regulations as by then we were over Red China and such communications were not allowed – I was informed rather dramatically by the pilot that we were in danger of being shot down. We eventually touched down at Hong Kong and were put up at the Hilton overnight, to await a relief Singapore Airline crew. I telephoned our flat in Tokyo, expecting no answer with a distraught Elizabeth still hanging around at Haneda Airport, only to hear her dulcet tones saying all was well as the Tokyo office of Singapore Airlines had kept her fully informed. I mention this incident as, other than to recommend Singapore Airlines, it demonstrates the complications which can arise from a last minute change in travel plans. My advice is stick to your original schedule.

Incidentally, while first class travel was a privileged 'perk' much appreciated by the management there was some justification from the Bank's point of view as, quite often, one's fellow passengers could prove to be useful business contacts. In those days the upper deck of the new Jumbo 747 was set aside as a bar, where legs could be stretched and cocktails served. On one such occasion I got into conversation with a South African by the name of Jack Goldin and we subsequently kept in touch and transacted some business on the banking front.

Jack was a thrusting, far-sighted entrepreneur who was one of the founders of a chain of stores in South Africa named Pick 'n' Pay – they are now the equivalent of Tesco. Having successfully launched the company he sold out, making in the process a considerable profit. Becoming bored with the idle life he then started up a pharmaceutical chain named Clicks – they are now the South African equivalent of Boots the Chemist. Enough was enough and with a substantial personal fortune, when last I heard, he had settled his offspring in Australia and himself and wife in California. If still alive he is probably now plotting to stamp his expertise on an unsuspecting USA. Wall-Mart had better look to their laurels. I certainly miss the case of wine he regularly used to send from South Africa as a gesture of 'goodwill and friendship' at Christmas.

While on the subject of travel by aeroplane I still hanker after the days when I originally sallied forth on the Bank's business in the '50s when taking to the air was a relatively uncomplicated business. Once on board there were but three buttons to master – one summoned the air hostess, the others manipulated the reading light and reclined the seat. Today, even travelling economy class, a descriptive booklet is handed out as to how to manage the surfeit of controls at one's disposal, whether it be working the TV screen or plotting the route of the aircraft as it surges across the globe. Apart from needing a Master's degree in Advanced Technology to interpret the instructions, there is little if any room to manoeuvre without upsetting fellow passengers. I have found that the solution is to eschew all such gadgetry and resort to the simple delights of reading a good book.

While taking our leave, en route to England, we stopped over in Dar es Salaam (Haven of Peace) to stay with Elizabeth's parents, where her father was in charge of the Caltex operation. They lived in a suitably impressive house sited along a clifftop drive overlooking the sea.

How it had all changed since my previous visit in the late '50s. In 1967 the President, Julius Nyerere, while in Arusha had declared his ideology of liberalised socialism a dogma justifying national theft. Thereafter the Government grabbed everything worth having – other than the oil companies. He was supported in getting rid of the vestiges of colonial rule by the Chinese, North Koreans and Russians. The Chinese who were helping to rebuild the railway exercised considerable influence and a condition of their aid was that Tanzania was flooded with second rate imports from China. About the only product in plentiful supply in the once well-stocked supermarkets were the 'bare' necessities, i.e. Chinese toilet rolls – the paper giving the impression of being pulped from incredibly knotty trees.

The tourist industry had collapsed and other than some well-muscled Brits we were the only patrons of the swimming pool of a new government hotel recently built on the outskirts of town. When I complimented our fellow guests on their dexterity in kicking a football around, they confessed to being the pride of Aston Villa who were taking on the Tanzanian team that weekend.

Apart from its virtually deserted fine sandy beaches and sailing facilities, Dar had little to offer and we were pleased to be on our way – shortly thereafter Elizabeth's parents retired to the west coast of Scotland.

177

From what I could gather socialism and self reliance had not worked. It is now fashionable to blame the Germans and latterly the British for introducing an alien culture and alien methods which have been said to have given rise to many of Tanzania's post colonial problems. Nevertheless the descent into grinding poverty, corruption, and famine must surely be placed at the door of 'J.N.' when he pressed the self destruct button. Perhaps this judgement is unduly harsh and the apparent prosperity and ordered calm of the '50s was delusory – only time will tell.

Despite the developed countries paying lip service by forgiving debt and providing increased aid there seems to be no panacea for Africa's insurmountable problems. With Zimbabwe along with most other African countries following the same route as Tanzania, Africa, the birthplace of civilisation, seems to have lost its way. In the words of the popular song 'Where have all the flowers gone – when will they ever learn?'

On moving back to Sussex with a growing family we decided to sell the Hove flats with a certain sense of sadness as they had provided happy memories. After much searching we purchased a family home close to Tonbridge on Bidborough Ridge. Apart from comfortable accommodation and well-maintained gardens complete with a small pond, it provided the most stunning views across the Weald of Kent. In fact, one of the daily pleasures was walking along the Ridge and collecting the paper from the village shop. There was nothing better on a spring morning as the sun scorched off wraiths of mist revealing an amazing vista stretching out to the North Downs with not a house in sight. The neatly hedged yellow-green of the meadows, the mauve clumps of trees merging into the distance, the chorus of birds and the sound of far away church bells. So different from the paddy fields of Japan, the vast sunbaked, seemingly empty, African countryside or the muezzin's call to prayer. Even when the weather was inclement it was fascinating watching the rain building up on the horizon like smoke and eventually drenching the apple trees and giving a new sheen to the crocuses, daffodils and tulips. It was difficult to believe we were living in one of the most crowded corners of England. A ribbon of motorway cutting through the North Downs was not without its attractions,

178

particularly at night, as the twinkling car headlights on the horizon competed with the stars.

Properties on the 'Ridge' were much sought after. One of our not-so-near neighbours was Don Revie, the England football manager. Despite being egged on by me, my sons never had the temerity to knock on his door and ask for their ball back.

To celebrate our purchase we hosted a number of dinner parties and on one occasion invited an old friend from Kenya along with his attractive new bride – David and Diana Rees. Other than chatting about the 'good old' days with David, I remember very little about the evening, nor for that matter did Mrs Rees. But, some twenty odd years later, playing at Rye Golf Club in a mixed foursomes competition our female opponent introduced herself as Diana Rees. For want of anything better to say I remarked that the only Diana Rees I knew was married to a David Rees. Diana confirmed the past tense. Although not part of this tale I was getting divorced at the time and, after a 'prolonged' courtship, I am delighted to report that Diana is now Mrs Bignell.

On safely getting back to Tokyo it was a continuous round of farewell parties. Also, of course, there was the obligatory reception to introduce my successor, David Murray John. The handover went smoothly, although David, with a larger, more adult family, had to move to a more spacious apartment.

The day of our departure from Tokyo was particularly poignant. It was a fresh spring morning with dawn's pale light shining through the blossom of the cherry trees that reached into our balcony. Our great friends, the Oshimas, insisted on coming with us to the airport to see us off. Their daughter, Anne, squeezed into our car and we played her favourite tape of Peter, Paul and Mary singing *Leaving on a Jet Plane* as we bowled along the upper freeway, filled with nostalgia. For once there was not too much traffic and we could drink in the view of concrete apartment blocks giving way to factories belching sooty smoke, and small figures scurrying along the streets below.

Amazingly, this riparian scene when viewed for the last time with the sun breaking through leaden skies and lighting up the waters of the port beyond took on a beauty one could not have believed possible – rather like a Lowry painting come to life. On reflection, Japan had been good to us. The warmth and friendliness of the people made it difficult to imagine the atrocities committed during the last war. For some reason the British were particularly respected; there seemed to be some special affinity, possibly because we were both island races and shared the same values of politeness, good manners and integrity.

Leaving brought back only the happy memories of sun-drenched days walking the trails of the Hakone National Park with the mighty snow-capped Mount Fuji rising above the surrounding hills, cherry blossom in the spring and the fabulous Japanese food – raw fish delicacies, tempura, sukiyaki, and mouthwatering kobe beef. One's mind somehow pushed aside the boredom of sitting in polluted traffic jams, the inability of understanding the classic Japanese dramas and dances of the 'Kabuki' and the 'Noh', the absence of sausages, pubs and test matches on TV.

When saying our final goodbyes in 1976 I was tempted to paraphrase General McArthur's 'We will return before Christmas'. But I did not, and, sadly, we have not.

Hong Kong

In the late '60s early '70s Hong Kong was still one of the loveliest harbours in the world, ringed by beautiful mountains, and the island wasn't the concrete jungle it is today. Victoria, the city, still had glimpses of greenery while across the harbour Kowloon and the New Territories were in the process of taking on greater significance. In fact the New Territories, a source of agricultural produce, were a picture of fields in cultivation and dotted with rural communities.

Flying into Hong Kong for the first time was quite an experience. After taking in the impressive expanse of the harbour, the approach to Kai Tak airport seemed hazardous in the extreme as we flew low over rooftops of crowded tenements with washing lines perilously close to the undercarriage. But land safely we did.

I generally stayed at the Hilton Hotel which was just across from the cricket ground – then the most valuable piece of undeveloped real estate in the world. The Hong Kong &

180

Shanghai Bank and the Bank of China dominated the skyline, although Jardine's new head office was competing for attention with its distinctive 'Swiss cheese' architecture of a façade full of holes. John Heywood, the dynamic young Managing Director at the time, mentioned that the staff had different views as to what the orifices represented, the connotations of which were not particularly complimentary to senior management. In fact, the edifice was known as 'The building of 1000 arseholes' and on counting only 990 the other ten were said to relate to the directors!

The tunnel joining the island to the mainland had just opened although the ferry was the most popular means of transport linking the Island and Kowloon. Rickshaws were still in evidence but were more of a tourist attraction than a recognised conveyance. Hong Kong was, and still is, a paradise for shoppers: Chinese carved ivory (yet to be banned), porcelain, antique curios – particularly snuff-boxes – and a plethora of duty-free goods kept one's cheque book busy. Hand-tailored suits and custom-made shirts could be had at bargain prices and it was well worth having decent clothes copied. Returning some thirty years later Ascot Chang still had my shirt measurements on record – although certain adjustments were needed.

With the Dao Heng Bank expanding its business and Japan increasing in importance, Head Office decided to relocate our Regional Director to Hong Kong. Colin Kerr and his charming wife, Anna, duly pitched their tent and could not have proved a better choice. Colin was a bit of a 'smoothy' and the Kerrs quickly integrated into Hong Kong's carefully structured society. Importantly for me, he was most supportive of our efforts in Japan.

At the time of my arrival the Bank had financed a couple of tugs and, if my memory serves me right, while they were Japanese owned, they were fronted by officials of the dock workers' union in Hong Kong. Whether or not we were dealing with some Triad society was never established but our clients certainly seemed to exert undue influence as to how and when the tugs were utilised. Mr Oyama, our Japanese client, despite a very shaky balance sheet, had somehow – presumably by exercising leverage in the right quarters – acquired the central section of the newly built Kowloon container complex. Having run out of funds to pay for the finishing touches (cranes, etc) over lunch at the Okura Hotel, he suggested through his interpreter that Grindlays refinance the whole deal. When I enquired how much he wrote down a figure in my diary which covered two pages before he ran out of noughts! To be fair he was thinking in yen but it was still a significant amount of dollars running into many millions. Having been initially sceptical, the deal, on further scrutiny, had considerable merit and seemed bankable. In addition to taking a charge over the facility – Kowloon Container Wharf (KCW) – once finished, the whole income stream generated by the users – Scan Dutch, Zim Israel, etc. – would be banked, after costs, to repay the debt. Everything went swimmingly. Tom Cross-Brown in Hong Kong (he subsequently looked after Lazard's interests in the colony) processed the number crunching, our merchant bank in London took enormous fees and syndicated the loan and our insurance agency successfully placed the insurance cover. Added to which, Dao Heng Bank gained a major client.

It was a highly gratifying transaction. Several enjoyable trips were made to Hong Kong finishing with a final flurry when Elizabeth accompanied me to the grand opening – parties galore and a fleet of Rolls Royces at our disposal. All good things had to come to an end. Mr Oyama, buoyed up by this success, over-reached himself by expanding his fleet of 'feeder' ships (small container vessels), defaulted on a loan to a Japanese Bank and was put into receivership. Grindlays in London got cold feet and, I thought rather feebly, decided to realise KCW's assets in Hong Kong. These were auctioned off, Hutchisons being the successful bidder. All our debts were cleared, all the expensive legal costs paid and the only loser was Mr Oyama whose vision and influence had initially secured and developed the facility.

Hutchisons, of course, went on to make enormous profits from the venture. I could not really complain as by way of compensation we had enjoyed several pleasurable stays at the Peninsular Hotel, lavish hospitality at the race track and, on one memorable occasion, a tour of the nightclubs. A strong bond was also built up with the management of the Dao Heng Bank, which proved mutually beneficial when we opened our branch in Tokyo.

The Bank, in their wisdom, had purchased a couple of flats for the expatriate officers in Century Towers – a modern circular edifice at the mid level. Despite the expense of having to produce custom-made semi-circular sofas, these proved a wise and profitable investment as property prices were going through the roof. That said, it was difficult to match the regal accommodation provided by the old established banks, particularly the Hong Kong & Shanghai and Chartered Banks, whose senior expatriate managers lived in considerable style.

Modern steel and glass sky-scrapers were beginning to dominate the skyline (still constructed with bamboo scaffolding); city executives consulted their Feng Shui expert before arranging their offices. The harbour was filled with sampans, junks (often corporate), barges and ferries, all of which vied with the ocean liners. While many of the shopping malls were air-conditioned the true flavour of Hong Kong was still to be found in the noise and smells of the crowded local markets. At night a forest of neon lights, restaurants, bazaars and 'Susie Wong' style nightclubs jostled for attention. Nowhere was the cliché 'Work hard, play hard' more apt, although on my arrival I had a slightly easier ride, being offered some shares in a new issue in Slater and Walker at cost which I was able to sell some days later at a useful profit.

Hong Kong had the reputation of being a fantastic introduction to Asia and I was able to endorse this after being subjected to an amazing variety of culinary experiences as the Dao Heng entertained me at the top restaurants with 'dim sum' featuring prominently.

On one occasion, on a trip from Tokyo to Hong Kong we had reason to stop over in Taipei. There, in the first class lounge, I fell into conversation with a most attractive, expensively attired oriental lady. Coincidentally I was seated next to her for the remainder of the flight to Hong Kong. She enquired where I was staying and what my name was. I mentioned the Hilton Hotel and she said she would book a room there – for some inexplicable reason I gave my name as George. After settling in at the hotel I received a phone call from the lady in question suggesting a dinner à deux at the Mandarin Hotel as her guest. Over dinner she explained she was the 'lady friend' of a deposed Vietnamese high ranking official and he

183

had provided her with sufficient funds to set up a new life, in some luxury, in America, where he would join her. Unfortunately in the ensuing chaos in Laos her provider had apparently 'gone missing, presumed dead'. She was obviously in a quandary and at times our conversation tended to be confused and stilted, inhibited not only by her limited command of the English language but her insistence on calling me George.

It was only on my return to Tokyo that I think the penny dropped. Having given my newfound friend a spurious address, I was disconcerted to read in the Japan Times that George Bignell was listed in a column set aside for undelivered registered mail to foreign residents. Hoping that it had gone unnoticed, although it seemed to stare out at me in luminous capitals, I hot-footed it round to the Post Office. After much form filling – the Japanese official was mystified by my warbled rendition of *Return to sender, address unknown, no such number, no such zone* – the letter which had been sent from America was re-directed (unopened) to an equally spurious address in Australia. It was there that I said George Bignell had recently departed. By then I had deduced, rightly or wrongly, that my correspondent was seeking to legitimise an encounter to gain a passport which would enable her to enjoy a new and comfortable life either in the States or the UK. Not knowing the truth, it remains one of life's mysteries and reminiscent of a Thomas Hardy novel.

Korea

At the time of my visit Korea was in the process of leaving the ranks of developing countries and, with its economy forging ahead, was successful in competing with Japan for major construction contracts and in some cases dominating the market for electrical goods and similar items. I visited Seoul to explore the feasibility of opening a branch there and to promote business with our correspondent banks. I was invited out to lunch by one of our Korean correspondent banks. This involved sitting on embroidered cushions around low tables which I found somewhat uncomfortable, not helped by painful knee joints. Copious amounts of rice seasoned by a very hot pickle and the odd slice of fish did little to stimulate the palate –

184

apparently I had drawn the short straw as, back at the hotel, marinated beef and other delicacies were on offer and to be enjoyed. At another official function – men only – I was entertained to dinner at a private dining room where we were literally fed by traditionally costumed hostesses, who presumed, probably rightly, that our competence with chopsticks didn't match their own skills. I found the whole experience stimulating. Whether or not Head Office paid any attention to my paper on the subject I am not sure but we eventually took the step and opened a branch in Seoul.

For some reason which I have forgotten, a curfew was in force but, egged on by, and at the invitation of, Kleinwort Benson's representative in Tokyo, who was there at the same time, we decided to break the curfew and sample the delights of the night life. We failed, however, as on leaving the safety of the Chosun Hotel we were immediately stopped by the police and, after a heated altercation, returned under escort with a stern reprimand. On balance this was no bad thing as we decided to drown our sorrows in the Hotel's nightclub and found the entertainment well up to expectations and probably more reliable than anything we might have encountered had we successfully ventured forth.

A worthwhile digression was a visit to the art market, where Korea's budding artists display their works. Some of the copies of famous works by the French impressionists were amazingly good and one could also find still lifes beautifully detailed. For a very modest sum I purchased a couple of oil paintings for the Tokyo Office and thought them thoroughly worthy of wall space.

Philippines

The Bank, still in its expansionary mode, had taken a stake in a local bank in Manila and we had seconded George Cunningham (one of our senior managers) to protect and promote the Bank's interests. Colin Kerr, quite rightly, considered it would make sense to enlist the aid of Japanese partners to further enlarge the business. Having established strong ties with the Kyowa and Saitama banks in Tokyo we enrolled their support and increased the share capital.

To celebrate this partnership the Kerrs suggested I accompany them to Manila to foster the relationship. This proved a delightful diversion as we were sumptuously entertained by our local partners who lived in lavish style in Forbe's Park, a luxurious 'Wentworth Estate' style enclave on the outskirts of Manila.

The whole venture, alas, proved an expensive disaster; corruption was rife and our local partners were milking the Bank dry to support their extravagant lifestyle. What was worse, Grindlays merchant bank in London had suffered severe losses following the failure of the UK property market in 1976 and rumours were prevalent that Grindlays itself was on the verge of collapse. I was summoned by our Japanese partners and politely informed that they wished to withdraw from the venture. This we readily agreed to and closed down our operation in the Philippines never to return. All very sad for if one could ignore the poverty and gun-toting gangsters, it seemed to be a most charming country with a lot to offer. I have memories of the flamboyant 'jeepneys' weaving through the dense Manila traffic and the busy nightlife. These forms of transport are in themselves an experience, being converted jeeps abandoned by the US Army and lovingly restored. They are a blinding display of glinting chrome, a galaxy of lights and hand painted murals of questionable artistic quality. Rather like the shikaras in Kashmir (mentioned in a later chapter) they are all individually named. The names often revealed the driver's temperament and philosophy on life, though 'Last Chance Saloon', 'God is my guardian' and 'Fully insured' were not particularly reassuring as one set off to joust with the Manila traffic.

Filipinos love to party and they have an inherent musical ability. Their bands and vocalists are particularly expert at reproducing the latest sounds of international artists. Tom Jones and Frankie Vaughan seemed to be in fashion during our visit.

Fortunately, Citibank, as a major shareholder, shored up Grindlays in London and the Group managed to escape the financial crisis which hit the banking sector at that time.

Kuala Lumpur

My trip to Malaysia proved to be a bit of a jolly. Arrangements

186

were made for me to spend a couple of days working in and with our newly established representative office. This coincided with the Malaysian Open Golf Championship at the Royal Selangor Golf Club. Having been assured that I would meet everybody that mattered from a business aspect and socially in the gallery, we duly decamped to the club. To be fair to our man in K L, Desmond Whittall, we did seem to meet just about everybody, if not on the course at least in the bar of the clubhouse afterwards. One evening I was invited along with the Whittalls to dinner by the Manager of the HSBC at their very splendid residence.

What I saw of Kuala Lumpur seemed very orderly and civilised – lovely colonial buildings, an attractive cricket ground and, in those days, a relaxed lifestyle, encouraged by the oppressive humidity. It was noticeable how gleaming high rise office blocks contrasted with ornate temples, quaint Chinese chop houses and old world charm – a unique blend of the ancient and modern. I understand the skyline is now dominated by the twin Petronas Towers – the tallest buildings in the world.

Grindlays took a stake in one of the local banks, Merchant Bankers Berhad, but generally we were too late on the scene to make much impact, although the representative office was subsequently successful in developing off-shore products for the rest of the Grindlays Group.

IX

India

New Delhi

Our arrival in New Delhi was not particularly auspicious as, while we pitched up on cue, our luggage went straight on to London. British Airways did everything possible to rectify matters but, while I had fortunately travelled in a reasonably smart suit, Elizabeth was understandably put out that she didn't have anything to wear at the welcoming parties. She need not have worried as the local tailors were well up to the task and, given a decent pattern to copy and the requisite measurements, they produced a suitable wardrobe within hours.

On the health front all was not well as 'I flew with 'flu' which, shortly after arrival, necessitated a somewhat painful operation to drain the inner ear. I'm not sure if the over-enthusiastic surgeon got it right and still, some thirty years later, experience unexpected and unexplained attacks of dizziness.

As mentioned previously I was extremely fortunate in taking over from James O'Gorman (Paddy) and his charming wife, Mary. They had been a popular fixture in New Delhi for many years and had an enormous circle of friends, both expatriate and local. We were eloquently introduced at the many farewell parties in their honour – Paddy was returning to Ireland – and many of the introductions matured into warm friendships which we had the privilege of continuing during our stay.

The eight hour flight had borne us into a landscape, a culture and a climate that was literally half a world away from Japan. India is a land so rich in contrasts it could not fail to be other than an interesting posting and we arrived full of hope and expectation.

We were fortunate in our accommodation – by New Delhi standards a comparatively modern house with central air-conditioning (if it worked a blessed luxury). Although not particularly grand we still had a staff of thirteen servants – the subject of separate comment elsewhere. They and their families were housed in a block of flats at the bottom of the garden. We were never sure of the exact complement as relatives and children came and went. If the speed at which food left over after dinner parties vanished was any indication and the constant comings and goings I suspect the number was close on fifty.

The garden was walled and mainly given over to lawn, although there was one enormous tree in the corner and the surrounding flowerbeds were a blaze of colour with sweet peas, roses, zinnias and carnations to the fore. The white walls were splashed crimson and purple with climbing jacaranda and bougainvillaea. Although the house was sited opposite a nature reserve, the garden was virtually devoid of wildlife if one discounted the squirrels, birds of every variety and the 'buzzing' of a multitude of butterflies. Or so we thought, until one morning our Jeeves-like butler appeared, unusually agitated, to inform us that a python was wedged in the outside drainpipe. With its head spitting fury at the top and its tail thrashing around at the bottom it must have been enormous. A professional snake remover was hastily summoned and what remedial steps he took we know not as work and school took priority. Much to our relief on our return there was no evidence of the python, although the drainpipe looked the worse for wear and was buckled where previously it had been unbuckled.

Having decided at birth that my sons had the potential to become test cricketers they were put through their paces at an early age. With thirteen servants and their offspring there were always sufficient fielders on hand to provide realistic playing conditions. Unfortunately, the gardener's boy, a strapping youth of seventeen, thought he was the next Kapil Dev and, backed up by four slips, three leg slips, a silly mid on and the Ayah, a slightly wobbly silly mid off, with the wicket keeper standing back, it was quite an ordeal for my six year old when he went out to bat. Particularly as the bowler, to generate sufficient pace, started his run up by disappearing behind the tree in

189

the far corner. The pitch at the time didn't help with its uneven bounce. Having witnessed the perfection of the greens at the golf club I enlisted the assistance of the head greenkeeper to transform the lawn, the work to be carried out while we were back in the UK on home leave. On our return some seven weeks later there was a verdant strip gleaming in the sunlight and we duly invited some friends round for the grand opening. Unfortunately, on the big day, it rained and the pitch became an evil-smelling quagmire which had our rather upmarket neighbours telephoning the Delhi sewerage department complaining about burst pipes. Unbeknown to us, to provide a fertile foundation tons of buffalo dung had been dug in to the topsoil. Not only did this encourage the grass to grow but also provided an ideal breeding ground for the fly population of New Delhi. After that, garden parties, replete with colourful shamiamas (marquees), had to be confined to the dry season, but at least Guy and Adrian mastered the art of batting on a 'sticky' wicket. This stood them in good stead when they moved on to their English preparatory school.

Being by far and away the largest and most important foreign bank in India, Grindlays with its origins stretching back to the 19th century had a property portfolio envied by all; magnificent, if in some places dated premises and grand residential accom-modation. The White House, Alipore, Calcutta was one of the finest private houses in India and the Regional Director's apartment above the main office in Bombay was the ultimate in grandiose luxury. Apart from boasting three dining rooms it was the only private residence in my experience having raised seating round the billiard table; this enabled guests after dinner to watch the invariable ineptitude of the players.

It was always a pleasure to visit the branches under my control, staying in Bank houses steeped in history and set in beautiful grounds. One must remember, of course, that people pay good money to stay in New Delhi and explore the 'Golden Triangle' with visits to the incomparable Taj Mahal and the pink city of Jaipur.

While regular visits were paid to Bombay, and occasionally Calcutta, my parish consisted of branches in old and New Delhi, Kanpur, Amritsar, Simla and Srinagar (Kashmir). A greater diversity of business would be difficult to imagine, from

190

the industrial factories of Kanpur to the mountainous attractions of Simla and Kashmir. Fortunately, at this time all the branches were making record profits under the guidance of their experienced and highly capable Indian managers. Grindlays probably had the pick of the labour market with a cadre of top university graduates applying for a strictly limited quota of junior management positions. A number of our Indian staff, when posted overseas, were head-hunted and, having moved on, invariably reached the top of their chosen profession.

Northern India was prospering with local industry expanding and beginning to compete on the world stage. Tractors were being exported and Rambaxy laboratories is now a major player as a leading and innovative pharmaceutical company. Tourism was flourishing with the Golden Triangle of Delhi, Agra and Jaipur a major attraction. The delights of Kashmir were still on offer and not inhibited by political constraints.

On one occasion I was invited by Brigadier Chopra, Chairman of Reckitt and Colman, India, to make up a four at golf. Apparently, a retired major general from England, a keen golfer, was passing through, along with friends, and they were arriving from Agra that morning. I was told to be on the first tee, which had been reserved, punctually at 14.00 hours. Chopra, to give the moment a sense of pageantry, had conscripted a squadron of mounted lancers in ceremonial dress with pennants fluttering to line the route to the clubhouse. Come 15.00 hours with pennants drooping and no visitors a disappointed Brigadier suggested nine holes, dismissed the mounted cavalry and we drove off down the fairway into the sunset.

It transpired, and I was only to learn the names of our proposed opponents later, that Major General James Majury and Colin Rowan MC (both of whom I knew well as past captains of Royal Ashdown Golf Club) had been detained in Agra where one of the wives had gone down with the dreaded 'Delhi Belly'. A great pity as I know James, in particular, would have enjoyed the pomp and circumstance conjured up in his honour.

Kanpur

As with most industrial towns situated on the banks of the

191

Ganges, Kanpur was not pleasing to the eye. Neither was that particular stretch of the Ganges as it rolled sluggishly by, the colour of milky coffee, mud churning on the currents and, just to add to the rather depressing scene, I witnessed the bloated body of a dead cow being dragged ashore by some perplexed fishermen.

In the late 19th century power-driven cotton mills, an offshoot from the Industrial Revolution back in the UK, were established in Kanpur and a flourishing textile trade resulted. I was escorted round some of the mills which still seemed to be using the original spinning equipment, most of it bearing a maker's name from Lancashire. By dint of regular maintenance and judicious oiling everything seemed to tick over reasonably smoothly to the extent that, while I was watching, bath towels were produced with my name woven into the fabric. The only element that seemed to clog up the works was a recalcitrant workforce prone to strikes. With union leaders of a similar bent, the Bank staff often came out in sympathy. If the walkouts coincided with a Test Match thousands of interested spectators used to congregate in the Bank compound where a giant scoreboard had, by tradition, been erected. To placate a possibly mutinous mob the junior management, not on strike, found themselves scurrying up and down ladders updating the score.

In the middle of the 19th century Kanpur had been the scene of an unforgivable massacre of British soldiers and European families by Nana Sahib who was subsequently defeated in equally bloody circumstances. The whole unpleasant episode continues to rankle and I had the lurking suspicion that some of the descendants of this infamous occasion were seeking, given a reasonable excuse, such as a collapse in India's batting, to keep their hand in.

The cricket ground at Kanpur was on the test match circuit and, with substandard hotels in town, those visiting players that could, arranged to get themselves billeted out in the expatriate bungalows. Apparently, it was not an uncommon occurrence to come down to breakfast and see some famous names tucking into bacon and eggs and other staple foods which allowed them to get through a period of play without regular repairs to the pavilion.

Most visitors, once off the recognised tourist trail, invariably

192

went down with irregular bowel movements. The maxim, 'Don't breath the air or drink the water' was ignored at one's peril.

Simla

Simla, somewhat off the beaten track for the international tourist, was still a major bolthole in the summer for the wealthy Indian families escaping the heat of the plains. Its reputation as probably the most famous hill station in India was forged well before the war, when the Viceroy's staff (the Heaven Born) emigrated in the summer with their families to escape the oppressive heat of New Delhi. It was called the 'abode of the high and mighty' and is spectacularly set at about 6,800 ft with splendid promenades, graceful colonial buildings, wooded ravines and surrounded on all sides by dense deodar and rhododendron trees which merge into evergreen forests with the snow-capped Himalayas as a backdrop.

When travelling around Britain, particularly in Tunbridge Wells, one tends to forget that the rhododendrons were originally found in the foothills of the Himalayas and are not native to the UK. No doubt, in days of yore, servants of the Raj, attracted by their flowering beauty, stomped through the foothills in their pursuit of botany and brought them back on retirement, transplanting them to their gardens or estates. They now flourish to the extent that in many areas they are beginning to dominate the landscape.

In those days it was a long and tortuous journey to Simla, and when Elizabeth and I undertook the trip it was equally hazardous but for different reasons. We were able to fly the first leg to Chandigarh but the perilous drive to Simla itself, perched on the lower slopes of the Himalayas, was particularly nerve-wracking. Our transport, a hired old Ambassador car (the best available – Valium not included) lived up to its reputation that the only part which did not make a noise was the horn. We drove in a flurry of dust. This seemed to hang over us for the whole journey but fortunately obscured the view which was of landslides and single track roads, with precipitous drops to valleys thousands of feet below on one side. On the other, sharp cliffs of rock hindered the avoidance of approaching lorries which seemed oblivious to any other road users. Great hunks of rock had fallen down the cliff edge and large chunks of the road were missing and where it existed the surface was severely pitted. I suppose we could have let the 'train take the strain' but, on inspecting this alternative form of transport, we decided that the car, such as it was, presented the lesser of two evils. We miraculously arrived relatively unscathed and unharmed, although every detail of that drive is kept fresh in my mind by recurrent nightmares.

Our transport deposited us some distance from Simla proper which was only accessible by foot, the luggage and all goods being carried by muscular porters up a series of terraces and steps to the Mall. Here a rickshaw awaited to take us to our hotel – the Cecil Oberoi – and the Bank. Many decades ago some far-sighted Viceroy decreed that the townsfolk of Simla should be able to enjoy the delights of an evening stroll along the Mall without the distraction of carriages – and this ban has remained in force, I believe, to this day. I'm sure, if given the opportunity, Mr Ken Livingstone would duplicate the Viceroy's idea in London. Once booked in at the Cecil Oberoi with a welcoming fire in the bedroom, we were able to observe from our hotel balcony houses and buildings clinging precariously to the steeply wooded hillsides spread out below. Most residences in Simla itself were devoid of gardens as the terrain on which they were built was too sheer to allow for more than a drive and small lawn.

It was more picturesque by night when lamps glittered in the darkness. By day it was a hotchpotch of corrugated roofs – mostly rusting – which presented a rather down-at-heel appearance.

After spending a day at the Bank we were able to explore further, when the attractions of Simla became more apparent. The Vice-Regal lodge was, as one would expect, a most impressive structure, despite the fact that it was now used as some form of educational establishment. From a grassy knoll on an outlying spur one could take in the breathtaking view of the rolling snow-covered waves of the Himalayas stretching to the outer reaches of Tibet. Banks of rhododendrons coloured the lower slopes in pink, mauve and red, along with many bright flowering plants whose names I have forgotten. The tops of the tall deodars, pine, fir and chestnut trees were dark against a cerulean sky.

A cocktail party was held that evening for our more important clients – mostly senior officers in the Indian Army who had, I thought with Machiavellian cunning, made this attractive hill station a major command post. In my capacity as a trustee of the Lady Hardinge Cottage Homes we also met a few Anglo-Indian memsahibs, relics from the Raj, who after independence had decided to 'stay on'. Unfortunately, their once acceptable pensions had been decimated by inflation and most were now surviving on slender means.

One lady had us round for lunch the next day to Rose Cottage (which resembled a setting from the TV series *The Jewel in the Crown*). The cottage was a veritable treasure trove containing some lovely furniture and paintings. The husband, long deceased, had been a colonel in the old Indian Army and there were many priceless mementos of the Raj. The garden, with its established rose beds and the snowy Himalayas providing a breathtaking backcloth, was sufficient reason in itself to persuade the owner to soldier on. Apart from listening avidly to the BBC World Service on an ancient wireless, she had severed all ties with the UK and there was no reason to return, particularly as she was well looked after by devoted, if slightly dotty, aged retainers.

The previous manager of our Simla branch, Punchy Sen, had been at Oxford before the war with Toby Low (Lord Aldington) and was the first Indian graduate to be recruited by Grindlays. Among many other achievements he was the ice-skating champion of India and had a splendid trophy to prove it. I suspect that he owed this more to his wife, as the senior judge, than his prowess on the ice rink, which was situated just behind the Bank. Another contributory factor was, no doubt, the fact that the trophy had been commissioned by his wife and challenges were accepted only when the Sens were resident in Simla.

Simla was redolent of the past. If anything, it was in a time-warp: out-dated etiquettes were still observed and very little building had taken place since the departure of the Raj. With the advent of air-conditioning there was now no longer the same pressing necessity to depart the oppressive heat of the plains and escape to Simla, not the easiest journey at the best of times.

The Mall was lined with antique shops offering dubious knick-knacks of uncertain age. I was never successful in my hunt for original Daniell's aquatints – which now fetch substantial sums at auction in London. The small Gaiety Theatre, complete with Green Room door, was a perfect small-scale reproduction of its London counterpart with engraved cherubs and boxes originally installed for the senior officers and wives of the Raj. There was a small exhibition of old programmes for productions (mostly Victorian melodramas) in which Lady 'this or that' played the lead. There were also some faded dance programmes: one page listed the dances and tunes that accompanied them, the facing page provided space for people to write down the names of partners they were booked to dance with. The example on show had a 'dashing' young cavalry officer monopolising the page in question. I wonder if his persistence was ever rewarded. The window of a nearby photographic studio still displayed sepia portraits of beautiful young English ladies attired in turn-of-the-century ball gowns; alongside were photographs of carefully composed groups of Indian families togged out in their Sunday best. Presumably, this display was designed to promote the versatility of the cameraman and provide evidence that, if one forgot the negatives, it was possible to return many decades later and get a copy.

When I visited the theatre the stage was being used by an Indian 'Captain Mainwaring' detailing the day's manoeuvres for the not inconsiderable army presence in Simla.

Time precluded our visiting Wildflower Hall, formerly the home of Lord Kitchener of Khartoum. This rather grand residence (since modernised) involved a further climb up to approximately 8,000 feet and reports suggested the views were well worth the effort. Possibly next time.

We thoroughly enjoyed our visit to Simla, apart from the drive, but it is now best left to its memories when it was an important haven of tranquillity for senior officers in the Indian Civil Service in the days when the Raj governed India. To paraphrase Henry James on another place, 'It is the loveliest of small towns overflowing with everything that makes for ease, for plenty, for beauty, for interest and good example.' Although the porters might disagree!

Amritsar

Amritsar is the spiritual and religious 'Mecca' of all Sikhs and the Golden Temple, the holy shrine of the religion, is a major tourist attraction.

Grindlays was first established in Amritsar in 1900.

It was, of course, the site of an infamous massacre in 1919, which was sparked off when a female missionary was knocked off her bicycle and beaten insensible. British troops, under the command of a fiery-tempered General Rex Dyer, were ordered to ban all public gatherings. When a large crowd gathered at a meeting ground, Dyer took a squadron of troops and armoured cars and ordered them to open fire without warning. There was no chance for the gathering to disperse as the meeting ground was hemmed in by four walls with only one narrow entrance. In a short burst of sustained shooting 379 demonstrators were killed and many more wounded. During the disturbance the bank was ransacked and the manager – a Mr Stewart – lost his life, whether at the hand of a vengeful demonstrator or an irate customer history does not recount. Interestingly, having disposed of the management, the rampaging mob made an abortive attempt at opening the cash safe with a battering ram, not realising that all they had to do was adopt the more scientific approach of turning the door handle.

The rights and wrongs of this incident have been discussed at length in books by politicians and historians, and recently in the press, and it would be wrong for me to add ill-informed conjecture to this debate. Suffice to say that all seemed forgiven for when Elizabeth and I arrived we were, in keeping with the charming fashion of the country, garlanded with flowers freshly picked from the Bank garden.

About 50% of all woollen products made in India are manufactured in this region and Grindlays has garnered most of the worthwhile business on offer. It is thus an important profit centre.

Amritsar is situated only seventeen miles from the border with Pakistan and, when it was open, a useful entrepôt centre facilitating trade between the two countries developed. This has now virtually dried up. After having visited the factories of major clients, we were, in the evening, given an instructive tour of the Golden Temple.

197

Life in Amritsar is still very much a mixture of the modern and primitive. The nine hole golf course, although it did not look particularly inviting, bore witness to the 'green' revolution, and the presence of a resident professional 'marker' suggested that tourism was being taken seriously.

The town has also recently received a certain amount of publicity as the location for the latest Bollywood blockbuster 'Bride and Prejudice'. Reading an article on the subject I noticed that little had changed, in the intervening years, in terms of the locals' direct approach to practicality. Outside the chemical toilets available for the leading actors was a heartfelt notice reading 'Please no number twos only number ones'. Strict adherence to this intimidating discipline has no doubt resulted in a 'number' of unscheduled show stoppers!

Jaipur

Old friends from Aden, Hugh and Sally Freeland, were staying with us in Delhi and we took the opportunity of their visit to combine trips to the Taj Mahal, Jaipur and the Amber Palace.

It was a perfect day to start the journey. The sun was just rising and the air was crisp although our departure for Agra was not without incident. Having booked a first class compartment and deposited our luggage on the train the menfolk decided to wander up front and inspect the two enormous steam locomotives. We were standing admiring these magnificent monsters, brasswork gleaming and steam hissing when some sharp blasts on a whistle interrupted our reverie and it dawned on us that the train was pulling out of the station. What followed would have done the Keystone Cops justice. Suddenly realising we were being left behind we had to sprint down the platform with the tearstained faces of our wives just a blur as they passed. To regain our compartment, or at least the train, we had to hurdle over or plough through the luggage coolies, food vendors, beggars, potential passengers and other assorted vociferous bodies (which became more vociferous on impact). In other words the usual crowd of platform dwellers on your average railway station – a depiction in miniature of the social fabric of India. Not as dense as Tokyo, but certainly more varied as the Indian version was normally augmented by stray goats and cows for good measure. Fortunately, the guard's van at the rear had a platform on which we managed to leap. From there we wound our way back to the carriage, expecting to have to placate our distraught wives only to find them rolling around with laughter at our predicament.

Despite at times less than hygienic conditions, there were advantages to travelling by train in India. Transport by car involved avoiding bullock carts, precipitous drops and other hazards and it was difficult to drink in views of the surrounding countryside. Flying one saw very little except for the odd mountain peak, seemingly surrounded by a blanket of snow. If one was not aware of flying over India it could well be a sun-bleached Arctic scene. However, the illusion was destroyed by the dun-coloured fields, and more so by the bleak buildings as we came in to land.

The journey was not without interest, as the train cut through the early morning with its shadow keeping pace as we clattered along. Gazing out from our carriage window the scene was ever-changing with small dwellings dotted over what appeared to be a barren and impoverished countryside. As we rattled through the splintering sunlight the plains seemed to throb beneath the wrinkling heat haze. Womenfolk in colourful saris could be seen beating their washing on slabs of rock. I always found it puzzling that, despite the murky water, the clothes came out looking fresh and clean without obvious recourse to any known brand of washing powder. An added bonus came when the olive-drab, scrubby plains were relieved by a burst of colour from flamboyant trees, aflame with scarlet flowers standing out amongst the prickly vegetation. The occasional stream hove into view with water buffalo attempting to wallow and bullocks endlessly circling as they pumped water to irrigate the patches of vegetables which provided sustenance for the isolated villages. As we watched India unfold before us, small children appeared from nowhere and cheerfully waved as we trundled by.

We were well introduced at Jaipur as one of the brothers of the Maharaja, Jai (Joey), in one of his rare sober moments, had put pen to paper in Delhi and set up appointments with his stepmother, Gayatri Devi, and the Maharaja, Bhawani 'Bubbles' Singh. Gayatri Devi, once named the most beautiful woman in the world by *Life* magazine, was recovering from a spell in prison where she had been incarcerated on some trumped up charge of evading income tax. The fact that she was a leading member of the only credible opposition party to the Government was incidental.

We stayed at the Rambagh Palace Hotel, once the ancestral home of the Maharaja – a dazzling and opulent building which was a fine example of grand and ornate Rajput architecture. The palace is spread over rolling acres of beautifully landscaped gardens with hibiscus, jasmine and orange blossom much on display. We were accorded the executive suite, which could be described as daunting rather than cosy. It was a good thing that we were still relatively youthful as the en suite bathroom facilities were a taxing hike from the bedroom.

We were invited to lunch by Gayatri Devi at her minor palace, which was furnished in a mixture of styles, European blending with the Oriental. The drawing-room was dotted with photographs of Jackie Onassis and various members of the British Royal Family who had enjoyed ostentatious parties, including tiger shoots, as guests of the previous Maharaja. 'Bubbles', a polo playing friend of the Prince of Wales, and his beautiful wife put in an appearance – he had just resigned his commission as colonel commanding the President's Bodyguard. At the time he was a handsome and imposing figure. We saw him a decade later when he was virtually unrecognisable, so corpulent and bloated had he become. 'Bubbles' was given his nickname as a result of the gallons of champagne consumed at his birth.

It was a very jolly and friendly lunch. Alas, I have read recently that a bitter family feud has developed over who should inherit the estimated £400 million assets. Not having a son 'Bubbles' adopted his daughter's son and has named his five year old grandson as his heir. Predictably, his brothers have issued a writ demanding that the family's wealth be shared.

Even during my short stay in India it was amazing how many of the leading families' fortunes were the subject of dispute, with dynasties torn apart by petty feuding.

Jaipur, the 'Pink City', is always worth a visit for its many bazaars. Certain sections of the 'City Palace', an amazing edifice, are open to the paying public. From Jaipur we visited the ancient palace of Amber – notable for the need to take an elephant ride, not the most comfortable form of transportation, although our efforts at climbing on board did provide amusement for the queuing spectators.

India's last mounted cavalry regiment is headquartered in Jaipur. Needless to say, officers of the regiment provide the nucleus of the polo playing fraternity. We were privileged to receive an invitation to dine at their mess – all the trappings and traditions of a British Regiment were on display and still observed. The regimental silver glistened, toasts were drunk honouring the President and our Queen, and bagpipes skirled in the background. Despite being on a war footing with Pakistan a toast was drunk, at our suggestion, in honour of Hesky Baig (apparently all the senior officers had been at Sandhurst together).

After Jaipur we stayed two nights in Agra and witnessed by moonlight the wondrous Taj Mahal, the most extravagant monument ever built for love, returning in time for the equally stunning view at sunrise. An unforgettable experience but so well recorded elsewhere that I do not feel as though I could do justice to the overpowering beauty of the occasion. Rather like the prophet Mohammed on entering Damascus, Rudyard Kipling on seeing the Taj Mahal for the first time from a passing railway carriage vowed never to take a closer look for fear of spoiling the first breathtaking vision. A good thing, as the environs now are spoilt by the Industrial Area and pollution from a giant chemical factory is slowly eroding the marble. Moreover, souvenir sellers and other hawkers jostle for custom and spoil the approach to the Ivory Gate.

Unexpectedly, we found a visit to the deserted sandstone city of Fatehpur Sikri perched on a hill in the middle of a desert just as impressive. This city was designed for the Emperor Akbar as his capital and many splendid buildings and courtyards were built. Amazingly, it was only after it was finished that the architect realised there was no means to provide a water supply. It must have been in the days of early global warming as several successive monsoons failed and the tanks and wells dried up. With insufficient water for the citizens' needs, let alone for the Emperor, the city was abandoned. History does not relate what happened to the architect!

Kashmir. Srinagar and Gulmarg.

It was always a pleasure, as part of my responsibilities, to find an excuse for 'counting the cash in Kashmir'. Getting there involved a relatively straightforward flight from Delhi – very different from the pre-partition days when visitors had to follow the Grand Trunk Road, of Kipling fame, traversing the plains to Rawalpindi, then upwards to the hill station of Murree and onwards to the cooler climes of Kashmir.

Though political discontent was festering below the surface, the State was still a major tourist venue and a delightful place to visit. The Bank not only had a most attractive (and profitable) branch in Srinagar but also owned a number of bungalows, higher up in the mountains, at Gulmarg. These were allocated to senior management and their families, should they decide to take their vacations there – and many did.

Somewhat surprisingly, even in the spring, the vale of Kashmir at first sight is a grave disappointment, presenting an amphitheatre of treeless hills devoid of any evident charm. I had expected forested, snow-clad peaks reflected in the clear waters of Dal Lake. It is only when one crosses the Jhelum River with the adjacent fields a sea of almond and cherry blossom that its famed beauty becomes evident.

Whereas the British had 'discovered' Simla as a recuperative retreat, the marauding locals had sampled the delights of Kashmir well before the expatriate community arrived on the scene. The captivating attractions of the Valley of Kashmir were well-known as far back as the 16th century when the great Moghul Emperors moved their courts and all their trappings in summer from the sweltering plains of the Punjab to enjoy the cool, rejuvenating pleasures of this magical valley. In due course the British followed, drawn by the attractions of catching trout in the clear mountain streams and drinking the supposedly curative waters.

The area is, of course, famous for the fabled houseboats moored on the various lakes along the Vale of Kashmir. In the days of the Raj, Kashmir was a favourite holiday retreat and Dal Lake the most favoured rendezvous. Dominated by Himalayan peaks, the State is home to some of the sub-continent's most dramatic scenery.

It was one of life's great experiences to relax on the deck of a houseboat, sipping the first cool drink of the evening as the gathering mist cast a haze of ghostly light across the lake and the large red sun sank below the peaks throwing vermilion reflections over the water.

The houseboats, self-contained holiday units, were substantial vessels, permanently moored along the banks of the interconnecting lakes. Most boasted a couple of bedrooms with en suite bathrooms, dining saloon cum sitting room and a small deck. The larger houseboats had their own kitchens; others were equipped with a cook boat moored behind, where, depending on the ability of the chef, meals of varying quality were rustled up. Some of the more impressive houseboats had sufficiently large flat roofs to host cocktail parties. And indeed the Bank took one over for this purpose; when garlanded with lights it made a most fetching venue.

When Kashmir became a popular retreat for the British, the then ruling Maharajah decreed that Europeans could not own land in the state. This dictum was circumvented late in the 19th century when the first houseboat, *The Victory*, was designed and built by an enterprising Englishman. At the time of my visit there were over two hundred elaborate boats with beautifully carved interiors, which had originally been richly furnished by the owners. Some of these furnishings were still evident, if our buckled bed-springs were anything to go by. The boats tended to be clustered together to allow for 'social' intercourse and were a pleasing sight at night, lit by myriad fairy lights.

Each boat had a boat-boy who arranged for shikaras (gondola-like taxis) to ferry one back and forwards across the lake, through lotus flowers and floating gardens to the main jetty. The flashing jewel colours of kingfishers added to the beauty of the experience. The shikaras had unlikely and diverse names like *The Tempest* or *King's Ship* etc. The one thing they had in common were 'Full Spring Seats'. Provisions and flowers were brought each morning by competing punts selling their wares. It was an entrancing sensation to take one of the shikaras at dawn. As the mist melted the rippling water sparkled in the sun and a gentle breeze ruffled the flowered banks, sunlight catching the heart-shaped paddles, water reflecting the sky as the odd sluggish cloud drifted by.

The houseboats were, like the shikaras, individually named with grandiose titles such as *HMS Pinafore, Unfaithful Collette* or *Queen of Sheba* – many were staffed by aged retainers who could no doubt weave a tale or two around the trysts of bygone days. The visitors' books were in themselves worthy of close inspection, containing famous names from the past interspersed with the odd 'Mr and Mrs Smith'.

In the quiet darkness of the night the silhouettes of the brightly lit houseboats on the lake shimmered over the calm water. The only sound as one traversed the lake was that of the paddles as they sculled the water and pushed on towards their destination, while the occupants of the shikaras lay reclining on the cushioned seats, lost in their thoughts – or otherwise engaged.

Philip (Nobby) Noble, one of my Bank colleagues, could not have put it better when he wrote, 'People come to this peaceful corner of the earth to make music. The atmosphere is poignant with creativity.

'Or they come to restore egos devastated by disastrous love affairs – to relax mentally and physically, drifting and dreaming through the warm days and sometimes hearing, on the edge of audibility, a spectral soprano singing *Pale hands I loved beside the Shalimar.*'

The vale of Kashmir was extremely fertile: orchards produced a wide variety of fruits, herds of cattle grazed serenely in sap-green fields and flocks of sheep gave rise to a flourishing woollen industry. For the tourist, locally woven 'Bokhara style' carpets and exquisitely crafted lacquer-ware were much sought after. These could be purchased at the famous 'Suffering Moses' emporium. The Bank was situated in a prominent position on the bund (mall) and housed in a mock Tudor building with spacious residential accommodation above. We tried playing the local golf course but while scenically attractive the greens were in such poor condition that it made putting a lottery – my normal excuse.

From Srinagar one could climb even higher to Gulmarg, where picturesque Swiss-style chalets and guest houses had originally been built by senior Government officials. Many had been extended and modernised by wealthy Indians and at the time of our visit it had very much the air of a privileged resort, even if the 'box wallahs' had replaced the 'Heaven Born' in the social pecking order. In the winter, ski-lifts had been erected to cater for the burgeoning tourist industry. A small hotel, run by, I seem to remember, an eccentric white Russian émigré, catered for those without access to the holiday homes. In the summer a reasonably demanding, well-maintained golf course, reputedly one of the highest in the world, catered for those tourists seeking a rest from trekking the Himalayan and Karakoram mountain ranges which traversed the region.

The golf course itself was worth the hike and enjoys a breathtaking view of some of the most beautiful and unrivalled scenery to be found anywhere. Nanga Parbat at 26,700 feet is clearly visible and other major snow-clad peaks dot the skyline. While the greens were laboriously mown by antiquated hand mowers, the fairways and rough were kept in some semblance of order by flocks of sheep which were shepherded back and forth by diligent green-keepers. Not quite Augusta but nevertheless effective. Sadly, Gulmarg, the 'meadow of flowers' is totally without, as the sheep have yet to be trained to discriminate between grass and flowers. At the time of our visit there was a plan to purchase some gang mowers for use on the fairways leaving the flowers to grow wild in the rough and also tidy up and widen the many trout-filled streams criss-crossing the course. With the resumption of hostilities between India and Pakistan no doubt the flora is flourishing again. I suspect, however, that the golf course opened as far back as 1888 by Colonel Neville Chamberlain may be no more and Walter Hagen's dictum 'Not to forget to smell the flowers along the way' may no longer be relevant.

While staying at the Bank bungalow I was informed that an 'English gentleman' and his Indian associate were seeking a competitive round of golf. On rustling up a partner we met on the first tee only to find, to my amazement, yet another past captain of Royal Ashdown GC had strayed off the beaten track. Geoffrey Bedford (Chairman of the British and Commonwealth Steamship Company) and his wife had found some excuse to visit Gulmarg on shipping business! How successful he was in promoting his maritime affairs I never found out. He was, however, singularly unsuccessful on the golf course and found the rather complicated betting system of 'compulsory presses' to his financial disadvantage. He did, nevertheless, make sure of recouping his losses in kind by drowning his sorrows in expensive wines at a dinner party hosted by the Bank that evening.

The only disadvantage of staying on a houseboat was that since the departure of the British at the time of partition, nothing had been done to put in place a system for diverting the untreated sewage that 'flowed' from the houseboats. This, coupled with a water supply which was suspect, at best, meant that most meals had to be complemented with a daily intake of 'Imodium' (or its equivalent) to allow one to venture forth and partake of the numerous attractions on offer.

Fortunately, the Oberoi Hotel Group had recognised the problem and converted the Maharajah's palace into a luxurious hotel with all modern amenities. As a precautionary measure, we spurned the more romantic, but less hygienic, houseboats and stayed at the hotel on subsequent visits. This in itself was a pleasing experience with the palace gardens dotted with mighty chenar trees (under the shade of which the hotel would lay out a buffet lunch). As far as the eye could see tall poplars fringed the lake. At dawn, when the sun was still well below the surrounding hills and the sky, initially pale yellow, was turning blue, a light haze of mist hung above the lake and with the early morning dew glittering like crystals on the budding flowers and the awakening birds in full chorus there seemed to be, at the time, no better place in the world. At night when the gardens were lit by thousands of fairy lights reflected in the still water of the lake, it was indeed the most romantic of settings.

The partition of India created a political 'brouhaha' of such resonance it echoes still. The problem is of immense complexity. At the time of partition the Maharajah of Kashmir, despite a predominantly Muslim population, opted to throw in his lot with India. India was prepared to hold a plebiscite, subsequently rescinded on the grounds that it wished to show the outside world that it was a secular country and the inclusion of a Muslim state in a mainly Hindu environment proved the point. This changed stance obviously did not suit the Pakistanis. They logically argued that with access to Kashmir readily achieved from Rawalpindi via Murree and the majority of the population in favour of links with Pakistan, the state should be handed over. India, from a position of strength, disagreed and the ensuing stalemate has yet to be resolved. The ramifications are evident today as Kashmir is off-limits to visitors, other than heavily armed Indian army units who seem to be more or less permanently engaged in exchanging fire with their Pakistani counterparts or coping with civil unrest from the mainly Muslim population.

Bombay

Bombay was a vibrant, sprawling city, at first glance the epitome of chaos. Most of the population seemed to make their living on the streets selling anything and everything. Although not part of my parish I visited there frequently to attend business conferences and see major clients. The journey from the airport was always an eye opener. As soon as the perimeter of the airport was left behind one was engulfed in some of the worst slums in India, which for anyone familiar with Calcutta is saying something. One was confronted with a heaving mass of humanity, living in the most pitiful conditions. Nevertheless, regardless of adversity, smiling faces were to be seen while to alleviate the gloom the lamp-posts bore advertisements decorated by paintings of exotic birds.

Some of the other advertisements were less welcoming, such as those publicising establishments offering dental 'care'. These invariably depicted a grinning skull replete with a set of gleaming 'choppers', sometimes with a suggestive gap. The accompanying blandishments guaranteed that whatever the problem a cure was readily at hand.

Getting closer to the town centre, gigantic gaudy bill-boards, often promoting the latest Bollywood epic, dominated the side walks behind which rose cliffs of high-rise apartment blocks. The whole traffic nightmare got even denser with bullying convoys of growling lorries and buses driving on both sides of the road making life hazardous in the extreme. One could barely see the bumpers of the cars in front which were wreathed in dark clouds of exhaust fumes. However, as the sun came up, dappling the dusty roads with light, the city started to

207

come alive, if that is the right word, with the usual gaggle of tireless beggars, suffering every affliction known to man, starting to cajole their way amongst the grid-locked traffic, seeking a few rupees to eke out their daily existence. Despite the poverty and depression there was still a sense of optimism as the street hawkers went about their business thinking this might be their lucky day.

Amazingly, a few gaps appeared amongst the tenement blocks and even at the early hour of six in the morning every available space had a cricket match in progress with many games over-lapping. This must have caused the scorers some confusion with batsmen running all over the place, quite often not between the relevant wickets. Nearing the business sector things got better with a light breeze coming off the Arabian Gulf, and the buildings became grander, the 'Gateway to India' looming large – a most imposing edifice, close to the equally impressive Taj Mahal Hotel where I normally stayed. Otherwise, I was accommodated at the equally luxurious and grand Bank apartment above our main office. The Taj Mahal normally qualified, and rightly so, as one of the great hotels of the world.

One of the Bank's major constituents, the Bombay Dyeing and Manufacturing Company, was headquartered in the city and its chairman, Neville Wadia, was a distinguished member of the Bank's main board of directors. Bombay, initially famous for being a centre of the cotton industry, is now better known for being the Bollywood of India and hundreds of films are produced there every year, some to international acclaim.

Bombay, as with most Indian towns, is a city of marked contrasts. If one could ignore the desperate distress of the majority of the inhabitants it was not without its attractions. Luxurious apartment blocks have been built, with sea views, to accommodate the upwardly-mobile middle classes and real estate in prime locations is some of the most expensive in the world. Although swept by sea breezes it was nevertheless difficult to escape the pall and stench of poverty and it was a relief, certainly in the winter, to return to the greenery and cooler climes of New Delhi.

New Delhi

As may have been gathered from our travels, Northern India and New Delhi in particular was a very pleasant place to live. We had made numerous friends – some inherited from the O'Gormans. As a General Manager of the largest foreign bank in India and, in accordance with the status that went with the job, we were invited to just about every social occasion of note, whether it be diplomatic or commercial. On top of a fairly demanding job this excess of hospitality could at times be draining.

On one memorable occasion, when Elizabeth was back in the UK, I had been invited by the local director of ICI to attend a small dinner party in honour of his chairman who was visiting their factories in India. The invitation totally slipped my mind and I had decided to spend a quiet evening at home enjoying a really decent curry. Having finished I was about to repair to bed when an anxious hostess called enquiring my whereabouts. I made some feeble excuse for the delay, hastily dressed and dashed round to the ICI director's house where I tried to consume a five course dinner with apparent relish.

No chapter on India would be complete without some reference to the effect it had on one's digestive system. Having suffered from all sorts of ailments in Pakistan ranging from hepatitis to amoebic dysentery, I approached the gastronomic delights of Delhi with some trepidation. I need not have worried unduly as, provided one took elementary precautions – particularly with regard to unboiled water and uncooked fruit and vegetables, the dreaded 'Delhi belly'. could be controlled, if not altogether eliminated.

In fact, other than some unplanned pit stops in Kashmir my colonic irrigation system generally behaved itself. Interestingly, the food found in Indian restaurants in the UK bears little comparison to the fare provided in their authentic counterparts. In England, for example, to be able to stomach a fiery vindaloo washed down with copious amounts of beer is seen as more a macho test of virility than a culinary experience. We were quickly informed by our Indian hostesses that such a dish, along with chicken tikka masala, was a British invention. Genuine

209

Indian food 'should not be spicy but spiced which means aromatic and flavoursome'. For the ultimate vegetarian experience it was always a privilege to dine with the Birlas (one of India's great industrial conglomerates) who employed the finest and most imaginative chefs and whose offerings stimulated the most jaded of palates.

Most of our informal meals at home were standard fare with by-products from chicken and mutton featuring prominently. There was a great variety of delicious fruits available, the accompanying cream being sourced from the buffalo. When dining at Indian friends' houses numerous appetising dishes were produced and the standard practice was to proceed into the dining room, help oneself from the lavish spreads on offer and then retire to one of the 'entertaining' rooms and be seated in a cluster with other kindred spirits. Very rarely did we sit down to a formal meal. Conversely, expatriate dinner parties tended to follow the accepted UK pattern, when the table was set with the best bone-china and the seating plan reflected the importance of the assembled guests. The ultimate treat was to be invited to one of the embassies where decent wines were served, a luxury not normally available elsewhere. While at all functions the ladies invariably dressed 'up to the nines' with a bedazzling array of jewellery, very rarely were the men obliged to wear black tie. Standard suiting in the winter and a safari-style jacket in the hot season were the norm. I suspect many a member of the ICS (the 'Heaven Born') must have turned in their graves at such lapses in sartorial standards, but overall it made for a more relaxed atmosphere.

The golf club featured most weekends and apart from an abundance of snakes and scorpions in the undergrowth, expediently dealt with by fore-caddies, and the distraction of monkeys swinging away with gay abandon in the trees, I have extremely fond recollections of the course. Possibly unique amongst recognised championship courses a number of Moghul tombs, deemed immovable obstructions, added beauty and character to an already attractive vista.

We were also members of two health clubs giving us the use of the two best swimming pools in New Delhi – those of the Oberoi Hotel and Claridges. Our offspring, already competent swimmers, found these venues a great place to show off their prowess and meet new friends.

New Delhi is beautifully laid out with wide tree-lined avenues and expensive residences ranging from colonial style bungalows to modern air-conditioned villas. The Government buildings and esplanade, designed by Sir Edwin Lutyens and Sir Richard Baker, epitomise imperial architecture at its most stately. A wide road sweeps down from the old Viceroy's house, built on a ridge between an imposing pair of secretariat offices, and merges into a long, level avenue known as the Raj path. The red sandstone of the buildings is most attractive and takes on different hues at sunset. From a vantage point at the top of the rise, on a clear unpolluted day, could be seen the old forts, domes and minarets of old Delhi.

The Republic Day parade with massed bands, lancers and infantry decked out in the most colourful ceremonial uniforms, along with contingents from the Navy and Airforce, was a sight to behold. The day culminated with a grand fireworks display and a lone piper playing a lament, silhouetted on the battlements – similar to, if not better than, the Edinburgh Tattoo.

Delhi was a city of many contrasts. Most of the traditional tourist attractions were in old Delhi: the impressive Red Fort, Jama Masjid, India's largest mosque with its marble-paved front court and the Raj Ghat, to name but a few. The old sector also teemed with colourful bazaars and not-so-colourful slums. We were privileged to attend a wedding ceremony in old Delhi and, having ventured nervously down a dingy, ill-lit alleyway, we arrived at our destination and were faced with the crumbling façade of a dilapidated building. However, once safely through a heavy brass-studded door we couldn't believe the opulent interior within. An attractive courtyard, festooned with fairy lights, led to a well-preserved mansion with many important rooms leading off a galleried hallway. Apparently, some of the old dynasties had retained family homes from a bygone era and were reluctant to move from old Delhi, even if surrounded by emergent slums.

There were also tax advantages to the owners as, hidden away in these apparently depressed areas, they were able to disguise any trappings of unseemly wealth.

211

The climate during the winter months was near perfect and, provided the monsoons had not failed, the many magnificent gardens, both private and public, were a blaze of colour. The summers could be oppressively hot as the air dissolved in a quivering heat but if one had the advantages of an air-conditioned house and car life was bearable and, unlike the days of old, there was no need to make the trek to the cool comfort of Simla. In fact, throughout the year – even during the heat of summer when temperatures exceeded 110° Fahrenheit – my regular golf four teed off just after midday every Saturday. Not only did we have our chosen caddies but, as mentioned earlier, fore-caddies were employed to look for errant golf balls in the snake-infested bush. Depending on how much you paid them their prehensile toes came in useful for improving difficult or unplayable lies and many a par was achieved in most unlikely circumstances.

Looking at old photographs I see that it was more or less compulsory for all concerned to wear appropriate headgear to fend off the debilitating effects of the sun. Apart from pith helmets or topees, a spine-pad which hung over the back of the neck was an obligatory part of the tropical kit. British troops were obliged to wear protective headgear at all times during the day, whereas we sunbathed at every opportunity, admittedly by the side of a cooling swimming pool, and I never wore a hat, even when playing golf in the heat of the midday sun. Contemplating my grizzled countenance now, I should perhaps have been more careful. However, at the time there was no greater pleasure than to sit by a pool, warmed by the sun blazing from a cloudless sky and with a reviving drink in the hand. Occasionally, the pool in question was that of the British High Commissioner, Sir Michael Walker – a splendid diplomat of the old school who was in his spare time a keen, but not particularly talented, golfer. Some years later I met him at the West Sussex Golf Club where he was still persevering in an attempt to improve his game – from all accounts without success.

India's climate follows an annual cycle of three distinct seasons: cold weather, hot weather and the rains. The delights of the cold weather and the travails of the hot weather have already been mentioned but nothing has so far been said of the rains. The coming of the monsoon in the Punjab was always dramatic, prefaced by hot winds that came whistling across the plains, the banking up of storm clouds and an unbearable feeling of pressure. Then all was released and the rain thundered down in great drops, splattering the arid soil and releasing that seductive smell as the parched earth greedily lapped up the water like a vast sponge. Within days the thaumaturgy of nature caused lush green flora to materialise where before was just scrubby vegetation.

Overall there was a great sense of relief, and an all round lifting of spirits, although the golfing fraternity found fresh hazards. The rough on the golf course became impenetrable, even for the most motivated fore-caddies, and scores and handicaps rose accordingly. Strangely, I found playing in a torrential downpour not altogether unpleasant. Other than soaking clothes and equipment the warm rain was tolerable – although the caddies found it hard work and at times looked as though they would dissolve in a puddle of perspiration. The regular golfers kept to their schedules as though nothing had changed, apart from their wet gear and the constant replacement of saturated gloves.

Relief from the heat was always short-lived as the hot, dry climate was simply replaced by conditions oozing humidity. The rains also brought out a multitude of insects – cockroaches and mosquitoes taking on a new lease of life – and snakes appeared where they had not before. Nor was it the healthiest of times – skin infections, particularly prickly heat, were commonplace. In Delhi we were comparatively fortunate. In Eastern India, where the humidity was at its worst, conditions verged on the intolerable – what it was like in the slums of Calcutta one dreads to think. But once it was all over the advent of the cool season was bliss indeed.

After the rains came Diwali – the festival of light – when the whole of Delhi was transformed by illuminated adornments of every description. The traditional lights in little clay dishes with oil in them faced fierce competition from strings of multicoloured fairy lights. The whole effect was not far removed from Oxford Street at Christmas.

The skies also became a blaze of colour with kites of differing shapes and materials darting around the heavens and presenting

213

a hazard to low flying aircraft. Children of differing shapes and sizes became so absorbed in keeping their tackle aloft, as they ran around the flat roof tops, that they too were a grave danger to themselves and in this case the traffic below. There were presumably casualties, but not sufficient to inhibit this essentially peaceful pastime. Those in the know – and in control – considered it a philosophical pursuit. A good substitute for yoga.

Regardless of the climatic conditions, to venture forth to old Delhi was a time-consuming adventure in itself as the density of traffic was dire in the extreme. On leaving the relative calm of the modern streets of New Delhi one was immediately immersed in total chaos – motorised rickshaws, dilapidated taxis, ancient lorries, gaily-coloured horse-drawn tongas, all competing for space with stray elephants, buffalo and dogs of every description. Very few pedestrians kept to the broken-down pavements and the near impenetrable wall of humanity, animals and vehicles necessitated a flexible schedule if meetings were held there. Returning in the evening, with legs and bottoms sticking to the sun-scorched vinyl seats of the ancient taxis, one became aware that outside the light was fading fast, but the streets were still alive with a jumble of colour. The aroma of a hundred different spices and the smoke of charcoal burners combined to create a scent which remains in my memory and is always evocative of India.

The city offers an amazing variety of locally-crafted goods to tempt the unwary shopper. Bargaining is an art form in itself and, as a resident, one can haggle over a period of time. I was fortunate in knocking down the price of an antique 'ivory' chess set to an 'appropriate' figure. On having it subsequently valued at Spinks in London they confirmed it was a most attractive 'bone' chess set and, fortunately, valued it at a figure well in excess of the price paid.

While we were in Delhi, Lord Aldington decided it was time to retire and in 1976 handed over the reins to his much respected deputy, Nigel Robson. Lord Aldington had guided and expanded the activities of the Bank through some fairly turbulent times. His farewell tour of his far-flung empire was cause for celebration in terms of honouring the major improvements achieved under his stewardship. It was also a time of some poignancy for many

214

as, during his extended travels, he had made numerous friends at all levels within the Bank. We hosted a number of farewell parties involving the Bank's clients, the diplomatic corps and, not least, the staff. Fortunately, it was not the rainy season and the gardens of the Bank house provided a relatively 'bug free', picturesque and impressive venue.

During my years working for Lord 'A' I found his visits a daunting prospect. His curriculum vitae stretched to many pages and not only were appointments required on the Bank's behalf but also for the many other companies of which he was either chairman or a director. These ranged from G.E.C., Sun Alliance insurance, Westland Aircraft through to English China Clays and others too numerous to mention. His days as chairman of the Port of London Authority received great publicity as it occurred during a time of extreme industrial strife.

His family connections with Grindlays went back over 130 years. His wife, Araminta, was invariably on hand to provide stalwart support and, when not involved in the Bank's affairs, kept herself busy publicising and promoting her beloved Jacob sheep.

Despite winning substantial libel damages against Count Nikolai Tolstoy, the rights and wrongs of the affair and subsequent publicity dragged on causing considerable angst. During this difficult period he found solace with his family and staunch friends and was able to enjoy his retirement playing golf at Royal St Georges Golf Club, Sandwich, where he was president. Every time I am privileged to play there I glance at his portrait in the club house and many happy memories come flooding back.

My tour of duty in Northern India offered much both in terms of business satisfaction and quality of life for my family. However, in all idyllic worlds there is quite often a 'fly in the ointment'. In our case flies appeared on a number of fronts in the form of the Bank's director for South-East Asia and his wife. The gentleman in question, whom I had known for many years as a capable and decisive banker, had a management technique which was as uncaring as it was unthinking. To make matters worse his wife had assumed uncalled for airs and graces which she deemed in keeping with her husband's position. They insisted on the same front seats on all internal flights and woe betide the poor manager in our travel department if these did not materialise. When departing domestic airports they expected to be seen off in style by senior management who were required to remain at the airport at least 30 minutes after the plane took off in case it was obliged to return through some technical fault (not unknown).

The regional director's office was in Bombay, which had virtually taken over from Calcutta as the commercial capital. However, the seat of government was in New Delhi and all the embassies were centred there. We thus received a steady stream of embossed invitations to dinner with the British High Commissioner, Dutch Ambassador et al. The director, as the Bank's senior man on the sub-continent, felt that he was being sidelined and adopted the tactic of paying visits to Delhi to coincide with such invitations. We were put in the unenviable position of having to explain to our hosts the arrival of our 'distinguished' visitor, the result being that an extra place was found. On one occasion, an unscheduled visit coincided with one of our own dinner parties. The next morning Elizabeth was annoyed to find that our cook had received his 'marching orders' – his puddings, it seemed, were not up to scratch. This upset not only Elizabeth but had we not reinstated the cook it would have displeased his thousands of fans – he was the kite-flying champion of Northern India. (No mean achievement in a country where, come the evening, the heavens are awash with thousands of colourful kites gliding and soaring into the night sky.)

This was the final straw and, much as I would have liked to remain in India, with further contretemps looming on the horizon I requested a transfer. This was granted and after a spell of leave in the UK during which we took the opportunity to deposit Guy at his new preparatory school – Ashdown House – we set off (by Jumbo Jet) for the New World.

After my departure the dictatorial reign in Bombay came to a premature end – presumably my successor experienced similar problems. Adrian Evans was drafted in to take up the reins and proved a popular choice. Subsequently he switched to Lazards where he became the chief executive. Sadly, this highly, talented and amusing individual died at a relatively young age and his passing was greatly mourned in the City, where he had built up an impressive reputation.

216

The lasting memory of the sub-continent is a heady mixture appealing to three senses. The sound of tinkling temple bells and the hooting of horns, the strong unforgettable smells of burning wood fires and charcoal driven irons, and the sight of the colourful saris of the elegant and not so elegant ladies. The most abiding impression, however, is of the stupendous star-filled skies, the mighty snow-capped peaks of the Kara Koram and Hindu Kush and the unfailing hospitality of the Indian and Pakistani people.

After I left India an article was published in the Bank's house magazine. It was written by one of our newly recruited graduates who, after a brief spell at head office, was posted to New Delhi. The following recounts his first impressions of India. It is written in a style I envy and lucidly expresses many of my own sentiments. Regrettably the author is anonymous. In the context of this book it is worth reprinting the whole without alteration as it offers a more up-to-date flavour of events in Delhi. I also get an honourable (or should that be dishonourable?) mention. Here it is.

'Prior briefings on India seemed all to focus on the perils it held for the digestive system, and so my expectations for this posting were confused and uncertain. There was much ominous talk of vouchers and rubber stamps, of duplicates, triplicates and carbon paper; of curries, chillies and Delhi belly.

Friends worried earnestly that I might return with an embarrassed loss of self-confidence and a transistor radio in my hand – or perhaps some football tickets in my pocket; ancient relatives warned of disease at Suez and rough seas from Aden to Bombay.

In the face of this catalogue of problems and pitfalls it was difficult to anticipate or enthuse – it all seemed a bit of a muddle, and I was muddled about it.

The Bank itself in India was a surprise. How can one explain the workings of 40% of Grindlays staff to the 60% who are not in India? I had anticipated high-ceilings, white pillars, gently swinging fans and colonial elegance – a sort of Bignell in turbans. Instead there is the atmosphere, not of Raffles or the club, but of a paper-factory; Ladbrokes

217

on Derby Day perhaps, a cheerful confusion of proof-tapes, soiled bank notes, and heavy bound ledgers.

There is prodigious activity: ancient typewriters stamp out statements, mechanical calculators clatter and whirr, flimsy vouchers struggle out from under paperweights thanks to the fans, and drift down to the marble floor. Visitors wander in and out, whether the Bank is open or not – visiting friends, delivering letters, coming to mend peoples' bicycles.

Throughout there is an atmosphere of friendliness and welcome – hands shaken so often that one might imagine this was the presidential primary; helpfulness and cheerfulness and smiles. It seems a happy and refreshing place – there is not the pin-striped despondency of Cannon Street station but instead a positivism and willingness, as if life is always closer to Friday than it is to Monday morning.

And outside the Bank is the elegance and muddle of an Indian city – the dignity and confusion, the splendour and the squalor. Chaos among the traffic; not just bad driving but positive lunacy, as the buses try to terrify the cars, the cars the scooters, the rickshaws and everyone the bullocks, mules, donkeys and pedestrians.

It is a very weird and wonderful place – the beautiful flowers, wide tree-lined avenues, magnificent government bungalows, and a sense of grandeur and space.

Then on the other side of the picture, the slums and shanties, where people live in card-board and hessian homes, and where a polythene roof is a proud possession.

These sights are a great shock when one first arrives; perhaps more shocking is the frightening speed with which one comes to accept and ignore them. And everywhere the people – crowds such as one cannot imagine in England: Oxford Street before Christmas, magnified and confused, and scattered down every road and bazaar.

The age of the population is another worrying thing: we in England are so terminally geriatric that even some of the managing directors appear sprightly and youthful; here every other person seems to be a child under six; and the problem of the future amongst such growth is an anxious one.

218

It is a wonderful place, a rather awesome place, and it is never ever dull.

So this is a privileged posting; it is a treat to work among such people, and in such an environment. There are discomforts and there are problems – nothing ever works quite as expected, and the heat and dust of March bodes ill for June and July.

But when one is struggling through the traffic; covered in sweat and dirt, overwhelmed by the stink, quarrelling with the rickshaw-wallah, and longing for a bath you know will fail to run, it is as well to reflect on the compensations. There are no frozen points at Waterloo, never any sleet or hail, no umbrellas blown inside out, or puddles for taxis to spray on your legs. And everywhere, in contrast to the averted looks of England, a friendly smile, a frank curiosity, and a desire to please.

It is a warm country, a welcoming one, a happy place to live and work.'

A few further thoughts to conclude our stay in New Delhi. Although we were relatively latecomers to the scene we were fortunate in as much that the relics and prestige of the Raj still enhanced the status of the British in India, ahead of any other nationality. Its advantages in terms of respect and obedience were considerable provided one remained aware that there was a great deal of unjustified flattery involved. Sycophancy could be a considerable irritant but this was more than offset by genuine affection.

By the late 1970s work permits for foreigners were difficult to come by and Indianisation was in full flow. Accordingly I was extremely fortunate to be appointed to one of the few jobs still open to expatriates, particularly as the calibre of the Bank's Indian executive staff was such that a qualified and able replacement could readily be found locally. Without this element of good luck we would have missed out on experiences and friendships and never been aware of the beauties, charms and contradictions of this amazing country.

When I had visited Simla some 'old dear' who had 'stayed on' showed me a rather battered topee which she still wore when venturing forth in the midday sun. She recounted the

219

practice of expatriates, in days of yore, when leaving India for good – as they sailed out of Port Said into the cooler climes of the West, they paraded on deck and threw their topees into the sea as a ritual farewell. As she never intended to leave India she had clung on to her headgear.

Although in comparison to the old hands of the Raj we had spent but a short time in India and Pakistan, nevertheless we had made many friends among the local community and had many happy memories. While we said with some passion that we would be back, there was no sign that India was aware of our leaving or for that matter cared. In any event the 'exigencies of the service' probably meant we would never return. With annual home leave now the norm, voyages home by sea were a thing of the past. Furthermore, the restrictions of flying prevented any flamboyant farewell gestures. More fittingly, we had a valedictory drink as we crossed the Mediterranean. By the same token I left a copy of *Freedom at Midnight*, which I had belatedly read, on the aircraft in the hope that some literate cleaner at Heathrow would take the trouble to put it aside, read it and, like us, be the wiser for the experience.

X

USA and Canada

New York

I had somehow progressed up the Grindlays ladder, with no
formal training other than Part I of the Institute of Bankers
and the odd course to improve my management skills and the
art of communicating. Along the way I had been ably assisted
by skilled and seasoned teams of 'number crunchers', so my
rôle as a senior manager had revolved around my judgment
and innovative skills rather than the 'nitty gritty'.

At my request, and quickly endorsed by the 'powers that be'
(until then it had escaped their notice that I had progressed
through the system lacking a decent qualification), I was
despatched on an accountancy course run by Citibank in New
York. This seminar was designed to assess the ability of their
newly recruited CPAs (Chartered Accountants) and MBAs, a
group of highly talented professionals who had survived Citibank's
rigorous selection procedures. I was very much the 'father
figure'.

Having been given about 500 pages of reading matter to
digest one week prior to the commencement of the course –
covering every facet of tax law, accountancy, etc. I quickly
realised the course was not going to be a 'doddle'. This view
was quickly reinforced on the first day when we were told that
at the end of six weeks we would be graded along the lines
that the top 30% had a future with Citibank, the mid range
40% would have a job with Citibank and the bottom 30% if
they were wise, should resign and seek employment with the
Bowery Savings Bank, New York. A salutary thought.

Arriving fresh in the Big Apple I was originally booked in

221

at the Drake Hotel – a decent hostelry in mid-Manhattan – for a week to give me time to find cheaper accommodation more befitting my student status. Despite being a seasoned traveller I found NY overpowering – even on a bright clear day after three o'clock virtually all the streets were in semi-twilight with the daunting sky-scrapers blocking out the sun. The odd puff of steam coming through the kerb gratings indicated that all was in working order, as the subway trains thundered underneath. That said, the denizens of Park Avenue went to considerable trouble to make the thoroughfare as attractive as possible and the beautiful, if contrived, floral displays were re-arranged in keeping with the changing seasons.

Central Park offered many and varied attractions, although it was not the place to be after dark.

Lacking any guidance I eventually found a reasonably appointed service apartment next to Madison Square Garden and signed up for the duration. The course could not have been more taxing – after morning tuition at the training centre some distance away in Queens we were set complex assignments which necessitated burning the midnight oil, and had to be handed in the next morning. Some of the Citibankers shared lodgings and exchanged solutions but because of the competitive environment I found I was very much on my own. With very little sleep and having to work seven days a week my composure was not helped by the location of the apartment. After dark the district was the haunt of some particularly seedy characters and, judging by the constant wail of police sirens, they were augmented by muggers, rapists and other inhabitants of the darker side of life. I felt quite nervous stocking up at the local grocery store. On the occasion of a big fight or basketball game at the 'Square' at least there was safety in numbers.

Travelling by subway to downmarket Queens on grubby trains covered in graffiti I adopted the character of Larry Kramer, the assistant DA, as he travelled to the Bronx, in Tom Wolfe's *Bonfire of the Vanities*. In other words I tried to look the part of a down-at-heel tramp. If mugged I was prepared to offer up, without a fight, my text books on Business Finance and Accounting but not my carefully researched homework.

A brief but, in view of the pressure of the course work, not particularly welcome interlude was a visit to United Technologies

Group in upstate New York. United Technologies had been targeted by our merchant bank in London as a key prospect in view of their many diverse activities around the world. I was conscripted at short notice to give a presentation on business opportunities in India. If nothing else it brought home to me the difference in the Bank's internal cultures when Anthony Greayer, the director in charge of the project, hired a stretched Cadillac limousine to ferry the team around. On our return to New York a celebratory dinner was held at the upmarket Pierre Hotel, although I was not aware that we had cause for celebration. One of Anthony's band, boasting a 'half blue' for wine tasting at Oxford then proceeded to order the best vintages available with no expense spared. I enjoyed the evening immensely, safe in the knowledge that the cost of the festivities would be borne elsewhere.

The course came to an end with a flurry of exams and, much to my relief, I was placed just inside the top quartile. The most rewarding aspect was my final report on which I was described as 'the outstanding student in terms of the contributions and insights offered at class level'. At least I had not let Grindlays down and was able to tear up my carefully prepared application for employment to the Bowery Savings Bank and avoided a premature and ignominious end to my banking career.

The New York branch had evolved from the representative office, perched high up in the Pan Am building above Grand Central Station – an ideal location for those commuting from Westchester and Connecticut. The premises were spacious, airy and tastefully furnished in the modern idiom. As the business expanded we quickly ran out of space, however, and were fortunate enough to find additional accommodation along the corridor to house our treasury team.

When we arrived much was made of the crime-wave hitting the city and the need to take care when walking even the most public of thoroughfares for fear of being mugged. After a while, with nothing untoward happening it was easy to ignore this malaise. However, the dangers were brought home with a vengeance when one of the members of our staff, Gerry McKenna, was mugged at gunpoint in the staff lavatory. There were shared toilet facilities on every floor of the Pan Am building for the use of the staff of the various offices located on the different levels. Gerry (a major in the National Guard in his spare time) on being approached by what appeared to be a messenger boy 'caught short' helpfully used his key to open up the facility. A loaded revolver was then thrust against his neck and, once inside, he was forced into a cubicle and ordered to drop his trousers and deliver his wallet. Another member of our staff entered the washroom shortly afterwards and noticed in one of the closed cubicles two pairs of legs, one with trousers draped around the ankles but thought that, being New York, this was reasonably commonplace and departed without further ado. It was only later 'when all was revealed' that Gerry, sans wallet, gave his firm opinion that had they been interrupted both he and the other staff member would have been shot.

After this particular episode we took especial care when being accosted by strangers, for whatever reason. We were nevertheless delighted to read subsequently of a mugger who ripped a gold watch off a pedestrian in Park Avenue, but during the ensuing struggle, the pedestrian had managed to grab the gold chain adorning the neck of his assailant, who fled in some disarray as a crowd collected. The gold chain was genuine and the watch a fake, so justice was at least seen to be done.

'Nobby' Noble was the Bank's first representative – a most competent banker who had missed his true vocation as a writer of considerable talent and an amusing after-dinner speaker. Having prepared the groundwork prior to his retirement, Nobby was succeeded by Brian Barr. Brian's real expertise lay in the Middle East where he had been a regional director with the Ottoman Bank. Brian had married a charming American lady and with a family in the States it very much suited their book to finish his illustrious career in New York. While I was slaving away in Queens, Brian had recruited staff, completed the necessary formalities for the branch opening and, much to my delight, retained the Bank house situated by the third green of Winged Foot Golf Club's famous West Course at Mamaroneck.

The branch was successfully opened in 1978 with a glittering reception at New York's famous art deco hotel, the Waldorf Astoria. A high-powered team came out from London with

Alec Ritchie (our deputy chairman) and Adrian Evans at the forefront. Tony Wright popped down from our Toronto office and we were augmented on the ground by Tony Hambro, Tony Twohey (we seemed to have a lot of 'Tonys' – the Grindlay's Mafiosi) and Neil Sebag Montefiore, amongst others. The business quickly got off to a profitable start – mainly due to some judicious deals completed by our Treasury. This department was run with great flair by Tony Hambro and – a genuine 'Essex' boy – Gordon Lane, who had emigrated to the States under his own steam and had the confidence to secure a job (and a green card) without the assistance of a major corporate sponsor.

Domestically we all found America very much to our liking. Guy was safely and happily tucked away at his English prep school. Adrian found his local pre-prep, friendly and challenging and the icing on the cake was playing for the winning team in the local junior soccer league – the fact that they had four girls in the side seemed to improve his game.

Elizabeth for the first time in her life was not plagued by servants and enjoyed the freedom this gave her. The Bank house, which was centrally air-conditioned, was ample for our needs and had a most attractive garden – we purchased an extra half an acre while we were there, from a neighbour. The lawns and flowerbeds were tended on a weekly basis by a firm of 'Lawn Doctors' – a Polish patriarch and his sons who had a contract for all the houses in the neighbourhood. As was the fashion in America most of the gardens, however large, merged with the adjacent plots. The location was superb with the verdant, tree-lined fairways of the golf course adding an attractive panorama at the rear and views of a sparkling Long Island Sound to be had from the upper windows. There were quite a few celebrities residing in the district and Harry Winston – the world famous jeweller – lived on a 'plot' at the bottom of our lane.

Most of our neighbours were members of Winged Foot and purchased their properties as and when they became available. No less a person than Jack Nicklaus wrote, 'On a point system using a scale of one to ten, I guess I would give Winged Foot a rating of eleven – maybe even twelve. It is one of the most tradition-rich clubs in the country, and the golf course, even today, continues to be one of the most challenging. The beauty of the club, the golf course and the members are all reasons why everyone remembers Winged Foot for being so fine.'

Predictably, despite enlisting all our neighbours as sponsors I had to go on a waiting list and pending acceptance joined the Wykagill Golf and Country Club at New Rochelle. This was a splendid American-style country club with every conceivable amenity and the golf course was regularly used to host events on the LPGA Tour, but it was purely an appetiser for the main dish. In due course I passed muster and found membership of Winged Foot all it was cracked up to be. I was allocated to the 'lower locker room' and the head steward in charge paired players off on arrival to make up a four-ball. As a member I was privileged to play with captains of industry, oil tycoons and bank chief executives, which elevated my status in the community and opened doors for potential business. Thus, the bank received some return for the enormous fees it forked out in membership dues and minimum spending requirements. Being a golf club, pure and simple, tennis courts and all the paraphernalia of a country club were prohibited. However, one concession had been made and a most attractive swimming pool had been installed, tucked away in a distant corner. This proved to be a great amenity for my family in the summer months.

Visitors were not permitted to play the course unless accompanied by a member. Peter Alliss was faced with this predicament prior to commentating on the US Senior Open. The secretary admitted to having one 'Brit' as a member, so I found to my astonishment that I was making up a four-ball with Peter Alliss, Dave Marr (a previous winner of the Masters Golf Tournament) and one other. We played a mini-Ryder Cup in which Alliss was supreme.

Our neighbours, in keeping with the upmarket enclave where we lived, were not short of a bob or two – Cadillacs, BMWs and Mercedes adorned their drives and quite a number of them kept expensive power boats at the yacht club. An elderly couple lived behind us. The husband had retired from Exxon, he had been in charge of their operations in the Middle East and a governor of the American University in Beirut so we found a common link. More importantly he had an English wife. Their routine on Sunday was to dine at the Rye Yacht

226

Club and we were regularly invited to make up a four. On a lovely summer evening with the boats bobbing around in the harbour, tanned ladies dressed in the latest fashions and their menfolk in jade-green jackets with pink slacks (or the reverse) and tasselled loafers, it could well have been a scene from the Great Gatsby. With oysters on ice and champagne flowing, after a few glasses one slipped easily into the mode and all seemed right with the world – which in the circumstances it was. Another neighbour, a senior lawyer by the name of Clune, had imaginatively named his house 'Lair de Clune'. Further down the street we became very friendly with an attractive couple, Rick and Susan Wilson. For Rick, a young good-looking South African, it was his first marriage; for Susan her third. We used to have a regular weekly game of table tennis, followed by a cheerful supper at one of the local Italian restaurants.

In due course we received an invitation to spend a weekend at their house at East Hampton. On arrival we were taken aback by the understated opulence of the residence; we were even more impressed when we were invited to lunch by Susan's brother at his mansion in Southampton.

Her brother, Herbert Allen (junior), was the son of the legendary Herbert Allen who, along with his brother, had founded one of Wall Street's most successful partnerships. Their personal fortune was immense and they were one of the wealthiest families in America. At one stage they controlled Columbia Pictures, Syntex Chemicals and Pen Central Railroad. They had at times been bidders for the New York Mets (baseball) and the twin towers of the World Trade Centre – now, sadly, no more. Herbert junior recently held a seminar at his ranch in Idaho's remote Sun Valley – executives including Bill Gates and Warren Buffet and other leaders gathered for this annual week of schmoozing. On this particular occasion a mere forty people had been invited for lunch including Vice President Mondale.

The Allen, home on Long Island was a Victorian-style mansion fronting the Atlantic – between the house and the beach were beautifully manicured lawns, a tennis court, swimming pool, then a protective grassy bank on which had been built a modern bungalow with changing rooms and jacuzzi. A tennis professional was on hand to provide a game, if required. Guy and Adrian were impressed as they thought the family had their own tennis balls emblazoned with the Wilson logo. I was even more impressed to be sharing a jacuzzi with young starlets. Herbert's wife – his second – was a Hollywood actress of some repute. She played Albert Finney's wife in the film of *Annie*.

The most pleasant part of the whole experience was that for the six months prior to our visit to the Hamptons, the Wilsons had never indicated that they were other than comfortably off – we had been accustomed to split the cost of our Italian meals. Some months later we had dinner with Susan's father at his apartment in Park Avenue – a splendid set up with paintings by the French Impressionists adorning the walls. My first (and only) private viewing of Monet's *Water Lilies*. As a reciprocal gesture for a most pleasant evening, having first established that Herbert Allen was a staunch Republican, I sent him a bank tie with its distinctive elephant logo made from the finest polyester. In return I received a profuse letter of thanks. I wonder if he ever wore the tie – I somehow doubt it. Herbert junior, as befitting his image, kept a permanent suite of rooms at the Carlisle – the most prestigious (and expensive) hotel in New York.

They say that one bite of the Big Apple and you're hooked. Midtown Manhattan's international landmarks such as the Rockefeller Centre (with its ice rink), the Empire State Building and Chrysler Building tower above vibrant Times Square and the bright lights of Broadway and elegant Fifth Avenue shops. Uptown has leafy Central Park and not so leafy Harlem. Downtown are the fascinating neighbourhoods of Greenwich Village and Soho and, further downtown, Wall Street (where it all happens).

Then the twin towers of the World Trade Centre dominated the skyline and, off-shore, the Statue of Liberty was being renovated. One of our neighbours had the contract purely to provide the scaffolding – apparently worth a considerable amount of money. The view from the top of the Empire State Building was spectacular – on a clear day you could see for ever, and after dark one had a breathtaking view of the city's lights. If one didn't have the time or inclination the view from the Grindlays office, sited on the 42nd floor of the Pan Am building was nearly as good. As far as shopping is concerned

New York is styled the bargain basement capital of the world but it is also a showcase for new designs and luxury goods. Shopaholics are in danger of overdosing. New York is the home of the Yankees and Mets (baseball) and the Giants (American football) and after a short period of indoctrination we became loyal fans.

Our first Thanksgiving holiday was spent with the Mace Family at their splendid home in Darien. David was President of the Irving Trust Co. of New York and we had become firm friends in Tokyo. Darien was an upmarket dormitory suburb of New York in leafy Connecticut. Many senior executives lived there as, apart from good schooling, a first class golf course and a most attractive country club, many of the homes had direct anchorage on to Long Island Sound.

One of my sponsors for Winged Foot, Tom Sutton, who lived in Darien, hit over a hundred practice balls into the Sound from a tee in his garden every morning before commuting to his office in New York. One Sunday, at one of his famed brunch parties, he had arranged for those of his guests with power-boats to arrive and tie up at his jetty. He himself had sold his own boat some years previously. What followed was unexpectedly chaotic in the extreme as many of the arriving craft ran aground on shoals of practice golf balls. Apart from damage to propellers and rudders – and the dignity of his stranded guests – all was resolved as a rowboat was commissioned to deposit his visitors ashore.

We thought at the time what a wonderful quality of life America offered. Possibly we should have received greater exposure to how the other half lived on the other side of the tracks, before arriving at this conclusion!

One of our first freebies, courtesy of Irving Trust Bank, was a trip to watch the Yankees play, initially all very bewildering but the boys at least enjoyed the popcorn. On the drive home we took a couple of wrong turnings and unwittingly finished up in Harlem. Espying an open, albeit poorly-lit, gas station we thought we had better get some directions. Not being able to attract any attention on the forecourt I wandered round the back leaving my family defenceless, though they did have the last bag of popcorn, which I thought might come in handy in an emergency. Hearing the sound of voices in what I assumed

229

was the office I wandered in. The rumble of talk ceased on my entry. Through a cloud of smoke, hazy figures could be seen playing cards, taking their drink straight from the bottle and puffing I know not what. Pictures of boxers stared from the grimy walls and the actuality stared open mouthed from oil-cloth covered tables lit by a row of dim lights. Not the most welcoming of scenes and even less welcoming when a very large black man in a dirty singlet, a clone of Mike Tyson, detached himself and enquired my business. Fortunately he was as surprised as I was and when I politely enquired the way to Mamaroneck (I still hadn't learned how to pronounce it) the room, much to my relief, fell about laughing. My inquisitor eventually recovered and got out a map and instructed me 'never, but never' to stop my car 'in his neighbourhood again.' On this occasion, however, having given them a good laugh he said he wouldn't rape my wife, confiscate the car and leave me for dead. He then took considerable trouble to point us in the right direction. Apparently, I was the first white person to pull into his garage in living memory – and I could understand why. We never went back.

One weekend we sallied forth to New Jersey to have lunch with an old friend from Kenya – John Webb and his relatively new American wife. John had previously been with Brooke Bond but now worked in 'invisible zips and flavors and fragrances'. An interesting combination and a dream product for an advertising copywriter – 'on the whole it smells good' wouldn't be bad for starters! We still exchange Christmas cards and one day we will meet up at Lords as promised.

An old squash partner from Tokyo now based back in the UK, Christopher Taverner, used to visit us and the US regularly, purveying ready mixed drinks, such as gin and tonic, in small bottles. He carried his samples in one large suitcase which, when full, weighed a ton. One evening as we staggered across the concourse at Grand Central Station Christopher, an imposing figure in his pinstripe bespoke suit, grabbed some unsuspecting commuter who was scurrying for his train and, in commanding tones, addressed him along the lines of 'My good man, do you mind carrying this bag'. The poor chap was so taken aback he obediently obliged and humped the suitcase to our train. Many a tale could be told about Christopher, a larger than life

230

character – we still see him. He is now a successful wine merchant.

The ordered calm of the office, as we moved serenely into profit was fractured by a contretemps with the assistant general manager. The officer in question had previously been cautioned as to his liberal interpretation of the Bank's already generous terms of service, particularly with regard to expenses. While I was in the UK on leave he had used his new-found powers to push through, without proper authority, a number of extravagant and unrealistic charges relating to his personal welfare. This was not acceptable and moves were put in place to return him and his family to the UK without further ado. Predictably, with his wife comfortably ensconced in Connecticut and his children at preparatory schools in the UK he waged a campaign to stay put. As he was of sufficient seniority to cause ripples within the system the Bank correctly sent out a director, Roger Parsons, to listen to his appeal. Roger, a just and meticulous person, thoroughly examined the facts and agreed with, and implemented, the original decision.

I make mention of this fracas as it epitomises the problems of employing overseas staff at the executive level. While I had no sympathy for the miscreant the repercussions on his extremely pleasant wife and family were far-reaching – not least the upheaval of schools and accommodation. This made an already unpleasant management decision even more difficult. Incidentally, Roger Parsons in due course resigned from the bank and took over as chief executive of Rea Bros, an old established merchant bank which he successfully transformed and sold at considerable profit for his shareholders.

During our time in New York, much to Elizabeth's chagrin, our youngest son, Adrian, joined Guy at his preparatory school, Ashdown House in East Sussex. His first unaccompanied sortie back to the UK was not without incident as when we arrived at Kennedy Airport we discovered we had left Adrian's pristine new passport at home. Whether this was a ruse on Elizabeth's part to delay the inevitable I never found out. But to British Airways' credit they confirmed they would provide the necessary guarantees to the immigration authorities on arrival and all was resolved.

Despite initial misgivings even Elizabeth admitted after a

short while that the change in schooling was an unqualified success. When they first went there Ashdown House was a relatively small school with about 110 boys (all boarding) but to survive financially it expanded its numbers and took on an increasing proportion of girls so by the time Adrian had left the numbers had increased by approximately 30% along with enhanced facilities.

The school went through a transitionary period with a change of headmasters. Billie Williamson, who had built up the reputation of the school by winning regularly a clutch of scholarships to Eton and Winchester, retired and was succeeded by his protégé, Clive Williams. Clive, while maintaining the high educational standards, was a wonderful motivator and, being a natural games player himself, recognised talent and brought out the best in his pupils. He was ably assisted by the deputy headmaster, James Alexander, who ensured that exemplary standards were maintained both in the classroom and on the games field.

Whenever we were home on leave we derived enormous entertainment from watching the various matches while the team teas afterwards gave as much pleasure to the parents as they did to their offspring. Although, like their parents, neither Guy nor Adrian were musically inclined, both excelled at all games, so we got our money's worth. The pinnacle of their sporting achievement was against St Aubyn's School (replete with the Fleming brothers) when Guy took the first nine wickets with some hostile fast bowling and Adrian the tenth (caught by Guy who was in two minds whether to catch it or not). The scorer didn't bother to differentiate with initials so the record, somewhat suspect, appears as though it was a ten wicket haul for Guy. He carried on doing well at school level and opened the bowling for his public school for two years.

Prior to moving on he managed to break Damian Lewis's nose with a beamer while practising in the nets. Whether or not this has enhanced Damian's profile it is difficult to tell but he has gone on to take the lead in such TV epics as *The Band of Brothers* and *The Forsyte Saga*. It is even rumoured he could be the next James Bond. One of the more senior boys, Boris Johnson, has made his mark in politics and is also regularly seen on TV in some guise or another. His father at the time was an MEP and was also involved in a campaign to 'save the seal'. These parental influences may well have swayed young Boris's political leanings and stimulated his performing zeal in later years.

Adrian received his colours at all games and even won the golf tournament, having honed his skills at Winged Foot. Probably our proudest moment, later on, was when Adrian opened the batting for his school at Lords. On his second appearance he put on over a hundred for the first wicket – but despite my having splashed out on an expensive hospitality box, Elizabeth saw very little of the innings, her concern being that her presence ('Indian' eye) would be Adrian's downfall. She spent most of the time before lunch meandering around behind the stands, with the occasional peek to make sure Adrian was still at the wicket.

The great thing about Ashdown House was that our boys loved every minute of their time there (or gave us that impression). Whilst other parents were subjected to tearful, clinging departures at Kennedy Airport the Bignell clan maintained stiff upper lips, although Elizabeth was understandably downcast on the way home. Accordingly, when the Bank offered me the chance to head up the Private Bank back in the UK the chance of being closer to the family weighed the scales in favour of acceptance.

We very much looked forward to our home leave, evocative as it was of small hamlets nestling in the folds of hills, lush green lawns with flowered scent in the air, men dozing over endless cricket matches in the sunshine, a beer in hand, and the comforting sound of distant church bells. To achieve this idyll we decided to move further into the country and purchased Lower Stonehurst Farm. 'Farm' was a slight misnomer as by the time of purchase the land had been depleted to about twelve acres. But it did, amazingly, encompass three counties with the boundaries eating into Kent, Surrey and Sussex, stabling and a barn providing the requisite rural touch. It was very much love at first sight: a well maintained Elizabethan house, with decent ceiling heights downstairs – not so upstairs where the odd yelp punctuated the middle of the night as soporific guests took a wrong turning. A grapevine covered the south wall and an enormous ancient apple tree spilled blossom onto the landing; a gurgling stream cut through behind the house, spanned by a picturesque bridge replete with weeping willow. The house was fronted by sweeping lawns. In the fields, redolent with buttercups, cows chewed the cud; on the hedges hawthorn bloomed – it was as one imagined England should be. Exactly the sort of property expatriates dream about when sweltering in the heat of Africa or India.

We took the gamble of purchasing before finding a buyer for the Bidborough house and Elizabeth stayed on to complete the formalities. This proved more complicated than originally envisaged as we bought Lower Stonehurst from a McAlpine Trust with three daughters bearing the exotic names of Penelope (Poo), Nonie and Zerelda (Lalla) being the beneficiaries. The equation was not helped by the fact that we had three potential purchasers bidding for the Bidborough property. In answer to Elizabeth's cry for help I took the weekend off and flew home on Freddy Laker's airline with a view to returning to New York on the Monday morning. As fate would have it Laker ran into difficulties, and out of aircraft, and I didn't get back to the office until the Wednesday. Twenty years previously such dereliction of duty – absence without leave – would have been taken extremely seriously. However, fortunately there was now a more relaxed attitude at head office and there were no adverse repercussions.

Lower Stonehurst proved a splendid family home but presented commuting problems when I eventually returned to work in the UK and after a while we moved on with great reluctance, particularly as by then I had licked the lawns into shape.

Having travelled the world, the attractions of the American lifestyle nearly persuaded us to 'stay on'. The work was interesting and the quality of life as good as it got. At weekends barbecues burned and planes flew high in bright blue skies as we clutched our ice-cold Budweisers around sun-dappled swimming pools. In the winter the air was more often than not crisp and clear, a cloudless cobalt blue, and snow normally blanketed the ground at Christmas. All our neighbours, and in fact the whole locality, festooned their trees during the festive season with fairy lights and visiting friends in nearby Connecticut was akin to driving through a winter wonderland.

Over the school holidays the boys were able to ski across

the golf course. When the snow melted we were out like vultures collecting lost golf balls which had been abandoned by golfers caught in snow storms just before the course was closed.

My 'old friend', Ravi Tikkoo, had got fed up with the régime under old Labour and emigrated to the States, where he purchased an enormous mansion, Dunnellen Hall, at Greenwich, Connecticut. To mark his arrival in New York he threw a lavish party which received due publicity in the National Press. He must have used a professional party organiser as most of the cream of New York society didn't know how or why they had been invited nor the identity of their generous host. The purpose of the party, in addition to meeting the neighbours (this particular neighbourhood seemed to include not only Greenwich and Darien but Washington, New York and points west), was to launch a fund raising effort for the protection of the giant panda. The house was much admired, although there were sighs from some of the fashionables about the furniture, all of it, to the naked eye, unmarred by time. One guest was heard to remark authoritatively that Mr Tikkoo preferred reproductions to 'beaten up antiques'. The sighs increased in intensity. Ravi continued to run his successful shipping business from New York but pined for the English racing fraternity and, after a brief spell, he became sufficiently disillusioned to return to Hampstead.

Ravi sold Dunellen Hall to the immensely wealthy hotelier, Harry Helmsley. His wife, Leona, then achieved a measure of notoriety by spending millions renovating the 28 room 'Jacobean' mansion and offsetting the cost incorrectly against her tax liabilities. She was duly prosecuted and found guilty. At the time, of the seven owners who had lived there, two have been indicted, and, according to the press, at least three have lost the house following financial troubles. It was even compared to the Hope Diamond in terms of bringing the owners bad luck. Ravi never admitted to being other than happy there!

One day we received a visit in the office from William Bond Elliott flourishing a bankers draft for $200,000 drawn on our Kampala office. Apparently he was having difficulty finding any bank to cash it in New York. I recognised the authorised signatories, one being Barney McEnteggart, an old friend from the past, and we duly opened an account for WBE. This chance encounter led to a lasting friendship, which has had many ups and downs but never been boring. William is a genuine original. When we first met, coffee quotas were in force. To beat the embargo he had been indirectly employed by Idi Amin to transport Ugandan coffee in an old transport aircraft (with Red Cross markings) to neighbouring African States where it was repacked and exported under licence. For his troubles he had been paid $200,000. On the proceeds he adopted a lavish lifestyle, rented a splendid house on Long Island and a ski lodge in Aspen and acquired an attractive girlfriend.

We saw him socially on the odd occasion but the next point of contact was when I returned to London. Then he sought me out to obtain a loan for £10,000 to purchase a second-hand Rolls Royce. This was needed for image purposes as he endeavoured to establish himself as a reputable trader in second-hand aircraft. He certainly impressed someone along the way as before long he had acquired two 727 jets which he converted for private use (installing bedrooms, bathrooms, cinemas, etc.) and sold one to a Saudi millionaire; he had plans to sell the other to a South African tycoon. To promote this business he took a stand at the Farnborough Air Show and acquired a Lamborghini. He then met and fell in love with the beautiful Amanda, got married with a splendid reception at the Belfry Restaurant in London and honeymooned on a private yacht off the coast of Florida. His aircraft conversion business went bust and, to boost his finances, he hired Wembley Stadium, no mean feat, and brought over the Pittsburgh Steelers and Dallas Cowboys to play. I believe this was the first full scale version of American football in the UK. The anticipated gate, in the region of 50,000, would have shown a decent profit but only about 30,000 showed up on the day.

With an expensive flat in Wilton Crescent, an expensive wife to support and no money in the bank his future looked bleak. He then somehow cobbled together an amazingly lucrative deal with Air Lanka, which more than paid off his debts in the UK and enabled him to purchase a lovely house in Eaton Terrace together with the adjoining mews and, not least, sponsor a high goal polo side. Further deals with Air New Zealand and Air Canada contrived to support an amazing lifestyle. Harry's Bar and Annabel's nightclub were their regular haunts. His polo side, Santa Fe, with three of the world's top players rivalled Kerry Packer's and won some of the most prestigious high goal tournaments, including the Queen's Cup. William practised conscientiously but was a modest performer and preferred to bask in the reflected glory of his team mates.

By now he had a fleet of some of the finest vintage cars in the UK and an additional retreat of a mansion in Sunningdale. While he was asset rich he never seemed to have any cash and was always juggling his finances to keep his creditors at bay. After my divorce and a cash crisis as a result of horrendous losses at Lloyds, I somehow got myself entangled with an American heiress who had arrived at Southampton on the QE2. The Elliotts, curious to inspect 'my intended' put their helicopter at my disposal to fly her up to London with dinner at Annabel's. This was duly achieved but when I tried to extricate myself from the relationship on the grounds of poverty I ran into problems. So too did the Elliotts whose marriage was breaking up. William decamped to Palm Beach, amazingly debt-free in the UK, and Amanda continues to live in some style with their attractive daughters in Ascot. They keep in touch with each other, I keep in touch with both of them, and all seems well. I have recounted this tale at some length as I have never known anyone achieve so much with so little – long may the mystery remain.

Back to New York. To improve profits a decision was taken to build up the Treasury side of our business and with this in mind it was critical that we established lines of credit and reciprocal arrangements with some of the large domestic banks, which, at the time, were precluded from opening branches outside their state boundaries. This initially involved much travel across the length and breadth of the USA. It was very much a team effort and I was normally accompanied on these trips by Tony Hambro or Gordon Lane, members of our Treasury team.

Wherever we went we were received with the utmost courtesy as, while the banks visited were substantial financial institutions in their own right, many had very little business outside their state boundaries and were somewhat parochial in outlook.

Tony Hambro accompanied me on a trip to New Orleans, not having first disclosed that he had been a member of an 'upmarket' jazz band back in the UK. We had a memorable, and for me instructive, evening, sampling the delights of Bourbon and Basin Streets. New Orleans – pronounced 'N'Awlins' by the locals – is synonymous with jazz and the nightclubs and bars are legendary haunts of great players. It drips with originality and eccentricity, not to mention the humidity. If not of a musical inclination there are plenty of strip joints to remind you it is also a rowdy port. Food too is relished here – Cajun and Creole dishes provide alternative temptations. Tony somewhat belatedly informed me that he had spent several months of his youth with a leading law firm in the city and thus knew the best restaurants and dives. In between visiting the local banks we were sidetracked at lunchtime to Jackson Square where all sorts of weird street entertainers, fortune tellers and portrait painters vied for our attention. For me it was all a new experience.

On another sortie to South Carolina – real *Gone with the Wind* country – having enjoyed a hearty lunch with our host bank I was surprised prior to coffee to be invited to sample the house speciality, 'Lamb Pie'. Politely declining on the grounds of a burgeoning waistline, I was surprised when they brought on slivers of a tasty pastry with a 'lemon' filling. What was on offer was in fact lime pie – the confusion arose in the deep South accent, which is something different!

On visiting Chicago with Gordon Lane we found our booking at the Hilton Hotel had gone astray and, with a convention in town, no rooms were available. Gordon, in good Essex boy style told me to fade into the background and having button-holed the manager berated the Hilton Group on their inefficiency. He mentioned that it was imperative that they find a suitable suite for the chief executive (me) of a major international bank. Faced with the prospect of adverse publicity, the hotel duly opened up the opulent Hilton family penthouse which covered the whole of the top floor. There we were installed at no extra cost with our own private lift and a well-stocked bar, compliments of the management. Gordon, there and then, reinforced my view that he had all the attributes of a successful trader.

Chicago is a dynamic lakeside city with a wealth of striking architecture, including some of the world's tallest buildings. The city's banks, while being significant players, never really successfully competed on the international front with their New York counterparts. As mentioned previously Geoffrey Kent, an old buddy from Kenya, had married Jorie Butler and thus into one of the great Chicago families. Butler Aviation and the Butler Golf Course were well recognised names and Jorie Boulevard was one of the main thoroughfares. The Butlers were great supporters of polo and Jorie's brother had financed the musical *Hair*. With this fiscal backing behind them, their travel firm, Abercrombie and Kent, prospered, and Geoffrey's high goal polo side went on to win the world championship at Palm Beach.

California was an essential port of call, its economy and banks booming in tandem. A trip to San Francisco provided a colourful, charming and, at times, downright bizarre experience. Set in roller coaster streets (familiar to all those who go to the cinema) bounded on three sides by water with the famous Golden Gate Bridge much in evidence and the island of Alcatraz on the horizon there was much to see and digest. On the digestive front the restaurants offered every imaginable cooking style and Fisherman's Wharf and Chinatown were worth the visit.

I met up with my ex-secretary from Tokyo, Nobuko Christie, and her husband, George, who had transferred to Wells Fargo Bank. They gave me a Cook's tour of the city and dinner at their home, perched on a steep hillside. As George remarked, 'When you get tired of walking around San Francisco you can always lean on it.' I didn't see much evidence of 'Flower Power' but in every other respect San Francisco very much lived up to expectations.

While in San Francisco I found time to look up my old friends Iain and Caroline Aitchison (ex-Uganda, Japan, etc). Iain, predictably, inveigled me into playing a golf match at his Country Club. It was a lovely, manicured course and expensive villas with the statutory sparkling pools were set well back from the tree-lined fairways. On the 16th hole, a par five with the match all square, I nearly drove out of bounds. Iain was well down the fairway and I took out a three wood for my second, hoping to remedy matters. Unfortunately, while I made solid contact the resultant slice veered off at right angles over the trees to finish with the sound of breaking glass. With the prospect of an expensive repair bill we slunk off down the fairway to be pursued some three minutes later by a portly red-faced gent in brief swimming trunks waving a golf ball. Expecting the worst we were about to enquire what the damage was, when our pursuer beamed a smile and said that in all his twenty years no-one had managed to register a hit so far off target and did we want our ball back!

A tight schedule precluded any sightseeing in Los Angeles – the so called 'Capital of Glamour' – although we did drive past the famous Mann's Chinese Theatre where the stars have been honoured with their hand- and foot-prints in concrete. If one strays from the beaten tracks to the seedier districts other parts of one's anatomy could well finish up in concrete. The HOLLYWOOD sign erected on a steep hillside dominated the city – during my visit a letter was missing and I was told times were hard in Tinsel Town. Apparently, one can strike lucky by being spotted by a talent scout as one walks the streets and get signed up, at least as an extra, in the current epic being filmed. My best Robert Redford impression, however, fell on stony ground.

A visit to Washington DC was obligatory; it has all the trappings of a great capital. The city has a wealth of imposing buildings and monuments as well as several outstanding museums. The Smithsonian was particularly impressive, spanning everything from dinosaurs to space flight. I called on the British Embassy and met up with an old golf partner from New Delhi, Michael Pakenham, who gave me a comprehensive run down on the commercial and political scene. His career, quite rightly, has prospered and he is now the British Ambassador in Poland.

While in New York we opened a 'brass plate' agency in the Bahamas – this entailed keeping separate books in New York using stationery headed up with our accommodation address in the Bahamas. We used Barclays Bank, Nassau to handle the procedural matters. The Dao Heng Bank had put together a scheme for their clients in Hong Kong whereby, using our agency, the payment of tax in any shape or form on the interest on their deposits was avoided. The sums were significant and we took a fee, based on the volume of business transacted. All the clerical work was handled in Hong Kong and we purely issued the certificates of deposit.

To obtain the requisite licence necessitated a visit to the authorities in the Bahamas – no great hardship. I was to some degree guided by Jim Cockwell, President of the Imperial Bank of Canada, New York (a fellow member of Winged Foot). He provided letters of introduction to his lawyers and friends resident at Lyford Cay. This snooty enclave was something special boasting a beautiful golf course surrounded by grand plantation houses and pink-washed cottages. Behind white brick walls and waving palm trees one espied the roofs of colonial mansions – all the private roads had perfectly mown edges and at the club marina Chris-Craft and other elegant power boats were moored. At the entrance to the estate was a barrier manned by an immaculately dressed security guard. With membership strictly restricted one could only buy a house on the estate by knowing the right people. The club's rules had to be strictly observed: whites on the tennis courts and formal attire in the clubhouse after seven o'clock.

The only downside as far as I could see was that as a result of all these restrictions most of the members I met were of a certain age and needed golf buggies to get them round the course. Even so, dinner at the club was quite a glamorous occasion with a fair smattering of 'trophy' wives conspicuously bejewelled as their elderly husbands sought to find the elixir of youth.

Reminiscing about Lyford Cay brings to mind a story, possibly apocryphal, relating to Richard Greenwood, an illustrious member of Royal Ashdown Golf Club and also Lyford Cay. As part of the keep-fit regime some of the more elderly members, of which there were quite a few, assembled at the clubhouse on a regular basis prior to breakfast to be put through their paces. These were mostly stretching exercises involving lying on one's back with legs waving in the air. After the lithe young trainer had duly demonstrated what was required she rather naively enquired if anybody had anything to say. Richard's penetrating voice was heard to come booming from the back saying that it was all perfectly clear, but could they open all the windows before commencement!

While in the Bahamas I met up with Bob Sinclair, General Manager of Artoc Bank. Bob I had known in Karachi and Kuwait. Artoc Bank was the brainchild of Peter de Savary, the main shareholder, and had a strong involvement with the Middle East. It never really got off the ground and folded leaving, I think, substantial debts in its wake.

During my stay in Nassau I sold the concept of membership of Lloyds to a number of US clients of locally based lawyers. Grindlays owned a Lloyds Membership Agency and it was part and parcel of one's job to 'cross pollinate' services. It has only occurred to me, some years later, that this would have been an ideal way to launder drug money, the supporting cash deposit being placed in Jersey and the resultant profits remitted back to the USA as a legitimate transfer of funds. If this in fact was the case, while it might have worked initially, subsequent massive losses at Lloyds would have wiped out any benefits and the 'names' in question would have got their just desserts.

Michael Taylor, manager of the Standard Chartered Bank, New York, and his wife, Moira, became good friends. They were members of the prestigious Westchester Country Club and we regularly played golf there, with a return match at Winged Foot. We both had children at preparatory school in Sussex, their two boys being at Ashdown House's main rival, Brambletye. The headmaster of Brambletye, Donald Fowler Watt, stayed with the Taylors in New York while visiting America on a recruiting drive. We were invited along to dinner to meet him and given a somewhat frosty welcome. Apparently, the previous weekend the Bignell boys had bowled out Brambletye for 12 runs in an under eleven match.

The Taylors shared our enthusiasm for the States and suggested we join up and retain some form of base to be used for holidays and eventual retirement. We had received a brochure from John's Island just north of Vero Beach in Florida and we were brought into the equation having passed muster as members of Winged Foot. Apparently, John's Island never advertise properties for sale as they have a stringent ethnic criteria. I went on a reconnaissance and came back duly impressed.

If one had unlimited financial resources, for me, John's Island would be the perfect second home, possessing three first-class golf courses alongside literally miles of ocean front and intra-coastal waters. All residences are subject to a strict architectural code, which is basically English Georgian interspersed with Bahamian Colonial – a mix which works surprisingly well. The

242

skyline remains void of unsightly poles, television antennas or power lines. Underground sprinkler systems are obligatory and landscaping needs to be approved by the authorities. Garage doors have to be designed facing away from the street. To get into the complex one has to pass through a series of security checks and once inside it's either a visual paradise or a luxurious prison depending on one's taste and appetite for golf.

The clubhouse resembles a stately southern mansion and the Beach Club incorporates squash courts, cabanas and, a must in tropical Florida, a lounge with a magnificent fireplace!

The Winged Foot members who introduced me to this contrived mecca had employed interior designers to furnish their Georgian homes with English antiques and fittings. According to the guidelines for joining, 'membership consists of people of accomplishment who have made their own equally significant contributions to communities from which they came and who now evidence their leadership capacities in the many organizations which exist in the John's Island environment.' What other reason could one want for joining – provided one had a healthy bank balance. The only drawback was the exorbitant membership fees and the fact that we could only let to tenants approved by the John's Island committee.

Michael investigated what was available elsewhere and we finished up purchasing a Spanish-style villa with views across yet another 'championship' golf course at Boca Raton. This gave us some pleasurable holidays and we managed to let the property during our absence at a rent sufficient to pay the mortgage.

Interestingly, when we came to sell, some eight years later, the value of the property had remained static while those at John's Island had more than doubled. The problem with real estate in Florida, as an investment opportunity, is that no sooner do developers build a golf course surrounded by attractive homes than a competitor reclaims some swamp-land not far away and duplicates the concept. Thus, there seems to be an inexhaustible supply of houses and flats on the market. The uniqueness and exclusivity of John's Island ensures demand outstrips supply and if one can afford the prohibitive dues then it provides an attractive investment.

Shortly after leaving America we were invited to return to

Winged Foot to attend the American Open Golf Championship. We accepted, thinking this would be a unique opportunity to watch the action close up within the ropes and distanced from the gallery. When we arrived it was only to find that the best official position on offer was in charge of car-parking. Having forked out a not inconsiderable sum for the airfares for Elizabeth and myself I thought we deserved better and were duly allocated less onerous duties. On what should have been the final afternoon, after spending five days (including the practice day) patrolling the course, Elizabeth, by no means a keen golfer, was becoming understandably tetchy. It all came to boil that evening in the clubhouse when I presumed we would watch the play off the next day between Greg Norman and Fuzzy Zoeller. Elizabeth had, not expecting a play off, hatched plans for a day at the beach and gave vent to her frustration at my lack of consideration in no uncertain terms. This led to a fleeting moment of fame, as unbeknown to us, we formed the backdrop to a TV interview involving Nick Faldo which was subsequently transmitted worldwide.

On our return to the UK we were inundated with calls from people, some of whom we hadn't had contact with for years, saying that they had seen us on TV, though not in the most flattering of circumstances. Come New Year's Day we and some friends were comfortably settled in front of the box when the BBC decided to show sporting highlights of the past year which involved the interview with Faldo. Much to our embarrassment, for the next few days the phone didn't stop ringing with kindly souls reminding us, if we had not seen it, of the moment when the fragility of our domestic life was exposed to an unsuspecting world.

With some considerable sadness, not long thereafter, we decided to go our separate ways. It is said that maturity brings selectivity. Love and relationships are tempered by compatibility – earlier intemperate affairs are put down to the excesses of youth. Some men, in an attempt to regain their youth and improve their image in public, take on 'trophy' wives. These women, however, once stripped of their accoutrements may do little to please. With Elizabeth I was most fortunate. Not only did she look good but proved a loyal and supportive wife and wonderful mother in the most challenging and changing circumstances.

244

Coincidentally, the Taylors on their return bought a property close to us in Sussex and joined Piltdown Golf Club where Michael became captain; he was also captain of the China Golf Society. Sadly, he succumbed to cancer a few years after retirement – a great loss to his family and many friends.

Life seems to be a series of coincidences and by travelling the world I seem to be constantly running into old acquaintances. In New York I managed to get a slice of the business of Kay Jewellers – a major retail chain – on the basis that I had become friendly with the chairman, Christo Van Ekris – when he represented a Dutch company based in Mombasa. We actually first met at the Gulu Club, which in itself was a sufficient bond to form a lasting relationship.

We used to meet the director of Barclays Bank, New York, Richard Carden, and his charming wife, Penel, on the social circuit. Some twenty years later Penel was the lady captain of the Royal Ashdown Golf Club at the same time as I was elected captain of the men's section. In our official capacity we were invited to play in a number of the club's traditional away fixtures. As Richard was invariably in Leicestershire fulfilling his duties as Master of the Quorn this did not lead to any discord on the domestic front. Other Ashdown members who visited us in New York were Graham and Margaret McCallum (ex-Tokyo) and Simon Radcliffe with his stunningly attractive new wife, Tania (née Mallett), in her day a top model and one of the original Bond girls.

On my return to the UK and further travels abroad this trend has continued and I am always amazed how one meets former friends and colleagues in the most unlikely circumstances. Mark Cato (ex-Aden) at Lords, Tony Wright (ex-Canada) in Muscat, Len Hendry (ex-Uganda) and Andy McLeod (ex-Tokyo) in Capetown. On a holiday in Kenya in 1995 some 28 years after departing the country I was sitting in the lobby of the Windsor Country Club when an American tour group arrived replete in Abercrombie and Kent safari outfits. As one couple passed I heard the husband remark, 'I wonder if the Bignells still live here.' The couple concerned were friends from Tokyo (Jim Hensell was the manager of the 3M Corporation); they had retired to Minnesota and we hadn't been in contact in the intervening 20-odd years. That evening we bored my wife and

Mike and Liza Jones, our travelling companions, by recounting tales of yore.

Toronto

We spent our first Christmas in the USA by visiting our old friends, George and Margaret Cook, who by then were based in Toronto, where George had opened a new office for the Bank. As a newcomer to the highly competitive banking scene he found the going tough. Nevertheless, building on Grindlay's connections with the sub-continent he had garnered some useful business from the large Indian community resident in Toronto. This proved a mixed blessing as a number of doubtful debts arose, particularly one involving the import of prawns from Bangladesh. This aside, Toronto was a most attractive environment and when we arrived the storms had passed through and the snow was deep and crisp and even. Driving to church on Christmas morning, it was as though we were passing through a traditional Christmas card with the trees and surrounding buildings covered in a mantle of snow offset by a clear blue sky.

While it was freezingly cold, icicles hanging from every building, it was nevertheless a most enjoyable break. Fortunately, both Toronto and New York are geared up for extremes of climate, and all the necessary equipment is in place to scrape snow from pavements, grit streets to keep the traffic flowing and free up the airports in the event of heavy snow-storms. Not normally the case in the UK where 'leaves on the line' are sufficient to cause endless delays on the railway and concomitant traffic chaos on the roads as people resort to their cars.

George took early retirement from the bank in Toronto and was quickly snapped up by the Chartered Bank. With the advantage of a Swedish wife he was made their representative in Stockholm. There he still resides but, in keeping with local custom, has changed wives and is now happily married to the charming Birgit.

XI

Servants

These deserve a special mention as some became good friends and others a hindrance. On my first tour of duty in East Africa as a bachelor they were normally in situ. Very rarely were they other than reasonable cooks and most were extremely handy with a charcoal-fired iron. All of them did, however, hit the bottle if the opportunity arose. Most servants were well trained in the use of a flit gun. This was a pump action cylinder, loaded with a pungent insect repellent – an essential precaution in locations where all sorts of strange, blood-sucking creatures foraged at night. While it produced a rather revolting antiseptic smell, it was nevertheless comforting and had the advantage of keeping servants on their toes as purely by sniffing the air one was aware if this vital duty had been neglected.

On the golf course I quickly acquired a regular caddy, who was able not only to club me correctly and read the greens but also, with deft use of prehensile toes, often improved my lie dramatically. Most bet their match fee on the result of the game and, amazingly, their loyalty went with their bag – regardless of the shortcomings of the owner. Fortunately, the results of most regular four-balls tended to even out. This code of conduct seemed to know no boundaries in the less-developed countries. The lady caddies in Japan were, however, impassive and acted strictly according to the rules, as did the professional caddies at Winged Foot and other courses in America.

I had my only woman servant in Entebbe, not surprising given the near all-female environment in which I found myself. She certainly aimed to please. In Aden I thought I had a most efficient and loyal Arab houseboy – until he stole a pair of valuable, much treasured, gold cufflinks. His replacement wasn't as good, but at least nothing else of value went missing (to the best of my knowledge). My syce (groom) in Kenya pinched a Swiss army knife but he was so good at his job that I allowed this misdemeanour to go unpunished.

Once I was married the acquisition and retention of servants became more problematical. Our initial experience in Pakistan was disastrous. We inherited our bearer (houseboy) from my predecessor, a bachelor. He had previously served under fairly senior officers in the old Indian Army. His letters of reference were impeccable, dating back many years and written in scholarly hands on writing-paper heavily embossed with regimental crests. Unfortunately, while my shoes gleamed as they had never gleamed before he refused to accept orders from 'the Memsahib' and even a request for toast and tea had to be channelled through me. This situation obviously couldn't last and he had to go – which he did and, with much saluting and clicking of heels, he disappeared, ramrod straight, into the sunset. We were not alone in our quandary as few bachelor bearers could survive the introduction of a memsahib into the equation – it was not the done thing for a 'European memsahib to rule her husband'. His replacement, a rather obsequious individual, served us well and gave my new young bride the odd lesson on how to cook a curry. Elizabeth in turn introduced him into the art of preparing a quiche, her speciality (inherited from her mother) and a dish very much in vogue at the time.

A driver and housemaid completed our complement in Beirut. The driver was indispensable, given our hectic social life, and he worked (and slept) all hours. He was a first class chap and navigated the tortuous Beirut traffic with élan. On the odd occasion when we got caught up in a wedding celebration or funeral and guns were going off all over the place, he somehow steered us through unharmed. Again, his diplomacy was to the fore at the time of President Nasser's death when he bedecked our car with black ribbons to get us successfully through the numerous road blocks set up to chastise any traveller not in sympathy with the cause. The original housemaid, on the other hand, was particularly inept: she cleaned our silver with a wire scrubbing brush – what is left still bears the scars. Her replacement was adequate and generally helped Elizabeth with the housework and looking after the children.

248

A similar establishment was our lot in Tokyo. In our somewhat smaller apartment, we had a minute maid's room in which we housed a delightful Taiwanese girl student (a family friend of our landlords). While she didn't do any housework (she didn't have to) she was invaluable as a live-in baby-sitter for our young family. Our driver, Kho Kataoka, was a key member of the staff; we would have been totally lost without him in every sense. He picked up visiting VIPs from the airport (which could take anything up to three hours), drove the children to their pre-prep schools, took Elizabeth to her ladies' lunches and ferried me around Tokyo to my various business appointments. Tokyo to any foreigner is an impenetrable maze and without Kataoka at the helm we would never have reached our chosen destinations. But on occasion even Kataoka failed and a letter of apology he wrote is reproduced here – it deserves wider publicity.

NATIONAL AND GRINDLAYS BANK LIMITED

OFFICE OF THE GROUP REPRESENTATIVE
RESIDENT IN JAPAN

C. P. O. BOX 2120
242 SHIN KOKUSAI BUILDING,
4-1, 3-CHOME MARUNOUCHI,
CHIYODA-KU, TOKYO, JAPAN,
TELEPHONE 214-4628, 4629
October 24th 1972 TELEGRAMS AVRENIM

Mr. and Mrs. Bigell

DEEPLY REGRETFULL EXPOSITION

On October 23rd 1972, you went to waste much time on your going way to your important party at the night I caused you.

As you remember, when I turned around and head for another direction, I had already found that it was wrong way. The more I tried to get correct way as soon as possible, the more I was coming into confusion.

If I could take easy mind as usuall, the way was not so difficulty, because I've known it and I've drived on those ways sometimes.

I was so poorest driver that I'm really regreting very much and I never repeat it again any more. I apologize you much trouble I caused you.

I really ask you to forgive me and understand me.

Yours sincerely

Kho Kataoka

Kataoka had to make the fraught journey from his home in Yokohama every day but was never late. All the doormen at the leading hotels knew his name and, on emerging from the numerous official cocktail parties I had to attend, I found my car sliding up to the entrance well ahead of the queue. When we left Tokyo we parted with considerable mutual sorrow and respect.

India was a different kettle of fish. When recruiting staff on the sub-continent it was always good practice to exercise caution when receiving letters of recommendation. It was also normally wise to take up references if offered. In most towns there was a flourishing industry of professional street scribes, helping the illiterate and unemployed and writing and typing letters to order. Invariably, a diverse selection of stationery was available with imposing letterheads of fictitious establishments, replete with sealing-wax if required. The one area not mastered by these counterfeiters was the reproduction of heavily-embossed crests. So, unless the notepaper was pilfered, it was normally safe to accept and act on a letter from an embassy or reputable regiment.

As detailed previously we had a veritable army of servants, who, in turn, had their own retainers. While we initially thought we were overstaffed, compared to the days of the Raj when a complement in the region of twenty was the norm, we were very much the reverse. In those far-off days the lowliest of Indian Civil Servants (the 'Heaven Born') or the Box Wallahs (merchants) were compelled to employ a whole range of servants to run even the humblest of ménages. As their pay and position improved so too did the number of their employees increase.

In our case we had a butler or 'khitmagar' (nicknamed King Rat after James Clavell's eponymous 'hero') whose sole job was to greet guests and whip his underlings into shape. Then we had a bearer who looked after our clothes and was a general dogsbody. An ayah attended to 'the Memsahib' and, more importantly, looked after our children. The virtues of a trained ayah were considerable, faced as we were with a continuous round of cocktail and dinner parties. In our case we were most fortunate as we had inherited an aged retainer who had been on the Bank's payroll for many years and was very much part of the furniture. She had correctly managed to hold on to her position as a trusted and valued servant. As a strong disciplinarian, full of wise counsel and with a fount of sleep-inducing stories, she was indispensable in looking after Guy and Adrian. During the day, when they were not with Elizabeth or at school, we could reliably leave them in her sole charge without any qualms. As a family we normally made a point of joining up during the week for breakfast and tea which was taken on the verandah; otherwise work and social commitments quite often precluded family gatherings in the evening.

The cook, when not flying his kite, was a rather idle individual whose comfortable dimensions were not so much a testament to his culinary prowess but more a reflection on his ability to hoover up any spare morsel retrieved from the table. When not cooking the books with the butler he was only galvanised into action at dinner parties. If sixteen guests were invited for dinner he invariably prepared food for forty. This made him a popular figure in the servants' quarters where he transported all the surplus food. We had a chokra to assist him with the washing up. A sweeper was employed to do the menial tasks which none of the other servants would deign to get involved in, such as cleaning the lavatories and other similarly unpleasant duties of which, fortunately, there were not many.

All the household servants wore white uniforms; the butler embellished his with some polished brass buttons and sported a cummerbund to add colour. The cook, who followed in the hierarchy, somewhat let the side down as his outfit was invariably bespattered with the dish of the day – or yesterday – depending on how busy the dhobi was.

Elizabeth had a derzi who sat cross-legged on the verandah behind a whirring Singer sewing-machine mending clothes for the household and running up the latest Paris fashions copied from dated copies of *Vogue*. A dhobi took care of our laundry. He was an absolute marvel and I took to wearing silk shirts safe in the knowledge that they would be returned intact and impeccably ironed.

Our extensive garden was looked after by a mali and his assistant. The lawns were mown with an antiquated mower, the mali pushing and his assistant pulling, but it somehow seemed to work. Apart from the jacaranda, bougainvillaea and blossoming trees most of the colour in the garden was provided by flowering plants contained in hundreds of pots. These were placed in clusters, some along the drive at the entrance in serried ranks, others in chaotic profusion providing banks of variable hues with chrysanthemums predominant in the winter. The overall effect was pleasing to the eye. To guard us at night we had a smartly turned out ex-army night-watchman – a chowkidar. His job was to discourage robbers and other nefarious persons from disturbing our night's peace but more often he was called in to provide assistance when our central air-conditioning plant broke down. Our establishment of thirteen was rounded off by two drivers. One car, a much valued second-hand air-conditioned Peugeot 403, was used for business purposes and the other, a locally made Ambassador, for domestic use. When our somewhat paranoid director arrived from Bombay he insisted the cars travel in convoy in case one broke down (I wish I could say that this never happened, but unhappily it occasionally did).

The other advantage of possessing two cars was that when we returned to New Delhi airport from a flight overseas, the first car whisked us straight home without delay, while the second car's driver negotiated with the customs to release our luggage which, after payment of a relatively small amount would be delivered some two hours later. It certainly saved a lot of hassle. Harry, the senior driver, was most polite and courteous and he was sensible enough to provide adequately for his children's education and encourage them to better themselves. It was cause for great celebration when his eldest daughter became a fully qualified chartered accountant and secured an executive position with an international bank.

As mentioned elsewhere, the foregoing were the individuals we had direct dealings with. In the servants' quarters (a block of flats at the bottom of the garden) a whole new world of intrigue, feuds and friendships existed. Occasionally we were asked to adjudicate in some domestic dispute but such matters were normally settled by our lordly butler.

And so to New York – and then there were none. Some reading this tale may have felt a twinge of envy at the privileged lifestyle of the expatriate. But, somewhat surprisingly, Elizabeth found that, free from the demands of an extensive household, she actually enjoyed being in total control. There were no arguments over inflated bills, no need for urgent medical assistance, no bickering over meals that had not turned out as planned, no grief at alcohol being watered down and personal items going missing.

America was a haven of calm and tranquillity by comparison.

EPILOGUE

Coincidentally, on my transfer back to the UK my relief was David Murray John who had taken over from me in Tokyo, so it was a relatively painless transition. David sadly, not many years later, died from a heart attack while skiing in Switzerland.

When I joined the Bank there was a house journal, *The Monsoon*, which had existed for many decades, mainly detailing 'hatches, matches and despatches' with the odd item of interest thrown in, mostly giving publicity to exploits on the games field. In the 1970s this was revamped and re-titled *Minerva* under the able editorship of Nick Cresswell and his assistant, Jill Trayner – both having been brought up in Kenya. The new magazine was a joy to read, full of entertaining articles and interesting photographs. It was professionally produced and won a number of awards. I mention this as reading some back copies has revived memories and helped add substance to this book.

Nick, unfortunately, died recently and Jill has gone on to establish her own successful public relations company in Chichester. I have a particularly warm spot for Jill. When I was first posted to Nairobi branch in 1956 and put in charge of Cash Department Jill, in those days a most captivating young girl, was recruited and, when free from her typing duties, used to dispense cheque books for new and existing customers. Such were her attractions that there was invariably a long queue at the cheque book counter, an area of the Bank's activities which had previously been largely ignored. If, as seems evident today, there had been a requirement to sell other services of the Bank – such as credit cards or insurance – she would certainly have reached the top. As it was she quite correctly switched to journalism.

On my return to the UK I was put in charge of private banking which became one of the Bank's major profit centres. However, shortly afterwards the ANZ Bank (Australian) became our major shareholder. While in most countries they retained the Grindlays name, the culture changed and there was a mass departure and shake-up of senior management. The marriage never really worked and Standard Chartered Bank have since bought out the Grindlays' operations from the ANZ. When I originally joined the National Bank of India, the Chartered Bank of India, Australia and China (as it was then known) was considered on par as a competitor and many a friendly alliance was formed. With the demise of the National Bank of India and Grindlays Bank it is sad to record that these two once great names are now virtually extinct.

When I started my career with the National Bank of India conditions at times were primitive and uncomfortable. However, as time progressed modern air-conditioning and comfortable air travel made the 'White Man's Burden' very much a relic of the past. Now it is no great hardship and very much a sought after privilege to work abroad.

After my adventures overseas I thought life would settle into a comfortable routine. Far from it. In a banking capacity I continued trekking the globe servicing the financial needs of private clients like Gina Lollobrigida and Natalie Hocq, the then owner of Cartier, amongst others. A change of job, divorce, 'financial hardship' as a result of the Lloyds débâcle, near marriage to an American heiress, appointment as financial advisor to the Prince and Princess of Wales and re-marriage to the delightful ex-wife of an old Kenya friend are surely the ingredients of a tale worth telling. Alas, the ink in the well of my inspiration has run dry; that said, if one had lived and worked within the confines simply of being comfortable this book would never have taken shape.

In retirement there are many excuses to take life easy and let things drift by, doing only those one enjoys the most: in my case golf, bridge, a spot of gardening and a lot of watching sport on TV with the odd holiday in the sun thrown in for good measure. I also enjoy painting watercolours and indulging in this pastime has given me a greater appreciation of colour and been of undoubted assistance in helping me visualise and

255

describe events and scenes from the past in other than sepia monochromes.

There is, however, the danger of going to the grave wishing one had done this or that and never actually doing anything. There is always a sense of inadequacy and the fear of failure and no immediate panacea for success. As an avid reader it never occurred to me how and why writers started writing. I presumed it was a God-given talent. That said, having scribbled out the first chapter I found the rest of this particular story came with a rush. The problem was, and is, making the prose interesting and readable. If I have achieved half of what I set out to do then I will rest content.

In recent years I have been fortunate to have the opportunity of revisiting many of the places chronicled in this journal. The changes that have taken place over the ensuing years have been quite extraordinary – many for the good but, regrettably, many for the bad. The Gulf States, spurred on by the enormous wealth generated by their oil reserves, have prospered beyond recognition. Good governance, relative stability and the ability to transform sea-water into fresh-water have totally changed the landscapes and many states are now major tourist attractions. The Lebanon, Cyprus, Aden (Yemen) and Egypt have not been able to overcome the political strife and their economies have suffered accordingly, while Libya has not made the best use of its oil wealth. Virtually all the African states have regressed – corruption, famine, political instability taking their toll – although Uganda is showing promising signs of progress after the wilderness years. Pakistan hobbles along. India at last seems to be making better use of its enormous reservoir of managerial talent and natural reserves. It is fast becoming the world's back office with call centres springing up, servicing the processing needs of many major international companies. Japan, surprisingly, is in the doldrums, the once mighty yen in decline. South Korea has, if anything, slipped backwards. Hong Kong is certainly changing, for the better or worse I know not. The USA, come hell or high water, stands supreme as the world's only super power, and will remain so.

I make these fleeting observations as had my sons embarked on a similar career their experiences would bear little resemblance to the story I have told. Fortunately, in their chosen professions they have succeeded where I would probably have failed. Guy seems settled at Knight Frank and is happily married. Providentially, he has given up the attempt to compete with his wife's brother-in-law, Bear Ghrylls, who, when not climbing Everest, is attempting even more implausible feats in Arctica. Adrian as a partner at Cazenove achieved his immediate goals, but has since moved on. At the time of writing the jury is out on a number of world events – so this seems a good point at which to bring this story to a close.

'Take up the White Man's burden –
Have done with childish days –
The lightly proffered laurel,
The easy, ungrudged praise.
Comes now to search your manhood
Through all the thankless years,
Cold-edged with dear-bought wisdom,
The judgement of your peers!'

Rudyard Kipling 1865–1936

INDEX

260

263

264

Musoma 42
Mussolini 118
Muthaiga 32
Muthaiga Club 10, 85–6, 88, 91
Mwanza 42

Nairobi 9
Nairobi Club 10, 79, 85, 90
Naivasha 18
Nakuru 18
Nana Sahib 192
Nanga Parbat 205
Napier, Sir Charles 97
Nasser, President 132, 155
National Bank of Dubai 78, 133–4
National Bank of India 4, 5, 6, 10, 17, 64, 151, 255
National Portrait Gallery 5
New Delhi 188
New Orleans 237–8
New Stanley Hotel 9, 94
New York 221
New York Giants 229
New York Mets 227, 229
New York Yankees 229
Ngugi, Lee 88
Nicholson, General John 107
Nicklaus, Jack 225
Nicosia 152
Nile River 25, 131
Nkrumah, Dr 81
Noble, Philip (Nobby) 204, 224
Norfolk Hotel 9
Norman, Greg 244
Nowshera 107
Nyali 36
Nyanza Province 39
Nye, Bridget 84
Nye, Jill 84
Nyerere, Julius 177–8

Oak-Rhind, Clive 84
Oberoi Hotel Group 206, 210
O'Gorman 'Paddy' 175, 188, 209
Okura Hotel 160, 182
Oldham, Allen 14
Oman 134–6
Omar, Khayyam 108
Onassis, Jackie 200
Ondaatje, Christopher 5, 24
Ordish, Liz 22

Oriental Hotel 158
Oshima, Family 160, 170, 179
Ottoman Bank 86, 114, 124, 138, 141, 149, 150–1
Oxford University 46
Oyama, Mr 181–2

P&O 57
P.I.A. 102
P.L.O. 147
Packenham, Michael 240
Packer, Kerry 237
Palin, Michael 26
Pan Am Building 223, 228
Pars Paper Factory 144
Parsons, Roger 231
Peacock Throne 145
Pearce, Stuart 151
Pemba 16
Peninsula Hotel 182
Percival, Philip 23
Peshawar 107, 108–9
Petra 146
Petronas Towers 187
Philby, Kim 128
Philippines 185–6
Phimister, Sandy 78
Pick 'n' Pay 176
Piggot, Lester 76
Pilgrims, The 163
Piltdown Golf Club 245
Pittsburgh Steelers 236
Port Said 51, 220
Portsmouth, Earl of 90
Powell-Cotton, Christopher 26
Powers, Gary 53
Presidents Bodyguard 106
Presley, Elvis 25
Price, Leslie 34, 95
Prince of Wales 255
Princess Margaret 123
Princess of Wales 255
Purves, William 164–5
Pyramids 50

Qatar 141
Queen Mother 35
Quetta 103

Radcliffe, Simon 169, 245
Rambagh Palace Hotel 200

265